Preface

There is still a tendency for efforts to widen participation in higher education to concentrate on the task of preparing 'non-traditional' entrants to conform – academically, socially and culturally – to accepted higher education norms. This *normalisation* process is often regarded as an essential pre-requisite both to their entry and their success in higher education. Pre-entry access programmes are frequently designed (as a conscious survival technique) to acclimatise potential entrants to an alien culture: post-entry programmes often involve mentoring or guidance schemes to speed up this acclimatisation process and smooth out any remaining rough edges of cultural non-conformity.

This publication, produced jointly by the Institute for Access Studies and the European Access Network, is based on quite a different premise – the need for higher education institutions themselves to change – so that they not only respect a pluralist culture, but also represent it. To achieve this will require a significant shift from the current ethos of selective normality to one of diversity and inclusion. This volume identifies the barriers to achieving this, shows how it can be done at institutional, regional and national levels, and reports on the resource commitment that is required.

The examples included here provide encouraging illustrations of what is being achieved by local initiatives: collectively they make a major contribution to shifting the debate away from a student deficit model towards one which recognises the necessity for cultural change in higher education itself. Without this change, whatever their professed commitment to widening participation, universities will continue to be distinguished by their exclusivity, rather than by their contribution to challenging social exclusion.

Maggie Woodrow
Executive Director
European Access Network

Foreword

As Chairman of the Higher Education and Research Committee (CH-HER) of the Council of Europe from 1992 to 1995, I look back with some satisfaction on the single-minded commitment of the member countries at the time to widening access and participation in higher education. Their singlemindedness is evidenced by the 1992 and 1996 Parma Conferences, organised jointly by the Council of Europe and the Commission of the EC, now EU, culminating in the Council of Europe's project on 'Access to Higher Education in Europe'. It is now reassuring to see the project well underway as a going concern thanks, in great measure, to the European Access Network (EAN).

Indeed, in outlining the project on 'Access to Higher Education In Europe' the Council of Europe described it as 'a regular work programme in education and culture, within the European Cultural Convention' and affirmed that 'an educated citizenry is a major pillar of democratic security'.

These are two very significant statements issuing from the 1992 Parma Conference. Previous meetings on the same theme, such as the 1967 Vienna Conference attended by Ministers of Education of the Europe Region of UNESCO were virtually self-contained events.

In fact the tasks set out by Parma and the consequent Council of Europe Access project have jump-started what has become a multifaceted European movement for promoting social inclusion through both formal and informal education. The EAN has released forces that are affecting every aspect of education provision right down to pre-schooling, especially current views on the central issue of individual empowerment.

At the start of the third millennium, there is now a growing awareness that the single-mindedness and assurance of the pioneering years are giving way to caution and circumspection in addressing the complex issues that wider participation in higher education and lifelong learning have thrown up. In the various initiatives taken by member countries to promote access among disadvantaged groups, new forms of social exclusion seem to be rearing their heads. There are mounting fears that lifelong education, involving as it does the whole education process, may inadvertently be promoting novel types of élitism. The privileged might very will go on accessing more. This is borne out by experience in some advanced western countries where lifelong learning has been capitalised on by already advantaged groups.

Changing the Culture of the Campus:

Towards an Inclusive Higher Education

edited by
Liz Thomas & Michael Cooper

Staffordshire University Press

Published by
Staffordshire University Press,
College Road, Stoke-on-Trent,
Staffordshire, ST4 2DE (UK)

First published 2000

ISBN 1 897898 65 7

Design, layout and setting
by Carmel Dennison

Printed in Great Britain
by Stowes the Printer, Longton, Stoke-on-Trent

Moreover potential contradictions are inherent in the main goals set by the two international bodies mainly involved. At Parma the EU Commission stressed the critical importance of a highly educated workforce to the economic future of its member states. It cited advances in technology as having 'raised significantly the knowledge and skill levels required by the workforces in European countries to maintain and increase economic competitiveness'. The Council of Europe, on the other hand, rightly aims to stimulate action in favour of access to quality higher education in Europe. Its main thrust is towards increasing and widening participation and retention rates particularly for under-represented groups.

The European Access Network strikes the right balance. It is developing a sound holistic approach to what is revealing itself as an increasingly complex undertaking. EAN holds fast to the guiding principles of quality and equity. It never loses sight of the central educational and democratic goal of individual empowerment, at one end of the spectrum, and opening up access across national barriers, on the other, thus promoting mobility and the European dimension. This accounts for EAN's growing political, economic, cultural and social relevance.

What is most noteworthy is that the access dialectic is one in which all the principal actors are themselves undergoing deep change:
1. a growing proportion of students are adult learners who make new demands, leading to drastic changes in university curricula;
2. a consequent assault has ensued on the concept of liberal education with learning taking place around one's professional activity;
3. the university's role is being challenged by workplace learning.

As can easily be surmised, the access dialectic is proving a potent catalyst for change, touching every aspect of mainstream, further, and higher education. I wish the European Access Network every success in meeting the formidable challenges that lie ahead.

Roger Ellul-Micallef
Rector of the University of Malta

Acknowledgements

The editors would like to thank Kim Slack for providing editorial support, and all the contributors who have patiently fulfilled the editors' requests in the preparation of the chapters for this book.

The editors would also like to thank the European Access Network (EAN), especially Maggie Woodrow and Roger Ellul-Micallef, for organising the 8th EAN Annual Convention, 7 – 10 July 1999, Malta.

Changing the Culture of the Campus: Towards an Inclusive Higher Education

Contents

Part Four: Institutional Responses to Promote Inclusion

Part Five: Targeting Specific Groups

Part Six: The Way Forward

Notes on the Contributors

John Blicharski

is head of the Wider Access Study Centre at the University of Dundee, Scotland. With a background in biochemical pharmacology and medical education, he transitioned to continuing education early in 1995. He currently directs four intensive higher education preparatory courses and tracks all students who complete them. The Access Summer School is widely recognised for successfully preparing and qualifying disadvantaged young people for higher education.

Bill Blunt

is an associate professor and deputy director of the Centre for Organisation of Academic Development, University of Port Elizabeth, South Africa, where he is responsible for academic staff development, higher education research and research supervision. He has published on student development, staff training and development, transformation in South Africa and affirmative action policy.

Patricia Callaghan

is head of Student and Academic Affairs at the Dun Laoghaire Institute, Ireland. Prior to that she was director and founder member of the Association for Higher Education and Access and Disability. She has published widely on access issues and her work has informed policy at both local and national level in the Irish education context. She is an executive member of the Confederation of Student Services of Ireland and of the North/South Conference on Higher Education in Ireland.

Amos Carmeli

is National Director of the Perach Tutorial Project, Israel; a position he has held for 18 years. He was educated at the Hebrew University of Jerusalem and the Institute for Senior Public Administration at the University of New York. He worked for five years as a Principal Aide at the Ministry of Education, Israel, with responsibility for the administration of the national kindergarten system and school planning and for five years as Deputy Head of Education in Agricultural School, Settlements and Rural Areas at the Ministry.

John Clarke

is Planning Manager at the University of Southern Queensland. John holds qualifications in Veterinary Science, Science, and Education. He entered the higher education sector in 1991 after a career in veterinary research. John is currently working towards his PhD in the areas of educational equity, and has published widely in this field.

Michael Cooper

is director of the International Office at Karlstad University, Sweden. He holds a degree in modern languages from King's College London and a research degree in English from Göteborg University, Sweden. Previously he was head of the School of Modern Languages at Karlstad where he lectured in English, in particular language and linguistics. Among his many other activities, he is currently President of the Compostela Group of Universities and a member of the committee of the European Access Network. He has worked extensively as a translator and language editor of scientific publications.

Geoffrey Copland

is Vice-Chancellor and Rector of the University of Westminster, UK. He holds a doctorate in Solid State Physics from Oxford University. He is currently special adviser to the North West London Training and Enterprise Council and chair of the Coalition of Modern Universities, a group of 30 universities which gained university status in 1992. He is an active member of a number of bodies concerned with the advancement of professional education in the London region.

David Davies

is a professor and dean of the School of Education and Social Science at the University of Derby, UK. David has spent much of his career working for wider access to educational opportunity and among other roles he has been a teacher-trainer at Reading University, an Open University staff tutor, and head of continuing education programmes at the Universities of Cambridge and Surrey. He is one of the editors of the Journal of Widening Participation and Lifelong Learning. After leaving the University of Birmingham, Westhill, as Deputy Principal he joined Derby as a new university committed to the integration of further and higher education.

Roger Ellul-Micallef

is currently Rector of the University of Malta. Prior to his election as Rector in 1996, he was Professor and Head of the Department of Clinical Pharmacology and Therapeutics at the University. Further he served as chair of the Council of Europe's Committee on

Higher Education and Research 1992-95. He has published widely in international refereed journals and has contributed to medical textbooks.

Margaret Heagney

is Student Equity Officer in the Student Equity and Access Branch of Monash University, Australia. She has participated in a number of collaborative research projects in the UK and Europe and has presented to the Australian Research Council and the Higher Education Council on student issues.

Paul Heywood

is head of Malta Equivalence Information Centre at the University of Malta and member of the Council of Foundation of the International Baccalaureate Organisation. He graduated from University of Malta: 1956 (BA), 1957 (Notary Public), 1958 (LL.D). From 1988-1994 he was Assistant Director of Education in charge of Post-Secondary and Adult Education and was appointed Director in 1994. He was Pro Chancellor and President of Council of University of Malta 1988-1996. His publications include Systems of Knowledge, a project for broadening the sixth-form curriculum.

Vivien Hope

is currently head of International Student Support Services at the University of Adelaide, Australia. She has a Masters in Australian Social and Political History and has taught Asian Studies in several Australian Universities between 1978-1992. She is also a qualified lawyer. Vivien now specialises and runs workshops in cross-cultural communication, cultural diversity and support services for international students.

Robert Jones

is a research assistant in the Institute for Access Studies at Staffordshire University, UK. He is researching widening participation, and working towards a PhD seeking to critically engage with the various agendas underpinning the current access milieu.

Anne Jordan

is manager of the Educational Development Centre in The Institute of Technology, in Waterford, Ireland. She was educated at the universities of Keele and Sheffield in the UK, and the National University of Ireland. Current work includes research into the Irish access movement and the role of guidance in facilitating access.

Renate Kosuch

gained her doctorate in psychology at the University of Hamburg. She was head of the project 'Motivating girls and young women to choose a technical career', which was set up by four universities of applied sciences in the northwestern part of Germany in 1993. In 1997 she helped to set up an 18-month project to improve and implement the summer school for young women to participate in science and engineering. Dr Kosuch is now working for the department of education at the University of Hamburg.

Robert Lemelin

was Director of Learning Assistance at the University of Southern Maine, USA, until his retirement in 1999. He has published widely in journals such the NADE Newsletter and the Journal of Developmental Education and in 1994 edited Issues in Access to Higher Education. He has contributed to many of the EAN conferences.

Ann O'Brien

graduated with an Arts degree from University College Cork. She spent a number of years teaching at second level and progressed into the field of adult and community education. She was awarded a Masters in Adult and Continuing Education from the National University of Ireland and holds the post of Access Officer in NUI Maynooth with responsibility for developing initiatives and policy in the area of access and disability.

Maeve O'Bryne

graduated with an Arts degree from Trinity College Dublin. For a number of years she worked in educational publishing before moving into adult and community education. She was awarded a Masters in Communication and Cultural Studies from Dublin City University where she currently holds the position of Access Officer. The main focus of her work is developing access strategies for school leavers from disadvantaged areas in North Dublin.

George Papadopoulos

is a freelance educational consultant. Until his retirement in 1990 he was Deputy Director for Education in the Organisation for Economic Cooperation and Development in Paris. In this capacity, he was responsible for the work of the OECD Education Committee and the Governing Board of the Centre for Educational Research and Innovation (CERI). His publications include papers, articles and addresses on a wide range of educational issues. He continues to be closely involved in the Council of Europe's work on the reform of higher education in central and eastern European countries.

Armand Policicchio

is an associate professor at Slippery Rock University, USA. He teaches study skills and directs a programme for access students. He is the chairperson of the International Access Committee of NADE and a member of EAN. His research interests include assessment of study skills and of access programming.

Nikolay Popov

is Associate Professor in Comparative Education at Sofia University, Bulgaria. He has published extensively on comparative studies on education in Europe. He chairs the Bulgarian Comparative Education Society and has undertaken a number of individual and collaborative research projects related to comparative education.

Glen Postle

is Associate Director (Academic) at the Distance Education Centre at the University of Southern Queensland, Australia. He has been working in the field of distance education since 1978 and has worked with various donor agencies (Asian Development Bank, Commonwealth of Learning, World Bank) in the areas of distance education, open learning and open schooling in Pakistan, Solomon Islands and India. Recently he was seconded to the State Department of Education in Queensland to manage the development of the Open Access Support Centre.

Julia Preece

is lecturer in higher education at the University of Surrey, UK. She is responsible for adult education and HE research with a focus on access and widening participation. She chairs the Society for Research into Higher Education Eastern European Network and has published several books and articles on widening participation for minority groups.

Heather Pudner

is currently employed as the key worker on an anti-social exclusion HEFC(W) project in the Penderry ward of Swansea, Wales. After a career in further education teaching and in Women's Aid she came into higher education guidance work in 1989. She was a member of the European Access Unit team that produced 'From Élitism to Inclusion'; she has also published on social exclusion and community-based progression routes and is particularly interested in work that integrates family, community, school, further and higher education.

Jarlath Ronayne

is Vice-Chancellor and President of Victoria University, Australia. He graduated in Chemistry from Trinity College Dublin in 1965 and obtained a PhD from the University of Cambridge in 1968. He has published widely in the science policy literature and is a Fellow of the Australian Academy of Technological Sciences and Engineering. In 1997 he was elected as an Honorary Fellow of Trinity College, Dublin. He was a Visiting Fellow at Oriel College, Oxford for Trinity Term 1999.

Andi Sebastian

currently works as an Equity Consultant in the University of Adelaide, Australia. She has a Masters Degree in Primary Health Care and considerable experience in organisational management and training in areas of equal opportunities and social justice.

Jan Smith

is a lecturer in post-compulsory education and education management at Sheffield Hallam University, UK, and has carried out research into aspects of student experience in further and higher education. She has previously worked in community, adult and further education, and as an adviser in post-16 education. She is currently acting as co-ordinator for a regional widening participation project led by Sheffield Hallam University.

Vera Stastna

is a senior official in the higher education department of the Ministry of Education, Youth and Sports of the Czech Republic. She is responsible for international academic programmes, co-operation with the Higher Education and Research Committee of the Council of Europe and the Czech contact person for the Bologna follow-up.

Janet Taylor

is a senior lecturer and co-ordinator of Academic Learning Support at the University of Southern Queensland, Australia, and has been involved in education and science for 18 years. Recent interests include flexible delivery of academic learning support programmes in mathematics and staff development for online environment. She has been the recipient of two national teaching development grants in the area of academic learning support.

Jim Taylor

is director of the Distance Education Centre at the University of Southern Queensland, Australia. He currently holds the position of Vice-President for Australia and Oceania of the International Council for Open and Distance Education (ICDE). Other professional activities include membership of the Higher Education Advisory Board for Education Network Australia and the National Council for Open and Distance Education (NCODE). He publishes in the fields of distance education, instructional design, human cognition, cognitive science and cognitive task analysis.

Paul Taylor

is a lecturer in sociology in the School of Humanities and Social Sciences at the University of Sunderland, UK. His main research interests and publications are in the area of the effectiveness of equal opportunities policies within higher education.

Liz Thomas

is senior research fellow in the Institute for Access Studies at Staffordshire University, UK. She graduated from the University of York, has an MA in social and community work (University of Bradford) and a PhD from the University of Sheffield. Liz is involved in a number of evaluation and research projects aimed at widening participation in further and higher education. She is managing editor of the Journal 'Widening Participation and Lifelong Learning' and is currently writing a book 'Widening Participation in Post-Compulsory Education'.

Colin Trotman

is currently Acting Head of the Department of Continuing Education at University of Wales Swansea. Formerly a National Union of Mineworkers shop steward, he studied for his first degree, as an adult student, in Sociology. He pioneered Wales' first community-based access to higher education course and initiated the Department's educational guidance work. He has wide experience of working with disadvantaged adult students and has published widely in this field. He was a member of the European Access research team which produced 'From Élitism to inclusion: Good Practice in Widening Access to HE'.

Part One

Introduction

1. Overview of the book

Liz Thomas and Michael Cooper

The desires to challenge social exclusion in general, and to promote access and wider participation in higher education (HE) in particular, have grown in importance in recent years in transnational, state and institutional policy debates. This edited book from authors who are practitioners, policymakers and researchers in Europe, Australia and the US examines these policies, and the associated practices.

    To reflect the various levels and aspects of the interest in widening access and participation, we have tried to give the book a logical structure by arranging the chapters in a series of progressive steps. The point of departure lies in a consideration of what social exclusion is, and the sort of contribution that education, especially HE, might be expected to make to help create a less divisive society. In part two the book moves to examining issues relating to greater diversity and inclusion in higher education. Much of the higher education sector is reactionary and élitist. The goal of greater diversity in participation in HE poses tensions and problems; for example, potentially there is conflict between greater access and the quality of the education provided in universities and colleges and between modernisers and progressives. After this more general approach, part three goes on to examine and illustrate national strategies and approaches to promote wider and greater participation. From this the focus is narrowed to a discussion of how individual institutions have responded to the challenge of promoting inclusion. The examples range from Australia and South Africa to Ireland and the United Kingdom with an interesting landing in Bulgaria. However, social inclusion is not just a matter of general principles and strategies; special measures are needed in particular situations and the book moves on to consider a number of case studies where specific groups are targeted. The survey reaches its conclusion in a short section which looks ahead towards the next steps that are necessary if we really are to change the culture of the campus towards an inclusive higher education.

Following on from this introduction, Liz Thomas and Robert Jones attempt to explore some aspects of the growth in usage of the term 'social exclusion'. This term is examined in relation to the notion of poverty – does the idea of social exclusion enhance or confuse understandings of poverty? Social exclusion may include poverty, and can take account of other factors, such as the degree of agency of those affected. Does higher education combat social exclusion by providing routes to the labour market, or through non-economic returns, such as the acquisition of social capital? There is a danger, as Maggie Woodrow points out in the Preface, that widening participation is part of a *normalising* agenda, rather than an *empowering* experience. It is with dilemmas such as these in mind that the book moves on.

Part two includes four chapters that reflect some of the conflicts of creating a more inclusive higher education system. Patricia Callaghan explores what an 'inclusive higher education' might consist of. She examines different notions of 'equality' and the institutional barriers encountered in promoting genuine social inclusion.

George Papadopoulos goes on to argue that despite the expansion of higher education, it has largely failed to change significantly the inequitable distribution of opportunities among social groups. New solutions are therefore required, and attention should be directed to the inadequate basic educational preparation of disadvantaged children and young people. This entails a massive shift of resources to combat school failure and to provide a variety of progression routes to both tertiary education and the labour market, and this must be supported by lifelong learning opportunities. Without such changes, there is a danger that lifelong learning policies may, in practice, actually exacerbate existing inequalities.

In one sense, David Davies takes this argument a step further when he considers the strategic 'drivers' for the growth of lifelong learning, and asks whether the reality is a progressive agenda or a mask for new forms of exclusion. He discusses the notion of curricular authority passing outside the universities as the globalisation of the knowledge and communication industries gathers pace. Finally, he wonders whether the democratic values of open access will be preserved if the modernist approach is adopted, and the extent to which non-learners will be blamed or pathologised within a deficit model of higher education.

In her chapter Anne Jordan engages with the recent debates about 'dumbing down' – a so-called practice of lowering academic standards to accommodate higher education participation for groups previously denied entry. Although this may not be a genuine issue but one hyped up to preserve an élitist system of higher education, the 'dumbing down' debate does raise serious questions. She examines academic levels and standards of some access courses in Ireland and UK Open University level-one courses and argues that participation can be extended to non-traditional students and that this does not compromise quality standards.

The chapters in part three represent a wide geographical spread, investigating national strategies in a diverse range of countries. First, Armand Policicchio provides an overview of mass higher education in the US in an historical perspective. He raises a number of key issues, such as who and how many should have access to higher education. Is the cost of mass education affordable? Is higher education an instrument of social exclusion, and should it be an instrument of social inclusion? What is the relationship between educational goals and societal goals? Finally he asks an important question: what can we learn from the American experience with mass education?

In the UK the Higher Education Funding Council for England is attempting to force the pace of change in institutions through financial incentives. Geoffrey Copland discusses the UK funding regime, which aims to widen participation in higher education, especially with respect to lower socio-economic groups and people with disabilities.

Ann O'Brien and Maeve O'Bryne examine access in the Republic of Ireland. The current economic boom in Ireland has heralded the advent of 'The Celtic Tiger'. While this has improved life for many, for those in socio-economically disadvantaged areas it is no better. Their chapter includes an overview of Irish access initiatives since 1994, a review of the current literature, and a focus on the new developments at third level and the links at community level. They identify emerging issues in the light of current economic conditions, outline future developments and pinpoint lessons learned from experience to date.

An example of good practice for wider participation in higher education that could be applied to many countries is the system developed in Israel under the name of 'Perach'. Amos Carmeli describes this nation-wide project, in which university students assist disadvantaged schoolchildren from under-privileged areas, through mentoring and tutoring. University students volunteer to spend a few hours each week tutoring, helping and motivating under-privileged children, and in return they receive a scholarship covering approximately half of their tuition fees. Thus pupils and students both gain under this arrangement, and it is an a-political project, where Jews, Arabs, Druse and other minorities participate side by side.

In the concluding chapter of this section Paul Heywood examines strategies to help create a mass higher education system in Malta. Currently, the University of Malta is the only HE institution. The author traces different possible routes to higher education, including links between the university and post-16 institutions, admission through vocational qualifications and the possibility of a binary system of higher education.

However good national HE initiatives are, their efficiency relies to some extent on the response from individual institutions and the strategies they put in place to achieve the aim of widening participation. A number of these strategies and responses are discussed in part four. The first example is a comparative study of restructuring to broaden access in four different countries. Julia Preece and her colleagues explore responses from institutions in these countries to recent policies on lifelong learning and widening participation. They use case studies to demonstrate how the institutional infrastructure caters specifically for 'disadvantaged' students, and give examples of induction schemes, bridging programmes, student support, and accreditation or curriculum initiatives. The chapter concludes with an analysis of the effect of the national and global context on institutions' decision-making for widening access.

Curriculum innovation naturally has a major role to play if institutions are to be successful in attracting a wider range of students. Jan Smith argues that traditional patterns of education and assessment in the UK have supported an élitist university system in which only particular forms of learning were valued. Recognition of changing social needs requires a different approach to attract a wider range of students and equip them with the knowledge and skills *they* need in the twenty-first century. This has led to some curriculum reforms, built on student-centred learning and transferable skills. Research at Sheffield Hallam University has tested some of the assumptions behind these initiatives and the findings are outlined in this chapter.

Another aspect of higher education relates to modes of delivery. Glen Postle and his colleagues demonstrate how the University of Southern Queensland has taken up the challenge of equitably distributing limited resources to flexible delivery initiatives in a manner which promotes both the optimum development of flexible delivery and inclusive teaching/learning practices. Decisions were informed by: the varying degrees to which student target audiences have access to different technologies, and the varying degrees to which the learning needs of different student groups were not being met. The chapter presents a teaching/learning framework developed in response to this challenge.

To be really successful institutions will probably have to develop an all-inclusive system. In his contribution, Jarlath Ronayne outlines initiatives undertaken at Victoria University in Melbourne, from ad hoc projects to a set of developed policies, which address the creation of curricula sensitive to the needs of its students, their communities and the broader communities the university serves.

Part four concludes with an interesting example of 'inclusivity workshops' for first-year engineering students. Vivien Hope and Andi Sebastian describe how collaboration between staff from engineering, equal opportunities and international programmes led to the development of an innovative pilot programme, intended to become the basis of a full curriculum. The pilot consisted of workshops in which participants engaged in experiential learning exercises built around issues of race, culture, gender, disability and sexual preference. The results from participants' evaluation sheets are encouraging and may justify developing the programme further.

To facilitate wider participation we also need to consider issues relating to specific groups. The needs and demands of those with physical disabilities differ from those of groups who come from socially disadvantaged backgrounds or belong to ethnic minorities. Part five presents a number of case studies targeting specific underrepresented groups, relating to issues of class, gender, ethnicity and restricted physical ability.

The first of these, presented by Colin Trotman and Heather Pudner illustrates the problems of social and economic deprivation associated with industrial decline in urban areas, by drawing on a collaborative initiative between primary, secondary and higher education to counter social exclusion. More importantly, it presents examples of good practice where a holistic approach to the community has delivered inclusive and successful experiences in locally based continuing education.

John Blicharski describes how targeting, tutoring and tracking potential undergraduates from disadvantaged backgrounds has, over the last six years, made it possible for nearly 400 disadvantaged young people from working-class backgrounds to prepare and qualify for higher education. Through partnerships, this course has allowed Dundee University to create a more inclusive and diverse educational environment. Tracking student progression has enabled the course to be improved and student outcomes to be monitored. The author outlines several transferable components of the course, which was recently selected as an example of best practice in research for the UK Committee of Vice-Chancellors and Principals (CVCP).

In Germany, as in most other countries, women continue to be underrepresented in science and engineering courses and professions. Renate Kosuch describes a project in which universities in Lower Saxony have developed successful programmes to encourage young women to enrol in non-traditional subjects. The activities include one-week summer schools for girls from 16+, and additional 2-3 day programmes in selected subjects during the spring and autumn vacations. Her contribution includes a presentation of the prerequisites, concepts and organisation underpinning the project, as well as the results of a study on the career decisions of former participants. Of particular interest is the necessity of keeping the programme of activities mono-educational, otherwise women will not participate.

Among the groups of potential undergraduates that need to be specially targeted are ethnic minorities. Paul Taylor argues that an inclusive higher education should start by creating an organisational culture which engages with previously excluded groups. The staff of higher education institutions should reflect the diversity that is sought within the student body. In this way potential students can be provided with role models. He uses the term 'engagement' in preference to the usual 'inclusion', which implies a sense of passivity by those from minority ethnic groups. Engagement also suggests that it is the responsibility of majority groups actively to engage with minority groups to overcome barriers to entry. These issues are illustrated by recent research in the UK relating to the recruitment of academic and non-academic staff.

The final case study in this section comes from the Czech Republic. In her contribution Vera Stastna of the Czech Education Ministry focuses on three areas of good practice relating to overcoming the potential limitations of physical disabilities. Her first example concerns centres for people with severe eyesight defects. The second relates to performance arts courses integrating students with hearing difficulties. The third example explores the work of a network of Czech universities in the area of integrated studies in adapted physical activities, where they have developed several very good international projects, the last helping people with post-traumatic stress caused by the Kosovo conflict.

In the concluding section, the book looks at what has been achieved and how we might go forward. Liz Thomas and Robert Jones focus on the role of higher education research. They argue that participatory action research (PAR) should play an integral part in the institutional response of higher education to combating social exclusion, and discuss the crucial role of research for practice. There is often a weak link between research and practice, but they argue, PAR helps to overcome the limitations of 'irrelevant' research. PAR actively involves intended beneficiaries and practitioners in the research process to ensure that research findings are useful and so are implemented to help make a difference.

The final chapter, by Robert Lemelin, on the past, present and future of access, reviews the development of access, the strategies used, and new problems facing access practitioners and researchers. In particular, Lemelin argues, the growing interest in access and social equity requires a more systematic examination of our new directions.

In conclusion we maintain that the present volume provides a wealth of background material and some pertinent concrete examples of changing the culture of the campus to make higher education more inclusive. Although it might be argued that many of the contributions have a basically Anglo-Saxon or at least an English-speaking background, there is much in the form of general strategy as well as specific case studies that may be applied in other contexts. We hope that the text will act as a stimulus to readers. We hope that *you* will feel challenged to critically examine aspects of access that you are involved with to help ensure that appropriate educational opportunities are accessible to a wider range of potential students – and that you will contribute to the sharing of information to expand our collective knowledge of these issues. Creating an inclusive higher education system relies not only on commitment, appropriate policies and good practice, but also on on-going research and dissemination, to avoid re-inventing the (potentially broken) wheel!

2. Social exclusion and higher education

Liz Thomas and Robert Jones

Introduction

In many developed countries there has been a shift in emphasis from use of the term 'poverty' to that of 'social exclusion', especially in policy circles. Whether or not there is a singular discourse of social exclusion is a question that should not detract from the more general point that, as a notion, it seems to be used primarily to signify more than material or financial deprivation. Critics of the term's use may suggest that governments employ it cynically, and that it serves to displace from political agendas debates seeking to address the redistribution of resources. The following tries to reflect on some of the ways in which the term has developed and attempts to relate them to the field of widening participation in higher education. The idea of social exclusion may offer greater insight into the causes of marginalisation and isolation that appear to be becoming more prevalent in late capitalism, and hence promote a broader and more effective approach to addressing such issues. Education and training are often perceived as a counter to social exclusion, in that they facilitate social 'networking', develop self-confidence and enhanced labour market participation. The chapters in this book contribute to an assessment of this perception and explore ways to create a more inclusive and diverse higher education system.

A number of so-called developed countries have, over the course of the past decade or more, used the term social exclusion to examine society and define segments of the population therein. Although these countries can be seen to have experienced increases in material affluence, significant proportions of their populaces have not shared in this growth. Concern about 'social exclusion' is evinced by European Union policy debates and anti-poverty programmes funded by the European Commission. The term was included in the Maastricht Treaty and written into the objectives of the European Structural Funds (see Room, 1995 and Duffy, 1995). Berghman (1995) comments that the Maastricht Treaty grew out of the following economic and social challenges within the European Union:

'Confronted with new social challenges, such as increased life expectancy, changes in the structure of the family, instability of the labour market and persistently high levels of unemployment, and being aware of possible social dislocations engendered by a more developed single market, the European Community was challenged to take a more active approach.' (Berghman, 1995, p12)

In the UK in August 1997 Peter Mandelson, then Minister without Portfolio, announced that there would be a campaign against social exclusion as a prominent plank in government policy. In December of the same year a new 'Social Exclusion Unit' was established in the Cabinet Office, reporting directly to the Prime Minister. The Prime Minister cited this as 'the defining difference between ourselves and the previous government' (Blair, 1997).

What is social exclusion?

Various studies (c.f. OECD, 1999; Atkinson & Hills, 1998 and Hayton, 1999) have noted the lack of consensus surrounding the definition of social exclusion. This has led authors such as Hodgson (1999) to conclude that the different perceptions of disaffection, non-participation and social exclusion often lead to 'different and potentially conflicting policy proposals for tackling them' (p11).

   With respect to notions of 'poverty' and 'social exclusion' it is useful to note the intellectual and political traditions from which the terms have developed. The term 'poverty' can be seen to originate primarily from British schools of thought dating back to the nineteenth century (e.g. Rowntree[1]). Conversely, the term 'social exclusion' emanates from continental social policy analysis. Thus, in France the term *l'exclusion sociale* has a comparatively long history (Hayton, 1999, p3). Social exclusion, rather than poverty, has been adopted as a term in Europe as some countries guarantee incomes that are deemed sufficient to meet basic needs. Definitions of social exclusion then link together a number of issues, such as material deprivation, the agency that individuals and groups have to affect changes in their lives and the social support or participation that they have. The UK Social Exclusion Unit uses the term in an attempt to recognise the impact of multiple disadvantages.

   'Social exclusion is a shorthand label for what can happen when individuals or areas suffer from a combination of linked problems, such as unemployment, poor skills, low incomes, poor housing, high crime environments, bad health and family breakdown.'
   (Social Exclusion Unit, 1998)

Graham Room provides a slightly more careful elaboration, however, contrasting poverty and social exclusion:

> 'The notion of poverty is primarily focused upon distributional issues: the lack of resources at the disposal of an individual or a household. In contrast, notions such as social exclusion focus primarily on relational issues, in other words, inadequate social participation, lack of social integration and lack of power.'
>
> (Room, 1995, p5)

> 'Where citizens are unable to secure their social rights, they will tend to suffer processes of generalised and persisting disadvantage and their social and occupational participation will be undermined.'
>
> (Ibid, p7)

The Organisation for Economic Co-operation and Development (OECD) also recognises the importance of social relations and 'social integration' in its definition of social exclusion:

> 'Exclusion involves a lack of social belonging and the absence of a sense of community. There are grounds for concern that lives are becoming more fragmented and less inclusive.'
>
> (OECD, 1999, p9)

Berghman (1995) notes the emphasis given by the European 'Poverty 3'[2] researchers to what they cited as two key aspects of social exclusion, these being its 'comprehensive' and 'dynamic' characteristics. And, from these, it is concluded that the term should be defined in relation to the following:

i). the democratic and legal system, which promotes civic integration;

ii). the labour market, which promotes economic integration;

iii). the welfare state system, promoting what may be called social integration;

iv). the community system, which promotes interpersonal integration.

Drawing on this schema the concept of social exclusion becomes sensitive to the denial or non-realisation of citizenship rights, or lack of access to the major institutions that give rise to these rights. This helps to take account of the multidimensional aspects of living conditions, which may be neglected by traditional or unsophisticated notions of poverty.

For Berghman, poverty then becomes '…part of - a specific form of – social exclusion. The latter is broader and should not necessarily always encompass an element of poverty' (ibid, p20). Where Room's conceptualisation of the distributional and relational elements of poverty and exclusion distinguishes their respective characteristic material and social components, Berghman does not rely upon this separation; instead poverty is more obviously a potential pre-condition of exclusion, and, by inference, could accompany or follow from it too. This, in turn, suggests the possibility of theorising causal links between them, yet retains a sense of contingency.

The elision, or at least, relegation of more familiar notions of penury from the concept of 'social exclusion' could be taken to imply that even the wealthy can experience some form of social exclusion, and, conversely, that one could live in abject poverty, yet be thoroughly included in – or by – society. But perhaps such logical objections merely obfuscate the fact that exclusion and poverty are most likely to be found together. Yet this would then seem to beg the question of why the terms should be separated in the first place. If, however, there is a degree of veracity in the OECD's view that communities can be 'materially poor but socially rich' (ibid, p 20) this question does not arise so readily.

Structural changes in the economy can be the cause of unemployment and poverty, but following the logic of social exclusion, these will affect individuals and groups with comparable economic circumstances differently. Mediating factors here will include, for example, the degree of cohesion in the affected community. Of equal, if not greater importance, are the means for democratic and political engagement (at community and national levels). These will reduce the impact of change and, where particularly well developed, the potential to influence its magnitude and tempo will increase. It may be that the comparatively strong communities and kin networks of some Southern European and Latin American countries contribute to lower rates of household unemployment, thus reducing the instances of social exclusion. In the UK, by contrast, traditional industries frequently provided community, as well as economic, infrastructure; hence the risk of social exclusion is greater.

Social exclusion may be viewed differently by governments, individuals, families and communities, and this will inevitably affect the formulation and implementation of policies aimed at prevention and/or remedy. Having given a brief overview of the concept of social exclusion, the following section examines the potentially ameliorative role of education and indicates issues and areas addressed in subsequent chapters.

The role of education in reducing social exclusion

'Educational policy has always had underlying social objectives, even though the focus of this social dimension has shifted' (Smith & Noble, 1995). In countries subscribing to the existence of social exclusion there is increasing recognition of the role that education may be able to play in creating routes from exclusion to inclusion.

> 'Learning is about opening access to economic activity and resources, and for promoting many aspects of social, cultural and personal life.'
> (OECD, 1999, p20)

In the UK the New Labour government sees education as a major tool for tackling social exclusion (Hayton, 1999, pvii) and within the member states of the European Union the educational sector has been targeted at all levels. Firstly, pre-school education has been a priority in some countries. The aim has been to provide access for all children to combat the effects of social disadvantage at an early, formative stage of development. Secondly, there has been an increase in the knowledge and range of skills developed through compulsory education. The trend has been towards delaying specialisation, and replacing this with basic skills (e.g. ICT) and broad knowledge areas. Thirdly, increasing participation in post-16 education, so that for the majority of young people the end of compulsory schooling does not mark the end of formal education and training. Fourthly, countries have tried to create positive opportunities for the 10 to 20 per cent of each age cohort who leave school with no or few formal qualifications. One instance of this is the UK government's 'New Deal' initiative, providing employment and training for the unemployed. Next, some countries have tried to overcome the divide between vocational education and training and general education, and develop more flexible pathways between them. Finally, states have focused on widening access to higher education, promoting lifelong learning and recognising learning through non-formal qualifications (such as APL and APEL).

Of course, education cannot address all the sources of social exclusion. But, if higher education and other forms of post-compulsory education and training are to play a role, they must be accessible to more than traditional élite students. Hodgson (1999) identifies a number of issues that have affected younger (under 25) and older learners, which have emerged during the last two decades in the UK.

Amongst younger learners the following issues are seen to be important:
- literacy and numeracy deficits and low levels of achievement at 16+ in relation to international competitors (Bynner & Parsons, 1997; Green & Steedman, 1997);
- polarisation of achievement with strongly differentiated performance for girls/boys, specific ethnic or socio-economic groups (Glennerster, 1998; Murphy & Elwood, 1997; Gillborn & Gipps, 1996);
- high school exclusion rates (Parsons & Castle, 1998);
- poor discipline at school (DES, 1989 – Elton report);
- disaffection with the current education and training system, particularly from 14+ (Dearing, 1996; Pearce & Hillman, 1998);
- persistent non-attendance at school (Education and Employment Committee, 1998);
- low levels of participation in post-16 education, particularly at 17 and 18+ (Green & Steedman, 1997; Pearce & Hillman, 1998).
(From Hodgson, 1999, p17)

Issues affecting older learners include:
- long-term unemployment, which in turn exacerbates the problem of securing future employment (OECD, 1996);
- basic skills deficits (Bynner & Parsons, 1997);
- negative attitudes towards participation in education and training (Kennedy, 1997);
- financial and other barriers preventing access to learning, e.g. childcare, transport etc (McGivney, 1993);
- differential economic rates of return from education (NCIHE, 1997).
(From Hodgson, 1999, p17)

In light of these difficulties, many of which are mirrored in other developed countries, there have been some efforts to recognise the connections between different policy areas, such as education, employment, housing, social security and health (see Howarth & Kenway, 1998; Mulgan, 1998 and Halpern, 1998). This is the 'joined up' thinking advocated by UK and European governmental neologians.

'Policies to address social exclusion involve, at least, access to employment that can be sustained, access to education, training and skills, changes in the housing sector, improved standards of living – including those locked outside the labour market – and an enhancement of social capital through improved social networks.' (Leney, 1999, p36)

An OECD report (1999) identifies three ways in which learning can help to counteract social exclusion: learning to meet basic needs, learning for labour market participation and learning to foster social action and participation. It is the latter two that higher education is potentially able to contribute to, but the former must not be ignored.

Basic skills

In most developed countries there are significant numbers of people who lack basic skills. For example, the Moser Report (1999) outlines the scale of literacy and numeracy basic skill deficits in the UK: it suggests that one in five adults aged over 19 have problems with literacy and numeracy. Basic skills, especially literacy, are crucial to learning, employment and social participation. At least minimal levels of literacy are required for everyday life, for example to gain information about housing, health, welfare, benefits and education. Improving literacy and basic skills is also likely to have a positive effect on self-confidence, and may contribute to greater community participation and activity.

Basic skills are a necessary first step towards closing the gap between the 'education-rich' and 'education-poor'. There is a real danger that social and educational exclusion will span generations (Machin, 1998). Gregg & Machin (1997) undertook analysis of data from the National Child Development Survey (NCDS), and found correlations between parental social and economic status, and that of their children, including educational achievement. Childhood disadvantage has a cumulative effect on educational achievement. Children with more educated parents, children with higher maths and reading ability at age seven and those in families that did not face financial difficulties in the years in which children grew up are more likely to have better school attendance and to continue in post-compulsory education. Furthermore, the impact of family financial difficulties is more influential than family structure. This is reflected in higher level educational attainment, which for the financially disadvantaged is considerably lower. Similarly, poorer people are heavily over-represented in the group of people that have no educational qualifications (Machin, 1998, p62). Similarly, Glennerster (1998) emphasises that, whatever the causal relationship, poverty and deprivation in children's families and the neighbourhood they grow up in tends to correlate with their school performance, and that there is a clear correlation between poor educational achievement and unemployment or low income.

To realise an inclusive higher education, institutions must provide flexible entry routes that acknowledge different life experiences and types of knowledge, taking account

of cumulative disadvantage. Furthermore, to ensure greater educational equality in the future, the appropriate providers must address poor basic skills of the adult population now, and compensate for disadvantage in pre-school and compulsory education. Simply providing a level playing field at point of entry will not overcome disadvantage and create a more inclusive higher education system.

Learning for employment

The Delors White Paper and the Flynn White Paper (European Commission 1993 and 1994) both envisage a key role for employment in combating social exclusion. Those seeking access to the labour market may, more than ever before, require specific and relevant training. If it is accepted that the labour market is undergoing almost unparalleled vicissitudes the role of post-compulsory education would appear to be assured (though what forms provision takes and precisely what is taught will remain contested). Succinctly, learning appears essential just to 'keep up', in order to avoid becoming excluded from both the labour market and wider society.

It is often argued that employers' apparently insatiable appetite for certificated learning has led to credentialism so that recruitment decisions are made on the basis of qualifications, which are taken as a proxy for relevant knowledge and skills. This has the effect of signalling to prospective job applicants that ever-higher levels of qualifications are a pre-requisite for employment.

'Credentials are increasingly necessary and decreasingly sufficient for successful labour market participation.'
(OECD, 1999, p22)

Higher education provides people with qualifications, and arguably skills, to access the labour market. Unemployment, especially involuntary unemployment undoubtedly contributes to social exclusion, but it must not be assumed that a return to work will necessarily foster social inclusion. The impact of employment is likely to depend on pay, job security and the intrinsic level of satisfaction.

In a culture of credentialism, graduation obviously increases employment prospects. Although graduates may experience some difficulty securing employment, in most countries, they are less likely to be unemployed than non-graduates (Teichler *et al*, 1988, p29). Furthermore, as Adnett & Coates (1999) note '...graduate status is one of the most important ways in which women can protect themselves against the negative labour market consequences of family formation in later life' (p13, see also Sommerland & Sanderson, 1997). Participation in education may also encourage a habit of lifelong learning. For example, those groups of people who are at the greatest risk of not participating in lifelong learning include those who left school with no qualifications. Participation in education can thus be viewed as a 'trigger', operating at a number of levels, to reduce social exclusion on an on-going basis.

It is, however, crucial to acknowledge the uneven nature of graduate recruitment. In the UK, for instance, research carried out by the Institute for Employment Research (1999) and published by the Council for Industry and Higher Education (CIHE) found 'extensive social class discrimination in graduate employment' (Taylor, 1999). George Taylor, the CIHE advisor on widening participation said 'the general message is that those from a socially disadvantaged environment are less likely to win through, even if their achievements are comparable with those from more traditional backgrounds'. Thus, although HE does facilitate labour market participation for some, the existence of credentialism and other forms of discrimination compromise its role in overcoming social exclusion. These effects may, at least in part, be reduced by the non-economic returns that accrue to participants.

Non-economic returns to participation in higher education

There is some recognition by the 'centre-left' governments in Europe that higher education can contribute to overcoming social exclusion in ways other than simply enhancing labour market participation. For example, the UK Green Paper on lifelong learning in England, *The Learning Age* (DfEE, 1998), acknowledged the value of education for its contribution to the economy, and 'for its own sake'. Here, learning is said to contribute to the social cohesion of communities and foster 'a sense of belonging, responsibility and identity', thus contributing to a more inclusive society. Such views often articulate with the idea of 'social capital', the development of which is said to be important for overcoming social exclusion and disadvantage. This term is used to signify the extent to which people have access to networks, their levels of political and civic engagement and membership of associations. It can be argued that, at least to some extent, those most vulnerable to exclusion are increasingly less able to call upon networks that yield some form of support.

'Measures to combat exclusion should be broadened still further beyond economic activity to include a greater array of social activities related to citizenship, voluntary action and culture. This is not as an alternative to employment but because

inclusion takes many forms. Successful participation in different social, community and cultural activities can also prove an effective bridge in building the skills, confidence and social capital that lead to labour market participation. Adult learning offers both preparation for such social participation and an element of it since education is a form of social inclusion itself.'
(OECD, 1999, p23)

Like 'social exclusion', the idea of 'social capital' can be seen to accommodate a range of meanings, some of which are at variance with others. Preece (1999) argues that disadvantaged people have access to networks and support, but that these are not recognised or acknowledged by dominant groups. Putnam *et al* (1993) also view social capital as a normative concept, but argue that not all social networks are productive. Conversely, Coleman (1988) believes that it is 'context-specific', and what functions as social capital in one situation may not work in another. Gamarnikow & Green (1999) recognise the tensions between different conceptualisations of the term, and identify a 'continuum of social capital manifestations'.

'At one end of the continuum, social capital embraces progressive, liberal and civic notions of co-operation, empowerment, participation and community action in the construction of needs and priorities... At the other extreme social capital may be realised in a normative order of traditional institutional forms, for instance, favouring two-parent nuclear families; locating the 'parenting deficit' in women's increased labour market activity; and arguing for a collective non-relativist moral regime of duties and responsibilities to which all are expected to conform, particularly those least well placed in the system... At this end of the continuum traditional forms of power relations, although invisible in the accounts, appear to form an essential feature of social capital, rendering citizenship ambiguous in relation to subjecthood.'
(Gamarnikow & Green, 1999, p49-50)

There is a danger that the process of widening participation in higher education is not about allowing people to develop the former liberal, empowering conceptualisation of social capital, but is more about covertly 'normalising' people, that is encouraging conformity with traditional, white, male and patriarchal, middle-class values.

In the UK and much of Europe 'Third Way' or middle way politics have employed the notion of social capital in attempts to overcome social exclusion. This has a rather eclectic view of society and utilises the rhetoric of 'stakeholders', 'partnership' and 'civic patriots', etc. The aim of policy interventions, including education and learning strategies, is to foster 'responsible families, thriving communities, strong norms, values and sanctions, dense social networks and social engagement' (Gamarnikow & Green, 1999, p51). But, regardless of the desirability of such objectives (e.g. what *kind* of family is acceptable? Whose norms are they anyway?), there is the serious question of whether policies formulated on the basis of a compensatory model are the most appropriate way to address issues, the origins of which lie beyond particular communities and locales. Hence Gamarnikow and Green note:

> 'Third Way' discourse, while trumpeting the oxymoronic rhetoric of 'excellence for everyone', may well be shifting us back to a deficit approach to educational underachievement.'
>
> (Gamarnikow & Green, 1999, p60)

If higher education is to provide routes out of social exclusion by aiding the acquisition of social capital, it must develop (through acceptable forms of research) and convey (via teaching and publishing) the ideas located at the former end of Garmarnikow and Green's continuum. Access researchers and practitioners will, of course, need to continue engaging with vocationality, academic élitism and apathy if the higher education sector is to become inclusive and contribute to an inclusive wider culture.

Some challenges facing higher education

Among the challenges faced by the higher education sector are the following:
- How do we ensure equality (taking into account earlier and intergenerational disadvantage), rather than equal opportunities at the point of entry?
- How can government policy promote wider participation?
- How can funding mechanisms support equality, and not continue to reinforce the position of the better off?
- How can the tension between access and standards be resolved?
- How can institutions alter their structures and systems to encourage and support diversity?
- Are the curriculum contents relevant to students from different backgrounds and for a range of purposes?
- What distinctions, if any, should be drawn between academic and vocational education?

- Are teaching and assessment styles appropriate, and what is the role of new technology?
- How can traditional attitudes be challenged and changed, both within institutions and beyond?

This book cannot provide simple, prescriptive answers to all of these issues – nothing can. But by drawing on international experiences of policymakers, practitioners and researchers, solutions and strategies are suggested.

References

Adnett, N. and Coates, G. (1999) 'Mature female entrants to higher education: matching theory, empirical analysis and policy', paper presented at *Access, the Changing Face of Further and Higher Education and Lifelong Learning*, Staffordshire University, April 1999.

Atkinson, A.B and Hills, J. (eds) (1998) *Exclusion, Employment and Opportunity*. CASEpaper 4. London, Centre for Analysis of Social Exclusion, London School of Economics.

Berghman, J. (1995) 'Social Exclusion in Europe: policy context and analytical framework' in Room, G (ed) *Beyond the Threshold: the measurement and analysis of social exclusion*. Bristol, The Policy Press.

Blair, A. (1997) *The Observer*, 23rd November 1997.

Bynner, J. and Parsons, S. (1997) *It Doesn't Get Any Better: The impact of poor basic skills on the lives of 37-year olds*. London, Basic Skills Agency.

Coleman, J.S. (1988) 'Social capital in the creation of human capital' in *American Journal of Sociology*, 94 (Suppl. 95), S95-S120.

Dearing, R. (1996) *Review of Qualifications for 16-19 year-olds: Full report*. London, School Curriculum and Assessment Authority.

DfEE (1998) *The Learning Age: A renaissance for a new Britain*. Cm 3790, London, Department for Education and Employment.

DES (1989) *Discipline in Schools* (Elton Report). London, HMSO.

Duffy, K. (1995) *Social exclusion and human dignity in Europe*. Strasbourg, Council for Europe.

Education and Employment Committee (1998) *Disaffected Children*, vol 1: Report and Proceedings of the Committee Department for Education and Employment. London, Stationery Office.

European Commission (1993) *Growth, competitiveness, employment - the challenges and ways forward in the 21ˢᵗ Century*, Bulletin of the European Communities, Supplement 6/93, Brussels.

European Commission (1994) *European social policy - the way forward for the Union*, COM(94)333, Brussels.

Gamarnikow, E. and Green, A. (1999) 'Developing social capital: dilemmas, possibilities and limitations in education' in Hayton, A. (ed) *Tackling Disaffection and Social Exclusion: Education perspectives and policies.* London, Kogan Page Ltd.

Gillborn, D. and Gipps, C. (1996) *Recent Research on the Achievements of Ethnic Minority Pupils.* London, Ofsted.

Glennerster H. (1998) 'Tackling poverty at its roots? Education' in Oppenheim, C. (ed) *An Inclusive Society: strategies for tackling poverty.* London, Institute for Public Policy Research.

Green, A. and Steedman, H. (1997) *Into the Twenty-first Century: An assessment of British skills, profiles and prospects.* London, Centre for Economic Performance.

Gregg, P. and Machin, S. (1997) 'Childhood disadvantage and success of failure in the youth labour market', mimeo.

Halpern, D. (1998) 'Poverty, social exclusion and the policy-making process: the road from theory to practice', in Oppenheim, C. (ed) *An Inclusive Society: strategies for tackling poverty.* London, Institute for Public Policy Research.

Hayton, A. (ed) (1999) *Tackling Disaffection and Social Exclusion: Education perspectives and policies.* London, Kogan Page Ltd.

Hodgson, A. (1999) 'Analysing education and training policies for tackling social exclusion' in Hayton, A. (ed) *Tackling Disaffection and Social Exclusion: Education perspectives and policies.* London, Kogan Page Ltd.

Howarth, C. and Kenway, P. (1998) 'A multi-dimensional approach to social exclusion indicators, Oppenheim, C. (ed) *An Inclusive Society: strategies for tackling poverty.* London, Institute for Public Policy Research.

Institute for Employment Research (1999) *Graduate Opportunities, Social Class and Age – Employers' Recruitment Strategies in the new Graduate Labour Market.* London, Council for Industry and Higher Education.

Kennedy, H. (1997) *Learning Works: Widening participation in further education.* Coventry, FEFC.

Leney, T. (1999) 'European approaches to social exclusion' in Hayton, A. (ed) *Tackling Disaffection and Social Exclusion: Education perspectives and policies.* London, Kogan Page Ltd.

20

Machin, S. (1998) 'Childhood disadvantages and intergenerational transmissions of economic status' in Atkinson, A.B and Hills, J. (eds) *Exclusion, Employment and Opportunity*. CASEpaper 4. London, Centre for Analysis of Social Exclusion, London School of Economics.

McGivney, V. (1993) 'Participation and non-participation: a review of the literature', in Edwards, R., Sieminski, S. and Zeldin, D. (eds) *Adult Learners, Education and Training*. London, Routledge.

Moser, Sir C. (1999) *Improving Literacy and Numeracy: A fresh start*. London, Crown Copyright.

Mulgan, G. (1998) 'Social exclusion: joined up solutions to joined up problems' in Oppenheim, C. (ed) *An Inclusive Society: strategies for tackling poverty*. London, Institute for Public Policy Research.

Murphy, P. and Elwood, J, (1997) 'Gendered experiences, choices and achievement – exploring the links', in *International Journal of Inclusive Education* 1998: 2, 95-118.

National Committee of Inquiry into Higher Education (NCIHE) (1997) *Higher Education in the Learning Society*. London, NCIHE.

OECD (1999) *Overcoming Exclusion Through Adult Learning*. Paris, OECD.

OECD (1996) *Lifelong Learning for All*. London, OECD.

Parsons, C. and Castle, F. (1998) 'Trends in exclusions from school – New Labour, new approaches', in *Forum for Promoting 3-19 Comprehensive Education*, 40 (1), Spring 1998.

Pearce, N. and Hillman, J. (1998) *Wasted Youth: Raising achievement and tackling social exclusion*. London, Institute for Public Policy Research.

Preece, J (1999) 'Difference and the Discourse of Inclusion' in *Widening Participation and Lifelong Learning*, 1 (2):16-23.

Putnam, R.D. with Leonardi, R. and Nanetti, R. (1993) *Making Democracy Work: Civic traditions in modern Italy*. Princeton, New Jersey, Princeton University.

Room, G. (1995) 'Poverty and social exclusion: the new European agenda for policy and research' in Room, G (ed) *Beyond the Threshold: the measurement and analysis of social exclusion*. Bristol, The Policy Press.

Smith, T. and Noble, M. (1995) *Education Divides: Poverty and schooling in the 1990s*. London: Child Poverty Action Group.

Social Exclusion Unit (1998) *Truancy and Social Exclusion*. London, The Stationery Office.

Sommerland, H. and Sanderson, P. (1997) 'The legal labour market and the training needs of women returners in the UK', in *Journal of Vocational Education and Training*, 49 (1): 45-64.

Taylor, G. (1999) 'Graduate recruitment and social class' in *Update on Inclusion*, Autumn 1999: 15-16.

Teichler, U., Hartung, D. and Nuthmann, R. (1988) *Higher Education and the Needs of Society*. (Translated by Vernon Ward). NFER.

Note

[1] In the 1970s and 1980s the concept of poverty was developed and used extensively in the work of Peter Townsend, greatly adding to the debate about disadvantage in the UK.

[2] Poverty 3 = the Third European Poverty Programme

Part Two

Higher Education and Social Inclusion

3. Equality, change and institutional barriers

Patricia Callaghan

Introduction

Achieving an 'inclusive higher education' system through changing the culture of the campus demands knowledge of the processes and problems of educational change as well as the differences in equality theories. Institutional processes are rooted in tradition and many of us who are pushing for change are divorced from the decision-making processes at executive and national level. Dealing with change is endemic to post-modern society and the fact that most educational structures and systems are fundamentally conservative is why so little real change has taken place.

If we assess the structures at the top of the hierarchy, we will find that there has been little if any change in their makeup for many years. The way in which teachers are trained, or not trained, as the case may be, the predominance of full-time courses, front-end admission policies, uniform starting times, funding arrangements for fees and student maintenance as well as the caste-system of the academic community itself (PhD – degree – certificate – second and primary level) – create a mindset that augurs poorly for any fundamental change taking root in the established higher education institutions.

No amount of strategizing for change will work if we are unable to achieve a mindset for change at all levels of the community – national and international – a mindset that sees the university as a learning community with a moral as well as an economic and social purpose. Productive change should be able to reconcile two important and equally legitimate goals in the context of higher education – namely, the achievement of equal educational opportunities for all and the preservation of academic standards along with the integrity of academic programmes.

Equality perspectives

The achievement of an inclusive higher education environment is premised as much on our working understanding of 'equality', as its application and relation to policy. Equality has various layers of meaning and interpretations, which derive as much from the different stages in which societies are on the continuum of human rights, as from the historical baggage which a society shoulders. There are at least three layers of meaning that can be ascribed to the moral and legal concept of equality. [1] They are 'Formal Equality', 'Equality of Opportunity' and 'Equality of Results'.

The first layer of equality is known as **Formal Equality** also referred to as '**Blind or pure equality'**. In its simplest form it entails a bald proscription against discrimination on stipulated grounds such as race, gender, age and disability (Quinn, 1994). It requires that all those who are similarly situated be treated alike. But because no two individuals are the same, reliance on formal equality is highly inappropriate in certain areas such as, for example, disability where the difference is real. The substantive issue is not so much the 'difference' *per se*, but the existence of a privileged norm which benchmarks issues of equality.

The second layer of meaning is that of **Equality of Opportunity** which requires a form of affirmative action or positive discrimination to make a real difference in the lives of people. In recent times, especially in the USA, affirmative action policies have been under attack where 'benign racism' is cited as a fall-out of equality of opportunity policies. Indeed 'benign racism' is an end result of equal opportunities for all, if measures are not taken to ensure that strategic action is targeted at both changing the culture and reducing discrimination simultaneously. Policies must evolve and adapt to reflect changing times. All policies, whether rooted in equality or not, must be transitional, especially as the scale of complexity accelerates in post-modern society.

In an article in *The Times Higher Education Supplement*, June 18, 1999, Martin Trow argues against 'positive discrimination' policies on two grounds, both of which have been well aired over the last decade. It is morally indefensible, he claims, to discriminate among citizens on the basis of their race or ethnicity, and incompatible with the norms of a democratic society. He continues to argue that it puts the achievements of all members of the 'preferenced' groups under suspicion even when they have not been recipients of any positive discrimination. What is important about this argument is the underlying mindset that equal opportunity policies themselves are the cause of the exclusion of other groups, and not the attitudes and the narrow focus on social justice that drives their implementation.

Martin Trow is not alone in this debate, as criticism, especially in the USA, against equal opportunities has been raging for some time now. In the higher education context, the main thrust of the argument is based on a closed interpretation of the concepts of merit, just desserts and fairness, as well as that of 'proportional representation'. In the USA there is a general belief that the stigma associated with 'proportional representation' could fuel, rather than debunk, stereotypical thinking and prejudiced attitudes. Other downsides of affirmative action measures at admissions level, for example, is the fear that it yields nothing more than tokenism – that is, once the requisite places have been filled the social responsibility has been met. All institutions should pay attention to the US experience, and avoid this kind of entrenchment of policy. We must be aware why affirmative action fails. Firstly, affirmative action will fail when it is seen as a policy end in itself, rather than a tool for policy development; and secondly, when 'deficiencies' are located within the individual rather than with the whole system, including its external and internal environments and policies. Finally, when affirmative action translates into 'special' initiatives, such as separate courses and certification, it will also fail. Marginal initiatives, regardless of how well they meet the immediate need of the recipients, will not change the environment and culture in education where discrimination exists.

The idea of preferential treatment based on ethnicity or race is repellent to many conservatives and liberals alike, but the case for preferential treatment based on class is now considered more acceptable. Class-based affirmative action, it is argued, could help defuse white racism, and would restore the principle of treating applicants as individuals and not as members of an ethnic group. However, there is a real possibility of past patterns and trends repeating themselves with regard to class-based affirmative action. Despite the arguments against 'affirmative action' we must not forget why they are in place and that this concept of equality is driven by the social goal of ensuring real participation in social and economic life by those who, through no fault of their own, have been excluded.

The third and final layer of meaning is known as **Equality of Results**, sometimes referred to as substantive or egalitarian equality. Equality of results is centred on the notion of equalising end results regardless of a person's ability to perform socially, politically, culturally or economically. Emanating from this meaning are such socio-economic rights as equality of access to health, education, employment and so forth. It is not surprising that this conceptualisation of equality has been the least advanced in our modern societies as it goes against the grain of market values and economic rights.

The meaning then of 'equality' in terms of how our laws and policies operate will dictate the quality of one's life and education experience. Any targeted positive action should be set in the broad context of strategic action both to change the culture of higher education and to reduce discrimination. Society does not necessarily owe a higher education to all, but because places are scarce social goods, there is an obligation to treat all citizens as equal (as opposed to equally) with respect to the distribution of higher education. The 'managing diversity agenda' is closely related in principle to the notion of 'Equality of Results' where the emphasis is on creating the conditions whereby people are enabled to participate in education to their full potential.

Equality and change

On the one hand we depend on an open interpretation of equality, as well as transitional policies, to correct an injustice at a particular stage of a higher education's history. On the other hand, we cannot legislate for change, change cannot come about by proclaiming new policies, or by new performance standards. Instead we have to engage in an elaborate dance of nurturing ownership of progress and chipping away at the walls of resistance.

Michael Fullan, Dean of the Ontario Institute for Studies in Education, who has done considerable work around the issue of change in the education context, remarked that:

> 'most changes, even the big restructuring ones, have a pacifier effect because they give the appearance that something substantial is happening when it is not.'
> (Fullan, 1993)

He also argues that despite countless efforts at change, they have failed because they do not impact on the culture of the establishment and the teaching profession. If we consider for a moment the amount of energy, commitment, hassle, and work, as well as the number of pilot projects, the number of bureaucratic hoops, the begging and grovelling that those of us working in this field have experienced, and match this with the level of change achieved, we must be inclined to agree with Fullan's *pacifier* theory.

Furthermore, traditional entry qualifications for access to higher education and approved parallel qualifying routes for adults are both still directed in the main to intensive preparation for full-time forms of undergraduate studies. It is amazing that it was possible for growth in higher education to be absorbed without fundamental change in the internal structures and processes of higher education. In an era of postmodernism, the diversity achieved in society is not matched by diversity in higher education where teaching styles and curricula are still firmly rooted in the élite tradition of higher education. The striking thing about higher education reform is the fact that real educational reform happens outside the sector at the local and community level. Higher education has followed, rather than led, the achievement of 'mass' level participation; it has been a passive rather than an active agent of change. We must strive towards the development of a unified system which eliminates the élite divide between non-traditional and traditional access routes.

Institutional barriers to change

In a post-modern society all citizens must learn to cope with change on a continuous basis, and one would expect that higher education would play a pivotal role in enabling this process of coping. Many of us have attended workshops and conferences on diversity and equal opportunities in higher education, and in the majority of instances it has been extremely difficult to transfer the knowledge and skills into practice in our own institutions. This is because there are major difficulties at institutional level and these include:

- ingrained patterns of institutional discrimination;
- educational culture swamped with technological changes and the demands of industry;
- Quality Assurance and the funding crisis; pressures on colleges to reach research targets, etc – equal opportunities too often are forced into second place;
- competition between academic excellence and the academic integrity of programmes and so-called 'soft' social justice issues;
- absence of collaborative work structures both internally and externally;
- isolationist tradition of teaching;
- the distrust between academics and senior administrators;
- unwillingness to synthesise the polar opposites of standards and access, unless it suits; for example higher education institutions are more than willing to synthesise opposites when there is a weak response for specific courses e.g. note the increase in foundation courses in engineering and technology disciplines in response to the weakness in demand for science-based and mathematics-based subjects. The decline in the number of students taking science and technology-based subjects at 2nd level has prompted higher education institutions to widen entry on the basis of vocational and non-standard qualifications;
- the lack of central support, recognition, and follow through of access initiatives and policies;

27

- unavailability of resources, and flexible working conditions;
- the pressure of too many competing demands and work overload, and
- staff development remains largely dissociated from learning.

Those of us who are advocating change rely on legislation and demand more resources and accountability, while those who resist change retreat into traditionalist arguments about diminishing standards and academic excellence.

For change to happen it requires top-down and bottom -up strategies. The idea of ownership of change is not new, it gained currency, for example, in community and women's education. Ownership is necessary and can only happen through the learning that arises from full engagement and recognition that you are part of a bigger on-going process. Professional ownership of developmental change is crucial. Many of us will recognise the mixed feelings of anger and pleasure when we hear our ideals and aspirations for which we shed blood, sweat and tears being reproduced as new and unique in the university provost's address at a promotional event. However, we cannot claim a right to equality issues and we must share, even relinquish, ownership of them.

Decision-makers can make organisational and curriculum change, but will not necessarily make progress without an inclusive institutional approach. The caste-system, which is a traditional feature of higher education, has left us with a huge negative legacy of failed reform. There has been a sea of pilot projects that have focused on difference, access and flexibility, and these initial projects that have produced visible concrete results should sustain the restructuring process. However, because of the absence of long-term funding and the half-hearted involvement of the academic community, the learning is shelved and the institutions retreat into the traditional safe methods of instruction and policy.

When we consider that the expansion and democratisation of the higher education has involved no alteration to the normal minimum requirements for entry to undergraduate education, at least as applied to young people, we would be correct to question the legitimacy of the lifelong learning agenda. Academic, meritocratic principles rather than affirmative actions have characterised the conduct of admissions in the majority of our higher education establishments. Alternative styles of certification for access is mainly for adults, while traditional qualifications are still the principal access route available to young people.

A study carried out by Conor, Pearson, Court and Jagger in 1996 bodes badly for the development of an inclusive higher education sector. The report presents a topology

Figure 1: A topology of universities and their future recruitment strategies

> (i) **The traditional élite:** a small number of universities, currently the more **prestigious ones,** which have hardly changed at all in the last five years as they have expanded in size. They are still recruiting mainly young 'A' level or higher students straight from school from a wide geographical catchment area.
> They expect to continue in the future to be able to do so without lowering their current academic standards, or making significant internal changes. They have little vocational orientation (outside the professional areas of medicine, law, etc.). Future growth is more likely to be at postgraduate level, in professional development and especially research.
>
> (ii) **The quasi-old:** a much larger number of universities which have traditionally recruited school leavers. They are struggling to compete with group (i) in this market, but have not initiated sufficient change to attract/admit sufficiently large numbers of new types of students, nor do they want to change the balance much in this direction.
> Their market is becoming more regionally based. They are developing more vocationalism in undergraduate study, and more flexibility in the curriculum and delivery of learning (e.g. modularity, CATS), but are facing internal tensions between traditional cultures and values and newer development which may be slowing the pace of change. They are less clear about their strategic direction and identity than group (i).
>
> (iii) **The quasi-new:** these former polytechnics and colleges have traditionally had a mixed student population and local focus but are trying to shed this in order to raise their image, both nationally and academically (improve standards).
> They are trying to emulate some of the older universities in their desired student profile, in particular their entry standards. At the same time, they are developing many of the new kinds of provision to continue to attract non-conventional students, their traditional base. The wisdom of this dual strategy is being questioned, and like group (ii) there is **lack of clarity** about future direction.
>
> (iv) **The real new:** these were the most innovative of the universities, at the opposite end of the spectrum to group (i). They are broadening their profile further from a wide base. They are strengthening local identities and links, moving further towards vocationalism, developing more access arrangements and a flexible range of delivery mechanisms. Their focus in the future is likely to be on teaching at various levels and modes.

(Source: *Qualifying for a Changing Higher Education*: Report on a Seminar held on 21st November 1995, prepared by Dr. Gareth Parry, University of Surrey)

of universities and their recruitment strategies of the future. This topology is worth looking at in some detail. While its subject is the UK, it is, with the exception of the local differences, applicable to higher education in the developed world. The report divides the higher education sector into four main categories: the traditional élite; the quasi-old; the quasi-new and the real-new. This is shown in Figure 1.

This type of topology of higher education is taking root and the most interesting feature is the hierarchical divide between traditional and non-traditional students as well as traditional and non-traditional higher education institutions. The mindset of (ii) and (iii) is overly subservient to the past and over-awed by tradition. They are afraid of the challenges of change. Type (iv), the real new, is the antithesis of type (i) and the teaching/research function copper-fastens the élite divide. One could argue that change in this context is the creation of something new, in opposition to, rather than in harmony with, the old.

Finally, to change the campus culture we must debunk some of the myths and re-think some of the rhetoric accumulated around the supposed inevitable sweep towards a 'learning community' for all. We are regularly informed that dramatic alteration in the student profile and student expectations will force traditional establishments to change. We are reminded that with increasing modularisation and the implementation of Credit Accumulation and Transfer Schemes (CATS) we can envisage a future where students will do most of their learning through an association with a different number of higher education institutions accessing resources from a distance over the Internet or other forms of information superhighways. We are also regularly informed that institutions of higher education that are rooted in the élite tradition with their cumbersome admissions structures and traditional academic programmes and structures will be left behind as (prospective) students will steer towards the more progressive and flexible higher education institutions. It is also widely believed that modularisation of curricula and credit systems will enhance access, extend choice and increase mobility for individuals in a lifelong learning system of higher education.

However, the above topology doesn't support the sentiment that the traditional establishment is facing imminent demise. The system still operates predominately in the context of front-end admissions where a great majority of students start at the same point in the system and exit at a fixed point. The Dearing Report (NCIHE, 1997) confirms this preference for traditional qualifications.

If this preference persists changing the campus culture will be a long, slow process as the élite qualifications continue to survive and dominate even in a context of more open and flexible forms of participation. The notion that higher education will always be provided on a physically identifiable campus to homogeneous groups of students is increasingly untenable as a vision of the future, yet reports of the impending death of the established structures are greatly exaggerated. Changing the campus culture requires not only restructuring, but also a massive shift in the established attitudes and mindset to bring about new habits, skills, norms, attitudes and values in higher education.

Conclusions

Our efforts to bring about change are complicated and stunted by the minimalist requirements of the law, and the inactive role of government agencies, as well as higher education's narrow focus on equality and social justice. This peripheral passive role and closed thinking has resulted in a patchy and incremental approach to the implementation of equal opportunities in most Western societies, as well as preserving the dominance of traditional élite education structures in our rapidly changing post-modern global society. In conclusion, we must recognise and resist the 'pacifier' effects of change as well as the promotional sound-bites of senior educational personnel of achieving equity and pluralism in our higher education systems. In a historical and philosophical sense *change* was understood as a new stage of coherent development (c.f. Marx, Hegel, Vico). Unfortunately, this meaning does not have resonance in the higher education context where change means the outside pushing in and the establishment shifting a little to the right or the left and making minor concessions while believing it has made a quantum leap.

References

Ahier, J., Cosin, B. and Hales, M. (eds) (1996) *Diversity and Change: Education, Policy and Selection.* London and New York, Routledge.

Conor, Pearson, Court and Jagger (1996) *University Challenge: Student Choices in the 21ˢᵗ Century, Report 306.* Brighton, Institute for Employment Studies.

Coolahan, J. (ed) (1994) *Report on the National Education convention.* Dublin, Government Publications.

Dearing, R. (1997) *Higher Education in the Learning Society.* London, National Committee of Inquiry into Higher Education.

Fullan, M.G. (1991) *The New Meaning of Educational Change.* London, Cassell Educational.

Fullan, M.G. (1993) *Change Forces: Probing the Depths of Educational Reform.* London, Falmer Press.

Gutmann, A.(1996) *Democratic Education.* New Jersey, Princeton University Press.

Lucas, C. J. (1996) *Crisis in the Academy: Rethinking Higher Education in America.* London, MacMillan.

Lynch, K. and O'Rriordan, C. (1996) *Social Class, Inequality and Higher Education.* HEA.

Mulcahy, D. G. and O'Sullivan, D. (eds) (1989) *Irish Educational Policy: Process and Substance.* Dublin, IPA.

OECD (1987)*Adults in Higher Education.* Paris, OECD Centre for Educational Research and Innovation.

Parry. G. (1996) *Qualifying for a Changing Higher Education: Report on a Seminar held on 21st November 1995.* University of Surrey.

Quinn, G. (1994) *Human Rights and Disability* paper presented at AHEAD Access Conference, Dublin.

Tight, M. (1996) *Key Concepts in Adult Education and Training.* London and New York, Routledge.

Trow, M. *The Times Higher Eduction Supplement,* June 18, 1999.

Notes

[1] For a more expansive interpretation of the layers of equality as it applies in particular to disability and human rights issues, please consult the work of Dr. Gerard Quinn, University College Galway, Ireland.

4. New resourcing strategies for an inclusive higher education

George Papadopoulos

Introduction

Despite the expansion of higher education in Europe, it has largely failed to significantly change the inequitable distribution of opportunities among social groups. In this chapter it is therefore argued that new solutions are required, and attention should be directed to the inadequate basic educational preparation of disadvantaged children and young people. This entails a massive shift of resources to combat school failure and to provide a variety of progression routes to both tertiary education and the labour market, and this must be supported by lifelong learning opportunities. Without such changes, there is a danger that lifelong learning policies may, in practice, actually exacerbate existing inequalities.

The problem

Counteracting social exclusion to create an inclusive higher education is a complex and many-faceted problem. One central issue however can be identified: primarily the persisting inequalities among different socio-economic groups in their share of higher education opportunities. Socio-economic groups themselves are greatly diversified, and this vastly compounds the problem. It is however only by prioritising the needs of lower socio-economic groups that equality will be achieved. A concern of governments, and also higher education systems and their constituent institutions is the extent that higher education is inclusive, as this is a strong antidote to social exclusion. In this resides the real meaning of the 'democratisation' of higher education – opening up the opportunities of higher education to all, not simply the élite.

Past failure to democratise higher education

Despite the moral and economic arguments for the democratisation of higher education, governments have so far largely failed to achieve this goal. In the halcyon days of equity *consensus* in the 1960s and early 1970s the massive growth of higher education coincided with the virtuous circle of economic growth and social consensus. Consequently a twofold response was witnessed. Firstly, the expansion and diversification of higher education. This included the development of new institutions, more diversified provision and delivery systems (e.g. the binary system and the Open University in the UK) and more flexible access procedures (e.g. U.S. Open Access and access for adults in Sweden). Secondly, the development of student financial support schemes, which were ostensibly socially directed.

These changes resulted in some progress being achieved, but this was limited. There was recognition and definition of regional disparities with regard to access to higher education, and this influenced the development and location of new institutions, such as the opening of Regional Colleges in Norway. Significant inroads were made with regard to gender inequality, although there are some remaining problems, such as female participation in particular subjects. However, no significant improvements were made in reducing socio-economic related disparities. There was an increase in participation by students from all social classes, but the gap between social classes remained fairly constant. For example, participation by the lower socio-economic groups is around 8% in most European countries and 25% in the U.S.A. There has been some progress with respect to social class in the 1990s, but the improvement is in no way dramatic or sufficient.

There are three inter-related reasons for the lack of progress that can be identified. Firstly the 'power of academic drift' that has sustained élitist values, best exemplified by the disappearance of the binary system, which has helped to exclude students from lower socio-economic groups. Secondly, the hijacking of student financing schemes by the middle-classes. But by far the most important issue is deep-rooted educational disadvantage, which is strongly linked to social disadvantage. This affects pupils throughout the education system, from the initial level of education onwards, with on-going cumulative effects. Thus, remedial measures to expand participation in higher education will only ever be of limited success at this stage.

The present context: an evaluation of past failures

Current participation in higher education reflects the past failures of the system. This is primarily caused by the dilution of the concept of higher education as a public service, which is largely publicly financed. In many European countries (e.g. UK and Germany) recently there has been a growth in private institutions offering higher education. Often these new establishments are profit-making, and therefore at odds with the notion of higher education as a public good to benefit society. Furthermore there have been substantial changes in the funding systems of higher education. Principally, this has involved shifting part of the costs of education to individuals through fees and loans. This has allowed a rise in the numbers of students participating in HE as there has been a reduction of per student public cost. The concept of the 'child in the family' has disappeared, and has been replaced by the 'individual investment' approach to the financing of higher education studies. There is a paradox between rich countries where the latter appraisal is becoming relevant and poorer ones where the former still prevails despite the lower levels of GNP available for distribution on public services.

These two changes both reflect and are reinforced by neo-liberal notions of 'economy' and 'efficiency', which favour market solutions to issues of planning and distribution. Consequently, higher education institutions are transformed into 'businesses', and this results in a new polarisation of higher education systems. There is a highly selective and well-resourced sector that caters for the élite; and a more open, but under-resourced sector for the masses. For example, this differentiation can be seen in the 'Californian model': the top 12% of students go to the University of California, 30% study at State Universities and the rest graduate through community colleges (c.f. Brint and Karabel, 1989; Dougherty, 1987; and Rouse, 1995).

In light of these observations it is not surprising to note that notions of 'equity consensus' are in decline, and there has been a halt in the policy discourses and associated research directed towards educational equality. For example, one can contrast the prominent place that educational disparities occupied in the 1970 OECD 'Review of Educational Growth' with the total absence of these concerns in the current 'Education at a Glance' annual publication of the organisation.

What strategies?

In order to start addressing the question 'what strategies are required to overcome inequitable participation in post-compulsory education by lower socio-economic groups', we should bear in mind the following three incontestable realities:
a) educational disadvantage is strongly rooted in socio-economic disadvantage;
b) those who benefit from post-compulsory education, in whatever setting, are those who are already well-educated;
c) funding from the public purse, however modest, remains crucial.

Equalisation policies are instrumental to change, but they must be conceived within a coherent longer-term strategic objective, the framework for which is now provided by the emergence of the concept of lifelong learning. Remedial measures, such as discriminatory student support schemes, incentives for higher education institutions in terms of rewards for accepting students from lower socio-economic groups, facilitating adult and non-traditional qualification-based awards, although useful, will only have a marginal impact, and will not significantly alter patterns of participation in further and higher education.

Radical conclusions must be reached. Higher education must be considered as an organic part of the total education system, with a corresponding need of a downwards shift, refocusing resources to attack the problem at its roots, namely: combating failure at school and improving post-school pathways to further and higher education and/or work.

Basic educational preparation

Positive discrimination measures are required to bring all pupils, irrespective of class or family background, to the same starting point at the end of compulsory schooling. These strategies should also seek to imbue in pupils both a capacity and an interest in learning to learn. Basic educational improvements would include extending pre-school provision, improving curricula relevance, creating individualised pedagogies, and implementing new classroom and school organisation. It must be recognised that high quality basic education for all cannot be had on the cheap, and therefore this will require significant financial support from governments.

Improving pathways

There is a crucial role for upper secondary schools to play in the social retention process, to facilitate more pupils from lower socio-economic classes to continue pursuing education and learning. In many countries there is a dichotomy between academic education versus vocational education and training, that effectively excludes pupils who pursue the latter from subsequently accessing further educational opportunities. This is best illustrated by the Germanic Dual System, which provides different academic and vocational pathways, one leading to higher education the other to employment.

In many countries there is a need to develop 'double-qualifying pathways', to facilitate access to higher education from vocational education streams, either immediately or subsequently after work experience. Indeed, there are currently pilot projects and experimentation taking place in Austria, Finland, Sweden, Netherlands and the UK. For example, the UK has seen the introduction of Advanced General National Vocational Qualifications (AGNVQ) for post-16 students. These are qualifications with a vocational emphasis, but they have a dual orientation, and can provide a pathway into higher education. In the Netherlands a similar approach has been developed, which is designed to facilitate transition to higher education of students from Senior Vocational Education (MBO). A related, but alternative approach has been introduced in Sweden through the 'adultification' of higher education, which, in essence, involves the verification of work experience as certified entry qualifications.

New admissions procedures and courses for higher education
The changes will have implications for admission procedures and criteria that are utilised by higher education institutions. Furthermore there will be consequences for the organisation and content of higher education courses, for example there is likely to be the need for a new type of first degree, in which vocational skills are academically recognised and can be incorporated in the general corpus of knowledge. Higher education institutions will therefore have to undergo processes of radical change.

Lifelong learning
Moves in the above directions are essential to the effectiveness of lifelong learning strategies. Lifelong learning must not be limited to training, but should include higher education and academic learning. The above strategies are required to ensure that 'lifelong learners' are not only those with the strongest educational base built up in childhood and youth. All people must have the opportunity to access higher education, and this requires enhanced basic educational preparation, the recognition of vocational routes into higher education and new admissions procedures and appropriate courses. Only then will lifelong learning promote social inclusion, rather than reinforce social division.

Affordability

The radical re-structuring of the education system will require that significant resources be made available. If the political will exists, and the incremental approach coherently applied, the resources can be found. There is scope for the redeployment of resources within the educational sector, although experience shows that this is not easy. There are financial and social advantages to be gained by transferring higher education from the campus to the community. Industry and the private sector more generally should be encouraged to provide financial support to education; it should be noted that at present firms under-invest in training, and do not invest in general education at all. In addition, there should be socially just systems of individual contributions, which do not penalise students from lower socio-economic groups and socially disadvantaged backgrounds. To create an inclusive and just higher education system additional public funds will also be necessary, indeed, this is already evident in the development of lifelong learning initiatives. A pertinent question however remains: are funds currently targeted at the right priorities?

References

Brint, S. and Karabel, J. (1989) *The Diverted Dream: Community colleges and the promise of educational opportunity in America, 1900-1985*. New York, Oxford University Press.

Dougherty, K. (1987) 'The effects of community colleges: aid or hindrance to socio-economic attainment' in *Sociology of Education*, 60:86-103.

OECD (1970) *Review of Educational Growth*. Paris, OECD Publications.

OECD (1999) *Education at a Glance*. Paris, OECD Publications.

OECD (1999) Chapter 4, 'Tertiary Education: Extending the Benefits of Growth to New Groups' in *Education Policy Analysis*. Paris, OECD Publications.

Rouse, C. (1995) 'Democratization or diversion? The effect of community colleges on educational attainment', in *Journal of Business and Economic Statistics*, 13(2): 217-224.

5. Lifelong learning in a global society: providential or pathological?

David Davies

Strategic drivers for lifelong learning

The challenge

For most of the post-war period, higher education institutions formed the pinnacle of the education and training systems in Britain and elsewhere. They recruited highly selectively from 18 year old school leavers (mainly male), and prepared them for secure and well paid employment in influential roles in society and the economy. Through its influence on school examinations, and its position as the end of the ladder of progression, higher education set standards for the rest of the education system. Through its teaching and research functions it defined what kinds of knowledge, skill and understanding were to be most highly valued in society.

All this has changed. In the UK the majority of entrants are now 'mature' at the point of entry (even if one excludes the very large number who participate in continuing education), whilst some 35% of school leavers in England and Wales now enter higher education and the proportion of women of all ages has increased rapidly. A degree is no longer a guarantee of high-status employment. Standards for the school system and vocational training are set by external agencies, and the role of the professional bodies is being debated. The traditional role of universities in defining and valuing knowledge is also less clear; in many fields new knowledge is created in commercial and industrial settings, and the right of the academic world to validate knowledge has come under challenge, politically from external forces and philosophically from within the academic world itself (Wills, 1998).

Knowledge and the global community

Among the many pressures changing the nature of learning in society, two trends are central. The first is the accelerating speed with which new ideas and knowledge move from conception to application, and obsolescence. This creates particular pressures on higher education, where academic knowledge was traditionally created, subjected to critical examination and transmitted to new generations of learners. Higher education in the future will have to process knowledge faster, and disseminate it to more people, more often and in radically different ways.

The second trend is the globalising of communication, and with it the redefinition and restructuring of cultural and social identities. On the one hand a shared culture makes us all members of much larger communities, but on the other it leads us to reassert more comprehensible and local identities, in terms of locality, national, religious or ethnic group.

One of the effects of these changes is global pressure to replace systems of central planning and control with devolved and fragmented market-led structures, which allow a more rapid and individualised response to changing needs. These pressures make individuals more vulnerable to change, and challenge traditional notions of authority, accountability and democracy.

Giddens (1990) has referred in this context to the ending of traditional epistemologies, whereby the authority and sanctity of knowledge and wisdom is rejected. This tendency can be seen as an aspect of the breakdown of tradition and the disembedding of individual lives from social roles and traditions. At the same time many people are being drawn into even larger economic and social structures whose rules, regulations and requirements for operating are arranged from very far away. Perhaps in reaction to this, there is also a counterbalancing pressure to assert local identities within nations, regions and within social, ethnic and religious groups. Cultural pluralism which allows the blossoming of many diverse, if not all, cultural phenomena exists alongside a more fiercely committed orthodoxy, where communities feel their identity to be at risk.

A changing economic and social reality has been accompanied by a rapidly changing knowledge base. The knowledge economy has expanded not only in relation to employment opportunities but also in terms of its structure and reach. New fields of knowledge and expertise are created continuously and expand beyond the old boundaries. The knowledge and information-based service industries have grown exponentially within the last decade and have merged in substantial ways into the leisure and entertainment industries. Clearly some parts of the higher education system are threatened by these developments. The traditional, affirmative cultural role of higher education could be said to be under threat. On the other hand, the simultaneous creation of local and global knowledge and experience is also creating a common culture of knowledge which may yield potential support for social and communitarian aspirations or for a kind of socially distributed knowledge production system (see Gibbons *et al*, 1994, Jary & Parker, 1998).

It is also the case that learning is being transformed by the artefacts of the 'information age'. The new communication technologies have disrupted the fixed realities of time and space (Giddens, 1990, 1991). This impacts on economic and social life in fundamental ways. According to Manuel Castells (1996-98), the economy has become globalised and is maintained by endlessly complex financial flows. The industrial corporation has become a network, as opposed to the Taylorist hierarchy of control and production of previous eras. Contemporaneously, social networks, as clusters of relationships, are no longer fixed in time and place and labour becomes disposable, literally across the world. In these circumstances, referred to as the 'network-society', individuals seek identity and meaning. We can surely identify here the need for a more educated and autonomous working population?

The economic arguments for global change and the growth of learning have been well documented (see Castells, 1996-98; Fryer, 1997; Finegold & Soskice, 1988; Finegold, 1992). Nevertheless, it is worth emphasising the fact that changes in the nature, structure, organisation and meaning of work are driving the demands for learning from different directions. The problem of change and de-industrialisation within the older heartlands of the advanced economies means there are few jobs now for life and insecurity within the labour market is endemic. The growth of flexible specialisation in the labour requirement has abolished many fixed boundaries between skills and jobs and a flexible 'core' labour force may have emerged locally, as well as a de-skilled marginal and 'disposable' element. Traditionally skilled and low-waged employees may be pushed to the margins of the labour market as the 'new' economy based on knowledge and information grows. More work is part-time, casual or freelance and more workers are women. Manufacturing employment in many places has declined whilst the professional labour force has exploded alongside the growth of higher education, (Jary & Parker, 1998).

These apparently contradictory trends demand on the one hand the further expansion of learning opportunities alongside the new, emerging organisational forms of living and working, whilst simultaneously, the millions trapped in economic poverty and backwardness are apparently confirmed in their exclusion. Modernity has brought with it a greater reflexivity and capacity for dialogue and communication, but also created unpredictability, uncertainty and exclusion.

The challenge of lifelong learning

The potential of lifelong learning is everywhere recognised, but nowhere achieved! A major cultural shift is alluded to in the writings of many analysts and pundits (Smith & Spurling, 1999; Watts, 1998; Fryer, 1997; Robertson, 1994) and there is widespread belief in both the inevitability and desirability of continuous learning. However, it is equally widely conceded that we have (in the UK) a chaotic system of post-compulsory education which is above all under-resourced and poorly funded in relation to the needs and potential demand (see Kennedy, 1997; Dearing, 1997; Hillman, 1996; DfEE, 1998). Furthermore, the system is overly institutionalised and paternalistic in its methods and approaches to modern learning needs. We are faced with a paradox: there is a burgeoning demand for, and growth of, learning opportunities – especially in relation to work-related activity – and 'entertainment'. The whole provider-led system has expanded over the last two decades in response to these factors yet there is simultaneously a widespread culture of exclusion with the large majority of the population effectively excluded or excluding themselves from the lifelong learning agenda. To many people, the lifelong learning prospectus makes little economic or financial sense and the 'rules of the game', that is, the meanings of what is on offer are not clear. In such cases, it can be argued, it is a false prospectus.

The challenge facing the protagonists of lifelong learning in these circumstances is to articulate clearly the needs of individuals, groups, local communities and collectivities of people (however constituted) and to translate these into key policy issues and themes from which a strategy may ultimately be derived. What then are these key policy themes or challenges and how might we respond? It is possible to attempt to summarise these under five themes.

1. Labour market needs

First, we need to respond to the realities of competitive economic forces and markets. There must be local strategies for developing the workforce, which target market failures and skill shortages. The needs of the employers, especially where small, local or regional companies are involved can be a paramount concern. It must be recognised that world-class competitive industry demands an ever more educated labour force and that as a corollary the 'marketisation' of learning, along with other 'services', has bitten deep into the collective consciousness of consumers and clients. Internationally competitive levels and standards of education and training are essential aspects of lifelong learning. The globalisation thesis cannot be ignored; neither can its localised derivatives, which may create severe dislocation and deprivation.

There are other distinctive aspects of learning contexts which demand our attention and understanding when we consider lifelong learning. For example, the concept of organisational learning has gained credibility in recent years (see Teare *et al*, 1997; Davies, 1999). It has been described as a growth industry for business and commerce, whilst paradoxically within higher education itself organisational learning proceeds at an almost glacial pace. In general terms a learning organisation can be conceptualised as a social system whose members have consciously adopted commonly held processes for generating and motivating individual and collective learning in order to improve performance. Such improvements will be expected to impact on all stakeholders in the system. University educators need to face in two directions here – outwards at the wider world of work and learning and inwards at the internal, institutional practices which may restrict what can be learned as well as the way in which it can be learned. A strategic approach to identifying and working with learning organisations in the marketplace is hardly likely to succeed for a higher education institution if its own system, structures and working practices are firmly anchored in the discipline boundaries and recruitment strategies of the last century (or even the one before that). Such features as interdisciplinary working, enterprise units able to respond and innovate quickly so that as Revens put it '... an organisation's capacity to learn must be to exceed the rate of change imposed on it ...' (See Wills, 1993) are not yet characteristic of the system. Perhaps it is not too extravagant to suggest that a key function for higher education will be to help transform organisations of learning into learning organisations? In doing so universities must continue to transform themselves as part of the global transformation of learning.

An additional context is that of the changing nature of work itself and its requirement for knowledge. If the wider contexts appear as either daunting or liberatory, we must nevertheless come to terms with the immediate realities within which the individual learner is likely to exist. The key trends here include the growth of the graduate labour market, the explosion of professional jobs world-wide, the entry of more women into such markets, the growth of continual job specialisation within the globalisation of the professional workforce and, as mentioned earlier, the emergence of new organisational structures of learning. In these sort of circumstances, according to James Quinn (1992) professional intellect will be the main wealth creator in the knowledge economy. The task of lifelong learning will therefore be to identify the requisite levels of intellect needed in the system and to create a value-added superstructure of different types of knowledge.

'Cognitive' knowledge will be allied with 'applied' knowledge so that our understanding of systems (knowing **why**) will produce creativity and enhance self-motivation. These key intellectual skills and competencies are likely to be crafted into a new type of 'knowledge base' which is focused on work-task(s) and which values and rewards creativity as the highest level of labour.

The application of creative labour, it can be argued, will take place increasingly within the new learning organisation structures. New skills will be at a premium and these can be expected to shift our current conceptions of what a professional worker or graduate 'owns' as skills and intellectual capital. Universities should thus be at the current boundary of debate on what it is to be personally and professionally educated and what is really useful knowledge (core or key skills) in this age (see Otter, 1997). The expectations of a range of stakeholders in this issue are undergoing transformation, including those of many individual learners who will expect to hold work-related qualifications in the future.

2. Lifelong learning is realised

Second, lifelong learning must be made a reality. This may mean re-focusing our efforts on learning rather than on 'education' and investing in learners rather than in providers. There is a clear need to stimulate demand for learning and to break out of the sometimes restrictive institutional roles which have been given for example to schools and higher education institutions. Schools could become centres of lifelong learning, the educational apartheid between academic and vocational learning could be abolished, degree structures could be reformed to be more open and workforce development plans which promote individual development opportunities could be vastly extended. The status of teachers could be raised as the key mediators in the learning processes which need to be available to everyone.

3. Social exclusion is addressed

Third, lifelong learning must extend and deepen its response to the issues surrounding social exclusion. Activity needs to be undertaken with employers to promote inclusive working and learning practices and work-based learning opportunities should be the entitlement and expectation of all. Learning in communities should be fostered and lead to sustainable opportunities within both the learning and employment markets. This may of course mean that resources are re-distributed to learners and away from **providers** of learning in order to secure the motivation of the more reluctant learners. Communities themselves may need to articulate their long-term learning needs which take them well beyond the short-term culture of 'projects' funded from outside the community but which inevitably diminish and (or) disappear as funds run out or are withdrawn.

4. Economic and community regeneration

Fourth, the regeneration of local economies and communities needs to be undertaken as part of a learning agenda for change. 'Learning communities' exist in the same way as 'learning organisations', promoting sustained innovation with continuous learning. For perhaps the majority of 'excluded' learners in fact, the context of community life is the critical factor in defining and supporting both individual and collective motivations to learn.

5. A dynamic curriculum

Fifth, it is surely not enough to assert the need for learning without asking what kind of learning is to be acquired? The strategic design of lifelong learning and its model(s) of delivery for mass participation need to engage with **what** is learned, **the way** it is learned and how this learning is **relevant** to those acquiring it or consuming it or actually generating it. In other words, lifelong learning demands a modern and dynamic curriculum (Teare, Davies & Sandelands, 1998). A dynamic curriculum first of all must incorporate the gains of recent years associated with modularity, credit transfer, student-centredness, IT-supported learning and part-time and access provision (Robertson, 1994; Davies, 1995). Furthermore, it must include the vital aspects of learning support, counselling and guidance (McNair, 1996; Davies & Nedderman, 1997; Watts & Stevens, 1999) on the one hand, and the requirement for 'performativity' (Lyotard, 1984; Edwards, 1998) and accountability on the other. The dynamic curriculum model recognises the existence and validity of different 'discourses' and 'paradigms' within learning activity and insists that they contribute to a progressive and democratic ethos. The elements of such a curriculum embrace and privilege experiential learning, action-learning methodologies and workplace and community-based learning. Shared learning, which recognises the individual and collective psychological sources of motivation to learn (and to act) is a vital component of the dynamic curriculum model. Such learning is to be found in cultural collectivities focused on ethnicity, faith and religion, neighbourhoods and increasingly in the context of work where experiential and academic learning are combined. There is a challenge to some conventional conceptions of knowledge ownership here because there is a recognition that learning takes place everywhere and increasingly is to be gained beyond the walls of the academy (Bruffee, 1995). For the providentially inclined there is huge potential in how experiential learning can further an open and democratic society.

> 'Until the present, the management of knowledge has been in the hands of those who, on the whole, subscribe to the fixed objective view of knowledge, and to the view that certain forms of knowledge which we obtain from the 'life process' are something quite separate. The consequence is that those who are initiated into the processes that count as knowledge themselves, become 'special' and distinct occupiers of positions in society which carry with them forms of power and control. In contrast to this, if knowledge is socially grounded, a large part of it arises from the simple fact of living over a total lifetime. Recurrent education then must place an emphasis on individuals having full participation in knowledge processes in society. If knowledge is firmly set in a context of **social interaction**, then life becomes a process of continuing negotiations through which we gain an open access to knowledge resources in society.'
> (Jones, 1974)

Jones' insight formulated over a quarter of a century ago, has resonance in the new millennium and for the idea of a dynamic curriculum. Surely an idea whose time is now coming?

Conclusions: lifelong learning – providential or pathological?

An outline has been presented of strategic issues which are driving lifelong learning. A series of questions has been asked concerning the challenges facing learners and providers, accompanied by some tentative answers. No simple trade-off as to the providential or pathological results can be attempted, though we can point to the inter-connectedness of contradictory and paradoxical events. Just as global events are intimately connected with local life, learning in modernity is dynamic, involving profound discontinuity and disruption of traditional life. Lifelong learning can be said to be an expression of what Giddens has referred to as the arena of unpredictability, whilst offering a vision of progress which can be benign.

Such a providential system will be defined not by its role in social selection, but by the ways in which it combines the creation and transmission of knowledge. It will be offered in many forms and locations, by a variety of agencies. It will be lifelong with the large majority of its learners engaged in recurrent learning throughout their lives, much of it in the workplace and community. Learning will be student centred, which will enable individuals to construct individual learning careers which reflect their personal ambitions, talents and changing circumstances whilst remaining intellectually coherent and challenging. A providential lifelong learning system will be achievement led, recognising and accrediting a wide range of learning, rather than seeking to maintain standards by exclusion, rationing and selection. The providers in such a system will seek to feed ideas, knowledge and skills into society and the economy, through both teaching and research, rather than waiting for demand to be articulated. The systems' purposes, criteria and outcomes will be clear and public, to enable potential learners to make wise choices, and to make the shape and operation of the system open to debate. It will have clear public statements of what individuals are entitled to in terms of access, equity, quality, guidance, curriculum entitlement and public financial support. Diverse purposes, forms, institutions, learners and programmes will be sponsored so that communities and workplaces are able to become learning organisations and so that employment can be humanised to support the needs of a knowledge-based society.

Those who maintain the counterview might argue that there has been a failure to apply human capital theory successfully to the problems of the modern economy. Attempts to drive economic progress through investment in skills and labour markets have certainly not eradicated the disparities in wealth, investment and progress which leave millions in poverty – even in the wealthiest of societies. In supporting the globalisation thesis, it is argued, the emphasis on work-related learning and skills diverts attention away from the pressing issues of social equity. Curricular authority passes to the business culture which can exert economic pressure on educationalists. In such a context, lifelong learning 'pathologises' the non-learners, creating a deficit model for those who are outside the global communication networks. The low-wage earners, the unemployed and the socially excluded are subject therefore to a form of bland and positive utopianism which can deliver little for them.

As far as the providers (teachers and educational institutions) are concerned, the pure knowledge they formerly sought is supplanted by performativity and the need to deliver accountability to ever more demanding and restrictive paymasters. In such a view, the modern explosion of communications served to facilitate control, rather than to liberate learning and teaching.

It is not sufficient to characterise this perspective as 'intellectual luddism' or simply as an attempt to re-assert the academy's monopoly status over what counts as knowledge. There are real concerns about the many, perhaps even a majority, who are left out by the modernist, communications revolution and the effective smashing of previous and traditional ways of life and the communities which helped sustain them. However, there can be little doubt that the development of human interests generates in turn knowledge and learning domains which address in new ways the nature of work, the scale of communicative activity and its meanings and how a democracy of access to knowledge can aid critical self-awareness, social progress and emancipation. (Therborn, 1971; Habermas, 1972 & 1974; Mezirow, 1981). Such knowledge is no longer confined (if it ever was) to the academy. Lifelong learning must therefore be grounded in communicative action and in reciprocal understanding which includes **all** the arenas of learning, including work, community, family, identity and the formal and informal structures and institutions which shape a life.

Lifelong learning is developmental and incremental – it is not a question of marketing a new logo. There is writing on the slate (as well as on the wall) and there are existing images on the monitor screen. We need to recognise that there exists a **process** of learning as well as a product and that learners will increasingly want to speak for themselves as part of gaining control over their own lives. This process cannot be bought at a supermarket. We, the teachers, are in a different business and must recognise that learners are the most powerful potential we have. They, the learners, are not just a 'product portfolio' or the pathological victims of a marketised culture.

If this is the case and is to remain the case for the future, then the language of market forces, of incentives, cost effectiveness, quality audits, performance indicators, unit cost analysis has to be tempered by a full-blooded statement of our purposes and values as educators. These values are in the public sphere and are not simply the domain of private gain. But if we do not professionally defend them they certainly will be! Lifelong learning is now everyone's business and, as this argument has hoped to demonstrate, it may still be located in the emancipatory domain.

References

Bruffee, K. A. (1995) *Collaborative Learning: Higher Education, Interdependence, and the Authority of Knowledge.* Baltimore and London, The John Hopkins University Press.

Castells, M. (1996-98) *The Rise of the Network Society. Volume 1. The Information Age: Economy, Society and culture; Volume 2: The Power of Identity; Volume 3; The End of Millennium.* Oxford, Blackwell.

Davies, D. (1995) *Credit Where It's Due: Credit Frameworks and Learning Outcomes.* University of Cambridge, Employment Department.

Davies, D. and Nedderman, V. (1997) 'Information and On-course guidance to Continuing Education Students' in Rivis, V. (ed) *Managing Guidance in Higher Education*. London, HEQC.

Davies, D. (1999) 'The Learning Society: Moving on to the Workplace' in *Journal of Widening Participation and Lifelong Learning*, 1(1).

Dearing, Sir R. (1997) *Summary Report – Higher Education in the Learning Society*, London, NCIHE.

DfEE (1998) *The Learning Age: a renaissance for a new Britain*. London, HMSO DfEE.

Edwards, M. (1998) 'Commodification and Control in Mass Higher Education: A Double Edged Sword', in Jary, D. and Parker, M. (eds) *The New Higher Education: Issues and Directions for the Post-Dearing University*. Stoke-on-Trent, Staffordshire University Press.

Finegold, D. and Soskice, D. (1988) 'The failure of training in Britain: analysis and prescription', in *Oxford Review of Economic Policy*, 3(4).

Finegold, D. et al (1992) *Higher Education – Expansion and Reform*. London, IPPR.

Fryer, R. (report) (1997) *Learning for the 21ˢᵗ Century*. DfEE, London.

Gibbons, M., Limoges, C., Nowotny, H., Schwartzman, S., Scott, P. and Trow, M. (1994) *The New Production of Knowledge: The Dynamics of Science and Research in Contemporary Societies*. London, Sage.

Giddens, A. (1990) *The Consequences of Modernity*. Cambridge, Polity Press.

Giddens, A. (1991) *Modernity and Self-identity. Self and society in the late modern age*. Stanford, Cal., Stanford University Press.

Habermas, J. (1972) *Knowledge and Human Interests*. London, Heinemann.

Habermas, J. (1974) 'The Classical Doctrine of Politics in Relation to Social Philosophy' Chapter 1 – *Theory Practice*. London, Heinemann.

Hillman, J. (1996) *A University for Industry: Creating a National Learning Network*. London, IPPR.

Jary, D. and Parker, M. (1998) *The New Higher Education: Issues and Directions for the Post-Dearing University*. Stoke-on-Trent, Staffordshire University Press.

Jones, K. (1974) in Houghton, V. (ed) (1974) *Recurrent Education*. Milton Keynes, Open University Press.

Kennedy Report (1997) *Learning Works: Widening Participation in Further Education*. Coventry, FEFC.

Lyotard, J. F. (1984) *The Postmodern Condition: a Report on Knowledge*. Manchester, Manchester University Press.

McNair, S. (ed) (1996) *Putting learners at the centre.* Sheffield: GALA – DfEE.

Mezirow, J. (1981) 'A Critical Theory of Adult Education' in *Adult Education*, 31(1) (Fall).

Otter, S. (1997) *An Abilities Curriculum.* DfEE, London.

Quinn, J. B. (1992*) Intelligent Enterprise.* The Free Press.

Robertson, D. (1994) *Choosing to Change: Report of the National CATS Development Project.* London, HEQC.

Smith, J. and Spurling, A. (1999) *Lifelong Learning: Riding the Tiger.* London, Cassells.

Teare, R. et al (1998) 'Developing a Curriculum for Organisational Learning', in *The Journal of Workplace Learning,* 10(2):95-121.

Teare, R., Davies, D. and Sandelands, E. (1998) *The Virtual University.* London, Cassells.

Therborn, G. (1971) 'Jürgen Habermas: A New Eclectism', in *New Left Review*, Number 67, May-June 1971.

Watts, A.G. (1998) 'The Learning Age' in *Adults Learning*, 9(8).

Watts, A.G. and Stevens, B. (1999) 'The Relationship between Career Guidance and Financial Guidance' in *Journal of Widening Participation and Lifelong Learning*, 1 (3): 8 - 17.

Wills, G. (1993) *Your Enterprise School of Management.* Bradford, MCB University Press.

Wills, G. (ed) (1998) *The Knowledge Game: The Revolution in Learning and Communication in the Workplace.* London, Cassells.

6. 'Smartening up' or 'dumbing down'? Academic standards in access courses

Anne Jordan

Introduction

The aim of this chapter is to examine the development of the access movement in the Republic of Ireland, and to consider the issue of standards in relation to access provision. 'Access' in Ireland includes entry to all higher education certificate, and diploma programmes, as well as degree courses. (Access courses in Ireland do not on the whole guarantee entry to these programmes but will improve the chances of entry. A recent national report, The Points Commission Report recommends that the title 'access' be dropped for this reason.)

My interest in standards on access courses arose from an examination of Irish access provision and qualifications for a report commissioned by the Irish Department of Enterprise and Employment. The method used to establish the findings for this report was a quantitative survey of twenty- three higher education institutions, and of the national Vocational Training Opportunities Scheme (VTOS). Responses to an initial questionnaire were followed by telephone interviews with Access or Admissions Officers from these institutions. In-depth individual and group interviews were also held with the first cohort of access students from the Access for Mature Students to Higher Education (AMSHE) course in the Waterford Institute of Technology (WIT) of which I was the co-ordinator.

In discussions of academic standards it is usual to distinguish between input standards, the quality or characteristics of staff and students; process standards, the quality of course provision, teaching and student supports; and output standards, the attributes and achievements demonstrated by those successful in completing a programme of study (Wright, 1996). It is necessary first of all however to describe the Irish access scene.

The Irish context

Access courses for adults are a recent phenomena in Ireland. There are currently nineteen access courses for adult students in the Irish Republic, over half of which are located in Dublin, with its concentrated higher education provision of four universities and four Institutes of Technology. There are four courses in the south and south-east of the country;

three in the west, and one in the midlands. The northern part of the country has, as yet, no access provision, (though access courses are planned for this region) and scant higher education provision overall. Proximity to higher educational institutions in Northern Ireland has meant that in theory southern Irish students can avail of provision there, though it is doubtful if many have taken this opportunity.

There is one national educational programme for unemployed adults, VTOS, which may also act as an access route to higher education. Additionally, the Irish government has developed programmes in response to industrial skills shortages in the area of information technology, which could be seen as access provision. The focus of this paper however will be on generic access programmes delivered in the third-level sector, rather than on access to specialised programmes such as those mentioned above.

The total number of access students studying on generic access courses in the Irish Republic for the years 1997-1998, was 827, in a population of 3.6 million (IPA,1999). This number can be compared to that in the UK for 1994, where more than 30,000 students were enrolled on over 1000 access courses, in a population of 60 million i.e. proportionately double the number of students. It is surprising to note that only four per cent of higher education students in Britain arrive through access routes, given the huge increase in the number of mature students over the last two decades, (Merrill, 1999) though Davies (1996) claims in her paper, 'Noise rather than numbers' that it has suited policymakers to present such 'compensatory' mechanisms as access in an over-favourable light.

The differing higher education participation rates between the two countries is significant. The UK has a participation rate of thirty per cent, (Harvey & Ashworth, 1995) as compared to a participation rate of thirty four per cent for the Republic of Ireland (IPA, 1999). However, if one looks at the participation rates for adult students the gap widens considerably. In Britain, mature students make up a third of the student entry to higher education, (HEFCE, 1996) whereas in the Republic it is less than five percent, (Clancy, 1995). Here, adult students have to compete with school leavers for higher education places in a system which utilises an adjustable points score as a selection mechanism, so that for 'high demand' courses like medicine or physiotherapy the points requirement is high and may be increased every year. School-leavers find it difficult enough to gain entry to their chosen courses, and it leaves little room for mature students possessing non-traditional or no entry qualifications. Ireland did not have a system of free secondary education until 1967, with the consequence that there are a larger number of Irish adults than in other European countries who have been denied secondary and post-secondary education, and are now looking for such opportunities (OECD, 1997a).

In the UK access provision is frequently a collaborative enterprise between further and higher education, but this is not the case in the Republic (Cox, 1997) with the consequence that, in general, higher education itself is responsible for the design and delivery of access provision. One explanation is the absence, until recently, of a further education sector. This further education sector however, has begun to grow since 1992 when the third-level non-university sector gained autonomy from Vocational Educational Committee (VEC) control. Ireland has now created a system of vocational qualifications through the National Council for Vocational Awards, of which Level Two can also be seen as an access to third-level qualification, though there have been some difficulties in persuading the higher education sector to accept this award as comparable to the traditional entry qualifications to higher education.

Twelve of the nineteen Irish access courses surveyed, have only been established in the last five years; the oldest, for students with disabilities, being set up in the mid-1980s. The National Council for Educational Awards (NCEA) - validated course, The National Foundation Certificate for Mature Students, set up by Waterford Institute of Technology in 1996 was the first response in the country to a call for nationally-accredited access courses. By comparison, the access course in Magee College, University of Ulster, Northern Ireland has just celebrated twenty-five years of access provision (D'Arcy, 1995). We are therefore roughly fifteen to twenty years behind the UK which was developing its access provision in the 1970s and 1980s, (Parry, 1995). A major impetus here came in the form of EU funding, from 1992 onwards, leading to access programmes such as the Women into Science courses developed in Cork Institute of Technology (NOW, 1994) and since offered in a number of other institutes.

The ultimate aim of these European programmes is to assist disadvantaged adults and groups gain access to the labour market, (WRC, 1997: p4). It is unclear however whether the development of access programmes in Ireland derives from a concern with social justice and inclusion, a liberal philosophy of adult and lifelong learning, or a late realisation on the part of policymakers that alternative routes for adults into higher education and thence to the labour market are needed if Ireland is not to incur a serious skills shortage and damage the sustainable growth of the Celtic tiger economy. The recent Irish education Green Paper 'Adult Education in an Era of Lifelong Learning' (1998) which promotes the concept of access, utilises an over-arching discourse of lifelong learning, but arguments for access and accessibility are couched primarily in economic terms. In one sense this may not be detrimental in presenting a clear rationale for action to policymakers, but raises the question of the entitlement of all adults to participate in higher education as their democratic right.

Input standards

It is obvious that access students will be unable to demonstrate prior academic or school-based achievement, given that middle-aged Irish adults may not have had the opportunity to complete secondary education. In fact literacy levels in Ireland are the second lowest of twelve countries surveyed for the International Adult Literacy Survey (OECD, 1997b). Moreover, little use is made of pre-testing as a diagnostic tool. Many institutions, including our own, interview to determine which adults will benefit from the access course offered, since access course numbers are generally kept small in order that students will receive more individual attention. In this selection interview procedure it may be queried whether we are replicating the stresses that students undergo in the standard Mature Student Application to Higher Education Interview, with its opaque quota arrangements and lack of explicit admissions criteria. One solution that we utilise ourselves in WIT is to offer instead a counselling interview in which students have the opportunity to talk about their learning ambitions, goals, strengths and weaknesses with academic staff and an educational guidance counsellor. This is followed by the offer of guidance as to the most likely educational routes to enable individuals to achieve their own personalised learning plans.

The other input standard that is a matter of concern is the staffing of access courses. A number of these courses, including our own, run on short-term European or Department of Education funding, and the tendency is to appoint contract or part-time staff to co-ordinate and to lecture on these courses. Access provision is therefore liable to be regarded as a marginal activity by the institution itself, and vulnerable when the funding ceases, or other initiatives take priority. This was clearly shown in Australia when the government there ceased to support access provision, with the expectation that the institutions themselves would take over the funding. Postle (1995: pp15-16) points out the tensions arising, especially in the newer Australian universities, between research and access activity. A parallel situation has arisen in the UK in the distinct alignment of the new and older UK universities, either to widening participation or to research, (THES, 1999).

An allied complaint, raised by our own AMSHE student focus group was that too many staff teaching on the WIT access course were part-timers, specifically recruited for this course, and without much expertise in college systems and procedures. It had been our intention that the WIT access course would be staffed by full-time academics, but circumstances required us to appoint on the basis of availability. Without the commitment and input of these full-time staff, the risk is of de-coupling access from mainstream academic teaching activity, so that students do not gain relevant 'college knowledge' (Fleming, 1997) nor insight into academic structures and culture. This danger was highlighted by Brennan (1989) with his claim that 'too great a contrast between the educational cultures of access courses and degree courses runs the risk of adjustment problems and the dangers of failure' (p60).

Process standards

The Higher Education Quality Council which now has responsibility for the approval of UK access courses has set the standard for the duration of full-time access courses at five hundred hours per year (Parry, 1996). The National Council for Educational Awards which is the main validating body for the non-university higher education sector in the Irish Republic requires a total of six hundred hours for a full-time access course. Of the nineteen access courses currently offered in Ireland, the majority demand between three hundred and six hundred contact hours, though some part-time courses have considerably less, running over shorter blocks of time, and one or two courses utilise considerably more hours. This raises questions as to the appropriate length of student learning necessary to gain the skills needed to progress to higher education, and how to measure an access course of nine hours a week as against one of thirty hours a week, which represent the extremes in the courses surveyed. Should we equate the process of 'smartening up' with the longer courses, or are we making it difficult for students by requiring unnecessary class attendance, when other flexible forms of learning could be explored?

The WIT access students include Waterford Crystal Company workers on our pilot 'work-based access to higher education' course. Many of these workers have to drive a round trip of sixty miles after shift-working, for three evenings a week of lectures. My own view now is that the requirement of six hundred contact hours is simply adapting access to standard requirements for full-time students in Ireland, rather than the considering the pedagogical needs of access students, whether work-based learners or not. Work-based access learners could be fast-tracked through the access process by the use of Accreditation of Prior Learning procedures to exempt them from modules where they could demonstrate prior achievement, as in Information Technology or Communications. Opportunities could also be developed for flexible learning arrangements so that students can complete the equivalent of these hours in their own time, and to some extent, at their own pace. The only danger here is the loss of the group solidarity and support which the AMSHE students identified as a critical aspect of access provision.

A contentious issue is whether access courses should guarantee entry to higher education. The situation here is different for the Irish universities and the Institutes of Technology. The universities, as autonomous bodies, are in a better situation to guarantee entry to their own undergraduate courses than the Institutes of Technology, whose qualifications are validated by an external body – the NCEA. When the NCEA first formulated its access policy in 1994/5, the intention had been that higher education institutions guaranteed places to successful access students, as in the Scottish SWAP consortium (Spackman, 1995). However, the competitive scramble for places has meant that the NCEA can only urge institutions to offer third-level places to National Foundation Certificate holders, or to view successful candidates in a positive light (NCEA,1998). (Note the UK Lindop Report's (1985) recommendation that access students should not be guaranteed entry to their own institutions on the grounds that academic standards would be compromised.) Of the nineteen courses surveyed only five reported that successful completion guaranteed entry to their own (university) institutions, and in no case did the qualification guarantee entrance to other third-level institutions.

If we are to look at other indications of process standards, we might consider students' retention on Irish access courses. Student retention figures in Ireland have been the subject of much publicity, with first year drop-out rates of thirty seven per cent in the Institutes of Technology, (Healy, 1999) making them amongst the highest in Europe (OECD, 1997a). Reported attrition rates for access students in Ireland are lower - twenty eight per cent was the highest reported, with a mean rate overall of seventeen per cent. Moreover, evidence from access students indicates that unlike their younger brethren they drop out not because of subject difficulties or mistaken choice, but because of personal or family problems, or the strain of juggling a multiplicity of commitments. It is of course the case that access students, like most mature students are better motivated, generally have a more personalised experience, in smaller classes, with study skills and counselling available, and perhaps extra tutorial help with difficult subjects.

A major interest in relation to access provision is the content and level of such courses. Of the Irish courses surveyed, most offered the five core subjects of study skills, maths/numeracy, information technology, communications and guidance/personal development, generally with a range of electives or 'taster' subjects. Many of the courses did offer a wide range of electives, in order to facilitate student choice at undergraduate level, but the Waterford AMSHE students were critical of too broad a range of taster subjects, reinforcing the findings of the Scottish SWAP study where students wished they had spent more time on the subjects chosen for their degrees, rather than experiencing a broader range of options (Munn, 1994).

The AMSHE focus group communicated mixed messages about study skills. Some were scornful of the value and time spent on this area, whilst others reported it to be the most useful subject. This group ambivalence taps into an ongoing debate about the effectiveness of generic study skills, apart from areas of time management, note-taking, and the organisation of material, which can be covered over a short time period. Perhaps study skills are best taught through specific subject areas, as in Open University Level One courses, after an initial and optional study skills overview. Another reason for some hostility to the subject is that better (more organised) students have frequently discovered their own study methods and styles, and do not need prolonged training in this, whereas poorer (less organised students) may be those who resist method, planning and self-analysis. However there is certainly a group for whom study skills and the opportunity to reflect on their own styles and practices is of great benefit in preparing them to be deep or strategic, rather than shallow, rote learners.

The academic level of access courses should be sub-first year undergraduate or National Certificate level, and the equivalent of the Irish Leaving Certificate or A level. Findings from the survey revealed that for most courses this was the case, though two university access courses were first year university level, and another five access courses were pitched between Leaving Certificate and first year undergraduate level. This was also true of the Science strand of the Waterford AMSHE course where syllabi in Physics and Chemistry were written at too advanced a level, with staff having difficulties in identifying the core subject knowledge required of access students. Some students have reported on-going problems with these areas because they lack the foundation knowledge, traditionally gained through secondary school. Research is needed in each subject area to determine what is the essential foundation knowledge needed to cope with studying the subject at a higher academic level.

Other process standards relate to the way that access courses prepare the students for mainstream college life. This 'preparedness' might relate to academic pedagogies and assessment techniques, or accommodation to the politics and power structures of academia. The AMSHE students claimed that the access course shielded them too much from the realities of college life with its large class numbers and anonymity, possible hostility to adult students by lecturers, and the unexpectedly heavy workload of lectures and assessments, echoing student concerns from the Scottish SWAP evaluation (Munn, 1994).

Most access courses surveyed utilised a mix of continuous assessment and terminal examination. Groups such as the Irish Working Class Access Network have called for greater use of continuous assessment, and more creative assessment methods, taking into account newer concepts of multiple intelligence, more use of project work and the abolition of examinations. However, the AMSHE student cohort welcomed the practice in examinations, and would certainly feel unprepared were they to lack the opportunity of such testing. This desire by students to retain examinations is in line with SWAP findings, where students expressed regret that Scottish access courses did not build in formal examinations (Munn, 1994).

In relation to the grading of access qualifications, the practice here is diverse. The NCEA, following UK access guidelines, utilises criterion-rather than norm referencing for its access certification. The universities however are unused to this form of grading, and tend to rank access candidates, as is their practice for all academic awards. One might ask what is to be gained from this categorisation of performance apart from that of rewarding high-flying students? One merit of criterion-referencing is that if work-based access to higher education is to develop, and with it the accreditation of work-based learning or prior achievement (APEL), then criterion-referenced assessment will be required.

The final area in which process standards might be developed related to student support. Four of the courses surveyed possessed mentoring systems, though the understanding and practice of mentoring ranges from the provision of personal tutorial support to a form of 'buddying'. The AMSHE students were each assigned to a member of the access teaching staff who took on a mentoring role, and even those students who reported not using this support appreciated its value. Students also highlighted the importance of extra tutorial help with difficult subject areas such as mathematics and reported the importance of peer support, both in building confidence and as an aid to learning.

Output standards

Student progression to higher education, how they cope there, and their success in gaining higher level qualifications is, of course, the major output standard. Munn (1994: p16) amongst her criteria for the effectiveness of access courses lists the improvement of participation rates in higher education by older students. It is too early in Ireland to measure access courses by increased participation, where single factors alone would not substantially lead to more adults in the higher education system. However, there is much informal evidence of the success of access students. For example, Magee College, Derry claims five hundred graduates since 1974 with a small number of PhD graduates as ex-access students. It is difficult however to gather national statistics on access student progression and ultimate success. My own findings are that over sixty per cent of students enrolled on Irish access courses have gone on to higher education, compared with a Scottish figure of seventy per cent (Munn, 1994). It is difficult to estimate however how many of them have gained degrees or other awards since there is no mechanism for tracking access students, and a number of the courses are too new.

My own small study, on the success of the first AMSHE students in national examinations is probably a reasonable guide to outcomes for students. It represents the first attempt at tracking this group, two years after their enrolment on undergraduate courses. The study shows that fifteen of the original twenty students are still in higher education, and of these, seven have gained National Certificate qualifications, two more have successfully completed the second year of degree programmes and the remaining five are repeating subjects. The system in the Institutes of Technology which allows a ladder through to degree qualifications by means of an add-on year from National Certificate and Diplomas is well-suited to access students, giving them an opportunity to leave or rejoin the system at specified points, and with recognised achievements and awards.

Other outputs such as the increase in self-confidence, direction or motivation to learn gained through access courses are difficult to measure, but the Waterford students identified a number of 'soft indicators' – the support and motivation gained by being part of a group; the awareness that they could cope with studying and were not stupid after all; the reflection on their own personal and career goals. These were also identified by those who had chosen not to progress to higher education, but saw the value of the access year as a valuable learning experience.

Recommendations

If standards are to be devised for Irish access courses, the following points should be considered:
- the Irish Department of Education and Science should set up a national access unit to consider the duration, academic level, currency and progression routes for access courses;
- diagnostic pre-testing should be utilised in order to identify students who need extra academic support;
- specific subject areas should be used as a medium through which to teach key knowledge and skills rather than isolating the key skills themselves. However, students need to be aware of how they learn critical thinking through reading and writing in specific subject areas;

- access courses should be more closely linked to mainstream higher education and undergraduate life. Initial scaffolds of support e.g. extra tuition, mentoring and additional academic help could be gradually withdrawn, so that there is a closer approximation to academic realities on full-time courses. A broad subject 'taster' input could be achieved by having access students sit in on full-time undergraduate courses and the use of other mature students or ex-access students to paint the 'real' picture.

Several questions were raised by the analysis of findings from this research. Is there a value in the articulation of explicit standards for access programmes when the criteria for the admission of adults to higher education in Ireland is neither explicit nor transparent? Should we in time seek the same kind of regulatory mechanisms as have been created in the UK and other countries in relation to access courses? Moreover, what is the value of a diversity of provision and practice, as opposed to conformity to a strict framework of standards and practice in relation to access provision? Malcolm Tight's 1989 article, 'Access not access courses' about the dangers inherent in the institutional appropriation of access courses, as opposed to a multiplicity of other access initiatives, is still a timely one here, in spite of its being written ten years ago, and in a British context.

References

Brennan, J. (1989) 'Access courses' in Fulton, O. (ed) *Access and Institutional Change*. Milton Keynes, SRHE/OU Press.

Clancy, P. (1995) *'Socio-economic disparities in participation'* in Higher Education Authority Access Courses for Higher Education. Proceedings of a seminar held on 31 January 1995 at Mary Immaculate College, Limerick.

Cox, D. (1997) 'Key issues in access facing the pre-1992 universities' in *Journal of Access Studies*, 12(1).

D'Arcy, F. (1995) 'Access courses: the Northern Ireland Experience in Higher Education Authority Access Courses for Higher Education. Report of a Seminar held in Mary Immaculate College, Limerick on 31 January 1995, Dublin.

Davies, P. (ed) (1995) *Adults in Higher Education; International Perspectives in Access and Participation*. Bristol, Jessica Kingsley.

Davies, P (1996) 'Noise rather than numbers: access to higher education in three European countries' in *Comparative Education*, 32(1):111-123

Edwards, R., Sieminski, S. and Zeldin, D. (eds) (1993) *Adult Learners, Education and Training*. London, Routledge/Open University.

Fleming,T. (1997) *College knowledge; power, politics and the nature of student experience.* Kildare, NUI. Maynooth, Adult and Community Education Occasional Series.

Harvey, R. C. and Ashworth, A. (1995) 'Mass higher education: a first stage model for the United Kingdom' in *Quality Assurance in Education*, 3 (4):6-13.

Healy, M., Carpenter, A. and Lynch, K. (1999) *Non-Completion in Higher Education. A Study of First Year Students in Three Institutes of Technology, A Report.* Carlow, Dundalk and Tralee ITS.

Higher Education Authority (1995) *Access Courses for Higher Education.* Proceedings of a Seminar held on 31 January 1995 at Mary Immaculate College, Limerick.

HEFCE Advisory Group on Access & Participation (1996) *Widening Access to Higher Education: A Report.* London, HEFCE.

Institute of Public Administration (1999) *IPA Yearbook.* Dublin, IPA.

Irish Department of Education and Science (1998) *The Green Paper: Adult Education in an Era of Lifelong Learning.* Dublin, DES.

Lindop, N. *(1985) Report of the Committee of Enquiry into Public Section Higher Education: Academic Validation in Public Sector Higher Education.* London, HMSO.

Merrill, B. (1999) *'Access - the UK context'* Unpublished conference paper. NUI, Maynooth, May 1999.

Munn, P., Johnstone, M. and Robinson, R. (1994) *The effectiveness of access courses: views of access students and their teachers.* Edinburgh, Scottish Council for Research in Education.

National Council for Educational Awards (1988) *NCEA Foundation Regulations.* Dublin, NCEA.

New Opportunities for Women (1994) Report of a Seminar on Women into Science Technology and Engineering in Third-Level Education, Dublin Castle, April 1994.

OECD (1997a) *Education at a Glance: Policy Analysis.* Paris, OECD.

OECD (1997b) 'Literacy Skills for the Knowledge Society' in *International Adult Literacy Survey.* Paris, OECD.

Parry, G. (1995) 'England, Wales and Northern Ireland' in Davies, P. (ed) *Adults in Higher Education; International Perspectives in Access and Participation.* Bristol, Jessica Kingsley.

Parry, G. (1996) 'Access education in England and Wales 1973-1994: from second chance to third wave' in *Journal of Access Studies*, 11 (1):10-33.

Postle, G. (1995) Australia in Davies, P. (ed) (1995) *Adults in Higher Education; International Perspectives in Access and Participation.* Bristol, Jessica Kingsley.

Spackman, A. (1995) Access courses in Europe: a look at the position in the Netherlands, Denmark and Scotland in Higher Education Authority Access Courses for Higher Education. Report of a seminar held in Mary Immaculate College, Limerick on 31 January 1995, Dublin.

Tight, M. (1989) 'Access, not access courses: maintaining a broad vision' in Edwards, R. et al. (ed) (1993) *Adult Learners, Education and Training.* London, Open University.

Times Higher Education Supplement (09.06.99) *'Finding New Ways to Measure Success'.*

WRC (1998) Integra Review Issue No.3 Summer 1997, Dublin, WRC.

Wright, (1996) Mass higher education and the search for standards' in *Higher Education Quarterly,* 50(1).

Part Three

National Policy and Practice

7. Mass higher education in the USA

Armand Policicchio

Introduction

Higher education in the United States of America has several distinguishing characteristics: size, diversity in type and purpose of institutions, level of participation by high school graduates, relatively high levels of autonomy, emphasis on general education (liberal arts), use as an instrument of social and economic growth and change, tradition of attention to the 'non-élite' student, the high level of support provided to students and the lack of centralized authority over the higher education sector. In many ways higher education is reflective of the American practice of democracy, the emphasis on local decision-making and the importance of individual rights.

A history of mass education

Three distinct periods can be seen in the history of American higher education. The first period, the period of Aristocracy, started in colonial times and lasted until the Civil War in the 1860s. The second period, the period of Meritocracy, was from the Civil War until the Civil Rights movements in the 1950s. The current period, the period of Egalitarianism, began in the 1960s (see, for instance, Clowes in Maxwell, 1994).

The willingness to make higher education available to 'non-élite' groups of students and underprepared students can even be seen in the period of Aristocracy. The first institutions, including Harvard, which was founded to train ministers, needed to provide tutoring for students in Greek and Latin. In a frontier nation there were few students with adequate preparation necessary to undertake a programme of studies without preparatory work (Maxwell, 1997).

During the Civil War, the First Morrill Act was signed into law. The act established land grant colleges to teach practical arts such as agriculture, mechanics and industrial arts. A land grant was offered to each state to establish a college if the state renounced slavery. With the establishment of these schools, 'new' students started to flood the universities (Maxwell, 1997).

Women were not admitted into American colleges in any large number until after the Civil War, when there was a growth in women's colleges. The late 1800s also saw the growth of colleges to serve African-Americans. It was apparent that these institutions were needed if African-Americans were to participate more fully in society. This period also saw the growth of private colleges, often founded by religious groups. These institutions served to educate people with particular religious affiliations and often served to educate different immigrant groups who were beginning to come to the United States in several great waves of immigration. The Second Morrill Act was passed in 1890. This act increased federal aid to colleges in the areas of applied science and mechanical arts. It helped to free colleges from their reliance on classical studies and helped form the thinking that every American citizen was entitled to some form of higher education (Maxwell, 1997). America was in a period of rapid industrialisation and needed trained and educated people for this industrialisation process.

At the end of the Second World War the GI Bill was signed into law. This bill provided millions of returning servicemen and women with the opportunity to go to college. Another flood of 'new' students entered the university. Many of these students were the first in their families to go to college.

The stage was set for a more formal move to mass education. The seeds were sown to accept higher education as a vehicle for social inclusion. Increasingly, higher education has been seen and used from colonial times until the cold war days as a way to a better life for individuals, as a way to raise standards in the socio-economic area and to improve the economy and national defence. Relative to many other nations, America's class structure was one in which there was a real possibility of upward mobility that did not depend upon birth. Its form of democracy (although imperfectly applied) advocated equality and inclusion. The education system was broad enough to serve a diverse group of persons and meet diverse needs. A spark was needed. That spark came with the Civil Rights movement that started in the 1950s and continued into the 1960s.

The drive to provide true equality for African-Americans, other minority groups, women and the disabled has had a profound impact on American higher education. Education was seen as a primary vehicle for social mobility and economic growth for disenfranchised people. The government formed many programmes that helped fuel the tremendous growth in the higher education sector. Millions of new students entered colleges and universities. Existing colleges expanded and new ones were founded. Enormous amounts of money in the form of financial aid were made available to help students pay for school.

Mass education had taken hold of America. It was seen as the right of every qualified American high school graduate to have the opportunity to acquire a higher education. Coinciding with the massive expansion of higher education in the 1960s was the movement of the 1950s 'baby boom' children into college. In the 1980s and 90s the children of the 'baby boomers' are ready to go to college. Parents want the same opportunities for their children as they had. As disenfranchised groups and persons organized and attained positions where they could influence public policy which produced funding and support for higher education, they increased access to higher education (Karen, 1991). The past several decades have seen universities and colleges transformed into institutions that are among the most important in determining status and opportunity for people (Orfield, 1990).

Impact of mass education

'The United States appeared to be on the verge of creating a right unknown in the world, a right to higher education for all who might benefit' (Orfield, 1990: p325). For the year 1998 the U.S. Department of Labor reported that 65.6% of all high school graduates were attending college. This was slightly down from 1997, when 67% of all high school graduates were attending college. When 6 out of 10 high school graduates attend some form of post-secondary education (White & Ahrens, 1989), it is indeed necessary to examine the impact of this and to try and discern what it means.

The increase in student enrolment since the 1960s was part of a great expansion in all aspects of the higher education sector. New institutions were founded and existing ones were expanded. Community colleges expanded so they could emphasise their mission to serve as open-door institutions.

The make-up of institutions changed. Women became a majority of the students enroled in college. African-Americans increased their presence dramatically during this period. Their enrolments tripled during the seventeen-year period from 1960 to 1976, from 7% to 22.6% (Karen, 1991; Astin,1982).

Massive amounts of money for financial aid, developmental education, access programming, student services and other expansion projects poured into the universities, especially in the late 1960s and early 1970s. The federal government expanded its role in higher education during this period. It became heavily involved by providing money and sponsoring programmes that promoted equal educational opportunity as well as support for programming that helped the economy and strengthened the national defence.

One impact of the move towards mass education that was perhaps unintended, or at least unanticipated, was the effect mass education had on economic growth in the 1980s and on into the 1990s. In the 1960s the economy still provided an ample number of good, well-paying jobs for many workers in the industrial and manufacturing sectors. Higher education was not a necessity for a high standard of living. The economy began to change in the 1970s and jobs in the industrial sector shrank. We saw the development of technology- and information-based jobs as the driving force in the economy. Observers of the economy and of education have theorized that America was able to take advantage of this change very quickly because the mass education of the 1960s and 1970s produced a readily available pool of trained, educated workers to move into these new jobs. These people were educated at a time when the economy did not need their skills immediately but, as the economy changed, they were ready to move in.

The cost of higher education rose at the same time as enrolments grew, the economy changed and the government changed its aid focus from grants to loans. This shift put a severe strain on the very students that public policy was aimed at helping gain access to higher education.

There was concern that large numbers of students were being admitted to the universities who were not adequately prepared to undertake their studies. The presence of these students sparked a debate in the universities and government about who should be admitted to what level and with what preparation. As more groups demanded more schooling, education assumed greater importance as a means of achieving social mobility (Robinson & Hurst, 1997).

Access has increased over this time period but access has not been distributed equally across the various segments of higher education. The top colleges have seen gains in enrolment from non-élite students but access students are still clustered in non-élite institutions (Karen, 1991; Paul, 1990). The class gap in the type of college that access students attend may have widened (Dougherty, 1997).

Conclusion

The massification of American higher education must be seen in the context of the uniqueness of the American experience. The view that education in America is a way to improve one's standing both socially and economically has strongly influenced higher education and its place in American society. Mass education must also be viewed in the light of the particular type and style of democracy that is practised in America and the relatively high level of mobility within the society.

Finally, in the light of the American experience, a number of questions may be asked which could form a useful point of departure when comparing and contrasting the approach to access issues in different countries:

- Who should have access to higher education?
- How many persons should have access to higher education?
- Can we afford the cost of mass education?
- Is or has higher education been an instrument of social inclusion?
- Should higher education be an instrument of social inclusion?
- How do we (or should we) reconcile educational goals with other societal or governmental goals?
- What can we learn from the American experience with mass education?
- What can we learn from the experience of others with mass education?

References

Astin, Alexander and others. *Minorities in American Higher Education. Recent Trends, Current Prospects, and Recommendations.* San Francisco: Jossey-Bass Inc., 1982.

Dougherty, K. J. (1997) 'Mass Higher Education: What Is Its Impetus? What Is Its Impact?' *Teachers College Record* 99, Fall 1997:66-72.

Karen, D. (1991) 'The Politics of Class, Race and Gender: Access to Higher Education in the United States, 1960-1986.' *American Journal of Education* 99, February:208-237.

Maxwell, M. (1994) *From Access to Success: A Book of Readings on College Developmental Education and Learning Assistance Programmes.* Clearwater, Florida, H & H Publishing Co.

Maxwell, M. (1997) *Improving Student Learning Skills: A New Edition.* Clearwater, Florida, H & H Publishing Co.

Orfield, G. (1990) 'Public Policy and College Opportunity' in *American Journal of Education,* 98, August:317-350.

Paul, F. G. (1990) 'Access to College in a Public Policy Environment Supporting Both Opportunity and Selectivity' in *American Journal of Education* 98, August:351-388

Robinson, R. and Hurst, D. (1997) 'A College Education for Any and All' in *Teachers College Record 99,* Fall 1997:62-65.

U.S. Department of Labor. *News Release,* June 24, 1999.

White, E. M. and Ahrens, R. (1989) 'European vs American Higher Education' in *Change 21,* September/October 1989: 52-55.

8. National funding policies to widen participation: a model from the UK

Geoffrey Copland

This chapter discusses a number of issues arising from the use of funding to promote widening participation, mainly in England, using examples drawn from the University of Westminster. This university has 20,000 students, half of them studying part-time, of which 51% are women, and 50.4% declared ethnic minority. People with disabilities are supported by the Computer Centre for People with Disabilities.

The early 1990s saw a major growth in the numbers of students entering UK higher education with the age participation index (number of undergraduate students aged under 21 who enter higher education compared with 18-19 year old population) increasing from 15% to 33% in the space of only seven years. This was driven by the government encouraging the expansion of higher education, but in an uncontrolled way, dictated essentially by the market. This expansion was heavily skewed in socio-economic terms to the higher socio-economic groups who were already the predominant group. Hence a position arose where participation is as much as 80% of the age group for the upper socio-economic groups and as little as 12% in the least affluent groups.

In 1997 the new Labour government set out an ambitious agenda for social inclusion to address the serious divisive separation of British society into those of the affluent groups who have access to good education, work opportunities, housing and social resources, and those who do not. A key aspect of this agenda is to improve educational opportunities and aspirations amongst the lower socio-economic groups, many of whom it would appear had either opted out, or at best, could not break through the barriers to opt into the education system. This is not simply a question of increasing participation by ethnic minorities. The participation from most ethnic minority groups is now higher than the representation in the population as a whole, but there are groups where there is under-representation, for example, Afro-Caribbean men, Bangladeshi women and white males from the lower socio-economic groups.

The imbalance of participation in higher education was one manifestation of the social exclusion problem in the UK. This was, of course, highlighted in 1997 by the Dearing Report. In its response to this report the government published a policy document 'The Learning Age' which set out its priorities for the future of higher education. This established a clear agenda to improve participation from under-represented groups, coupled with improvements in schools and post-16 education. The government does not wish widening participation to be coupled to any reduction in standards, so proper attention has to be paid to selection and quality of support for such students. Value must be accorded to alternative routes into higher education. This requires valuing the importance of innovation and the need to think about standards in access programmes in a different way, not perpetuating the view of some commentators that these are in some sense inferior.

The socio-economic profile of students participating in universities varies widely with some universities heavily skewed to the more affluent and others to the less affluent. In broad general terms it is those universities that were formerly polytechnics, becoming universities in 1992, that have the largest participation by lower socio-economic groups. The longer established universities have the higher groups predominating. It is more likely that students from the lower groups will live at home, be of mature age and study at a local university. A recent analysis gave information to universities of the composition of their student body by socio-economic groups relative to the average for the higher education sector. The analysis for a group of the post-1992 universities shows that the student body is significantly under-represented in the highest socio-economic group relative to the average and much more highly represented in the lowest economic groups. This can be seen to pose quite different problems in teaching and student support between institutions in the pre and post-1992 university sectors.

Government allocates funds to the Higher Education Funding Council England (HEFCE), on an annual basis and gives 'guidance' as to how this might be used to support its objectives. The funding allocated to each university for teaching takes the form of a contract between HEFCE and the university to grant a certain sum of money for a defined student population from UK and other EU countries, with funding weighted according to subject, mode and level of study for each student. British universities have substantial powers of autonomy and are free to set their own strategic plans and imperatives, subject to external audit and quality assessment. The government can influence policy but rarely, if ever, can it direct it, but funding mechanisms do influence institutional behaviour. Funding from HEFCE is governed by a Financial Memorandum.

So the government does have levers by which it can bring about change in the system. For the funding for 1999/2000 the government expressed its desire that HEFCE should use funds amongst other priorities to promote the agenda for widening participation. However a key principle adopted by HEFCE is that change must not be so rapid as to destabilise any institution in the short-term. This is helpful to institutions, but means that change can take a long time. It is also important to understand that the government, having set its priorities, may not allocate sufficient additional funds to meet these and thus funding may have to be 'top-sliced' by HEFCE from elsewhere to meet these objectives. So increased money for widening participation may mean reduced funding elsewhere. Money has been set aside to support increased participation: £1.5million was allocated in 1998/9 by competitive bidding for special initiatives to stimulate widening participation, this will increase to £7.5 million in 1999/2000; and £21million was provided to support existing activities.

The first attempts to stimulate improvements in participation from lower socio-economic groups were by special initiatives to improve access to higher education from these groups. These were based on bids from Higher Education Institutions (HEIs) for project funding. Some innovative projects have been funded in this way. This funding is for a fixed period only and the university is expected to continue this work from other resources after the end of the funding period. This does not always happen and interesting projects come to a premature end or have to be continued at the expense of other university activities. A successful project at the University of Westminster working with local schools to increase awareness of higher education for those from the lower participation groups had part of its funding from a third source, which suddenly withdrew its funding for all such projects mid-year. In order to maintain this project it became necessary to divert money from other activities in the university. This tests the real commitment of the university to this work and some institutions may be found to be wanting.

It is not enough simply to encourage students from under-represented groups to enter university. They may well need special support to enable them to thrive in this community as they are likely to lack the confidence of the traditional university student and may lack some of the study skills experience of more traditional students whose schools have assisted their development. There may be tensions between access students and traditionally-minded students and staff. Once these barriers, which may be more apparent than real, are overcome, these students will often perform as effectively as, or more so than, their peers. They almost certainly will bring different perspectives. HEFCE has now recognised this in principle by adapting the funding formula for allocation of funds to individual universities to give a premium on the basic funding to meet additional institutional costs of students from under-represented groups. This comes in two ways. There is a funding premium for students who are mature age on entry, registered disabled or who study part-time. There is a separate additional funding for students who are deemed to be from poorer families as defined by home address. It must be stressed that this is additional funding to the university to help meet its extra costs, not to the student.

Recent changes in funding of students themselves are working through the system. Tuition fee charges, about which there has been much publicity, do make provision for fees to be paid by public authorities for students from poorer families, for full-time study, through a means-tested scheme. There has been less public reaction to the removal of maintenance grants yet it is this change that probably has greatest impact on students from poorer families and mature students. Loans are available but those less confident of success in higher education are more reluctant to take out loans and become indebted. There are also some cultures which discourage strongly or even forbid the use of loans. There is concern that students from these cultures will be deterred from higher education, thus negating initiatives to widen participation.

The identification of students from poorer families is made by an analysis of the post code of the home address. These are allocated to areas to assist with automatic sorting of mail. These codes may identify individual streets, or parts of streets, in towns but in rural areas they may cover wide areas. There is an established socio-economic analysis of the characteristics of households in specific post codes used by, for example, insurance companies, retailers and advertising organisations for commercial purposes. HEFCE uses this analysis to identify homes which fall into the lower socio-economic groups and awards a funding premium on this basis to universities according to the addresses of their students. Institutional performance towards meeting this aspect of the government agenda will be measured using this information. There are serious questions about the validity of this approach which is echoed from other parts of the world. The University of Westminster will receive an additional £250,000 next year from this analysis, on a basic grant of about £35million for teaching, i.e. a premium of less than 1%. This is one of the larger sums to be paid in the sector as the university has a larger proportion of its students from the lower income groups than average. But this is nothing like the real cost of outreach activities or the additional costs of providing for and administering part-time or other non-traditional students. The analysis of the funding premium for all universities shows a predominance of the former polytechnics receiving the larger percentages for this widening participation factor. This is consistent with the analysis given earlier.

This additional funding was set up to encourage all universities to widen participation and access. How effective this will be remains to be seen as this is the first year of this initiative. There is no doubt that additional funding is a powerful incentive but there are signs that it may have unintended consequences. It is focused on the higher education institution, not necessarily the access provider. There could be a danger that a university that had a low participation from the target group would adjust its admissions policy to give preference to applicants with particular postcodes to improve its performance on this measure and thereby gain increased funding. But it may not make any particular effort to increase the number of applicants from these areas, only to try to take some of the existing pool. This may do something to balance the social mix of that university but will not increase participation overall. It will certainly do nothing to stimulate and support alternative qualifications and entry routes such as Accreditation of Prior (Experiential) Learning (AP(E)L) and selection interviews.

So the UK government has a clear agenda to widen access but only to those who will benefit without diminution of standards. It sees this as part of its social inclusion agenda. The funding arrangements for universities are being adjusted slightly to provide incentives. For these to work effectively, extra effort is needed earlier in the education system to raise awareness of the importance of higher education amongst under-represented groups and, once such students have been recruited, to support them sensitively to enable them to succeed. Funding incentives which encourage universities simply to seek applicants in areas where they have not traditionally recruited without making any other efforts to increase participation will not achieve the government's aim and merely distort any current arrangements that have stimulated interest in HE in those areas. There are signs that students still have not understood the new fee and loan arrangements and that some are resistant to taking out loans.

The UK approach is thus to use funding incentives to stimulate new initiatives to widen participation and to reflect success. The amount of funding available is not yet sufficient to meet fully the additional costs of nurturing students from non-traditional backgrounds to success. It is for the universities to make the case with properly costed assessments of the funding needed, recognising that this may lead to a matching reduction of funding elsewhere in the higher education system if the government is not prepared to fund fully the costs of its agenda.

Performance measures are being devised to reflect the importance of this widening participation agenda but it is likely that these will not be understood by non-expert observers. Commentators in the commercial press devise league tables of universities which ignore such measures, stressing instead the more traditional measures of conventionally qualified students. Such highly publicised tables do nothing to stimulate interest in widening participation. Indeed they can work strongly against this objective as they set out to measure something else. The culture of league tables has affected the culture of the campus. These ignore lifelong learning and widening participation and indeed use measures that work against the initiatives by concentrating on research and traditional A level examination input scores for full-time undergraduates, excluding alternative qualifications and flexible modes of study.

This model of special projects and funding of achievement is a start but does not meet fully the needs of the widening participation agenda. It has not yet gained the recognition it deserves in performance and league tables and there remains the potential for being manipulated to serve the purposes of the institutions, not the under-represented potential students.

References

DfEE (1998) *The Learning Age: a renaissance for a new Britain*. London, HMSO DfEE.

National Committee of Inquiry into Higher Education (NCIHE) (1997) *Higher Education in the Learning Society*. London, NCIHE.

9. Celtic kittens and fat cats

Ann O'Brien and Maeve O'Byrne

Introduction

Ireland's rapid economic growth of the past four to five years has had a dramatic effect on the living standards of many of the citizens of the state. The so-called 'Celtic Tiger' has bounded onto the world stage increasing employment opportunities for a young highly educated workforce and forging a new confidence in the economic and social climate. The impact of the new prosperity has been rapid and pervasive. Emigration trends, which have been a traditional feature of Irish life, have been reversed to the extent that some service industries have been forced to import labour from other European countries. Property prices in a nation of homeowners are in an upward spiral and are now the second highest in Europe.

Education is the gatekeeper to this new-found prosperity. Since the education reforms of the 1960s the numbers participating in higher education have been steadily increasing – between 1960 and 1980 new building programmes were undertaken in all third-level institutions to cater for the greatly expanded student population which increased by about 60% (Coolahan, 1994: pp134, 136). Factors such as the Local Authority Higher Education Grant Scheme and the abolition of third-level fees in 1995 have increased participation in general but have not filtered through to students from 'non-traditional' backgrounds.

In the Ireland of today, third level education is seen as the key to labour market success and is increasingly necessary for a good quality of life. While many kittens of the Celtic Tiger have thrived, a significant section of society has been less well served. It is clear that some groups and communities are under-represented in third level education, including students from socio-economically disadvantaged backgrounds, mature students, travellers, ethnic minorities, students with disabilities and women students in non-traditional subject areas. The main body of research on educational disadvantage has tended to focus on access to third-level by students from socio-economic disadvantaged backgrounds, and the recent Green Paper on Adult Education (1998) has raised the issue of access by mature students. Consequently, the debate on tackling educational disadvantage is understood in terms of the large disparities by socio-economic groups in access to third level, and these are the groups that have been targeted by the new initiatives put in place by third-level institutions.

This chapter proposes to examine the developments in access initiatives for the socio-economically disadvantaged from 1994 to 1999 with particular emphasis on developments at third-level and their links with the communities they seek to target. There has been a large learning curve on the part of third-level institutions and in that process, many issues have been raised that can only be properly addressed at government policy level.

It has been estimated that the Irish education system is highly effective for approximately 80% of the population. Addressing the needs of the remaining 20% poses a challenge as the economic boom continues into the new millennium. There is a sense from some commentators that this challenge and the increasing divisions in Irish society is one of the critical issues facing the nation.

The Irish education system – who goes to college? – statistical surveys

Broadly speaking the Irish education system consists of three levels: primary education (from 4 to 11 or 12 years of age), post-primary education from 12 to 17 or 18 years of age) and third-level education. Normally, post-primary education consists of a three-year junior cycle followed by a two-year senior cycle. A 'Transition Year' between the two is optional. Education is compulsory up to 15 years of age. Third-level education consists of degree courses in universities, or degrees, three-year diplomas or two-year certificates offered by Institutes of Technology or business colleges.

Entry into university is decided on the basis of performance in a competitive exit examination (the Leaving Certificate) and places are allocated according to a points system. Points limits are set according to the academic standards of the courses and the demand for a limited number of places. Fees were abolished in 1995. Financial assistance for third-level students in Ireland consists of a means-tested system of grants, but the main problem is that the maximum grant is less than one third of what it costs to survive for the nine-month academic year. If you are poor enough to qualify for a grant – by definition – you are too poor to survive on it.

Most of the research on access to third-level has related to socio-economically-disadvantaged groups. The work of Prof. P. Clancy of University College Dublin in particular has focused on an analysis of the student body in various colleges (Clancy, 1982, 1988, 1995). While not directly related to the third level experiences of young people, these large scale statistical surveys are useful in that they give an indication of relative participation. Clancy uses the concept of participation ratio. This allows him to show the degree to which each social group is 'over-represented' (a ratio greater than one), proportionally represented (a ratio equal to one) or 'under-represented' (a ratio less than one). Figures for his three studies are outlined in Table 1.

Table 1

Socio-Economic Group	Participation Ratio 1992	Participation Ratio 1986	Participation Ratio 1980
Farmers	1.35	1.45	1.22
Other Agricultural Occupations	0.60	0.48	0.22
Higher Professional	2.47	3.00	3.37
Lower Professional	1.47	2.14	1.92
Employers and Managers	1.86	1.72	2.38
Salaried Employees	1.48	2.30	2.93
Intermediate Non-Manual Workers	0.91	1.21	1.10
Other Non-Manual Workers	0.72	0.45	0.47
Skilled Manual Workers	0.71	0.51	0.47
Semi-Skilled Manual Workers	0.44	0.42	0.47
Unskilled Manual Workers	0.37	0.16	0.13

Source: *Clancy, 1995*

These figures reveal as Clancy puts it 'very large disparities by socio-economic group'. He does note that there has been some decline in inequality over the period but it has been far from substantial. A child whose father/mother is in the higher professional category has a seven times better chance of going on to third-level education than his/her counterpart whose father/mother is an unskilled manual worker.

Another interesting aspect of the issue, which Clancy examines, is the transfer rate of the various types of post-primary school. There are three types of post-primary schools: secondary schools, vocational schools and community or comprehensive schools. Secondary schools are in the majority and are normally run by religious orders or church authorities and historically these schools were fee-paying. Vocational schools and community/comprehensive schools are not controlled by religious interests but are controlled by boards of management or local education committees as part of the state system. While all three types of school are funded by the state, many secondary schools operate a system of selective entry. This can result in a disproportionate number of high ability students in secondary schools with a correspondingly lower representation in vocational or community/comprehensive schools.

The transfer rates, which Clancy examines, reflect the numbers going on to third-level from the various school types as a percentage of the numbers preparing for the Leaving Certificate in those various categories of schools. These outcomes are set out in Table 2. He emphasises at various stages in his report, that different schools and indeed different types of schools vary greatly in their retention rates to Leaving Certificate. The varying transfer rates 'represent only the final state of differential selectivity which is operational throughout the whole post-primary system' (1995: p80).

Table 2

School Type	Leaving Certificate Students		New Entrants to Upper Education		Transfer Rate
Fee-Paying Secondary	3,325	6.7	2,316	9.9	69.7
Non-Fee Paying Secondary	31, 075	62.2	15,724	67.1	50.6
Vocational	9,217	18.4	2,814	12.0	30.5
Comprehensive	1,171	2.4	1,977	8.4	38.2
TOTAL	49,960	100	23,423	100	46.9

Source: *Clancy, 1995*

A final interesting aspect of Clancy's work is that there is considerable selectivity within third-level in both the type of institutions attended and the courses taken by students from different social classes. Students from working-class backgrounds (Semi-Skilled and Unskilled) are far more strongly represented in the Institute of Technology sector than in the universities (Clancy, 1995).

Other studies in recent years show that social class inequality of participation at third-level has not improved (CMRS, 1992; INTO, 1994; HEA, 1995; Department of Education White Paper on Education, 1995; Clancy, 1995; Kellaghan *et al*, 1995). Despite an eleven-fold increase in enrolments in third-level from 1950 to 1990 the social class profile of participants remains the same (Clancy, 1995).

The work of Kathleen Lynch and Claire O'Riordain of the Equality Studies Centre, University College Dublin, has been concerned with complementing the many large scale statistical studies in Ireland on inequality in education, and including the perspectives of the key players. Their 1996 study, Equality and Access to Higher Education: A Review of Selected Access Programmes, arose out of a series of interviews with low-income working-class students attending college and those in the Leaving Certificate classes at post-primary school, as well as the views of teachers, parents and community workers who are working and living within marginalised working-class areas.

Their study identified three crucial constraints on working-class students:

1. economic constraints which are independent of education in terms of origin, but which impact directly on educational decisions;
2. institutional constraints specific to the education system itself and arising from the nature of schooling and the way in which the education systems are organised;
3. cultural constraints which arise due to conflicts in cultural practices between the lifeworld of the students and the organisational culture of schools as social institutions.

Of the constraints identified the research shows that all four groups (students, teachers, parents and community workers) regarded economic barriers as the over-riding obstacle to equality of opportunity defined in terms of equality of access and participation (Lynch & O'Riordain, 1998: p454).

The effects of relative poverty are multifarious from the priority of financial survival in low-income households to the relative performance advantage of the private education market for those who can afford it. The lack of money for grinds (one-to-one tuition paid at an hourly rate), a suitable environment for study and the need to work were major factors identified, as was the pressure to leave and the lack of ambition and aspiration for the future due to the economic constraints under which working-class students live. A major difficulty is the inadequacy of the Higher Education Grant which does not come near to covering the direct cost of participation, nor the opportunity costs from loss of earnings.

These economic barriers are compounded by a series of inter-related obstacles which are social, cultural and educational. Community activists believed that working-class culture is not valued in schools or elsewhere in society, while teachers believed that there is a 'cultural deficit' among students due to the fact that many parents had a negative experience of the education system. A lack of information about how the education systems works and about life at third-level in general was identified as another barrier leading to a fear of isolation among second-level students and a sense of alienation from third-level institutions. The middle-class culture of the school, teacher expectation and the quality of schooling in terms of curriculum and subject choice were identified as some of the educational constraints. At post entry level, working-class students identified the role of lecturers and support in college as very important as they came from families with little previous experience of third-level. The quality of educational facilities within colleges and the lack of resource facilities in schools were other issues.

The findings of this study unpack some of the mysteries about the differences in participation and have influenced some of the initiatives which have been put in place by third-level institutions concerned with widening participation and addressing ways to improve retention rates of students from target groups.

The third-level response: access initiatives 1994-99

The White Paper on Education: Charting our Education Future (1995) made clear recommendations with regard to how third-level institutions might begin to tackle the problem of unequal access. The Paper states that each third-level institution will be encouraged to:

- develop links with designated second-level schools, promoting an awareness of the opportunities for, and the benefits from, third-level education;
- devise appropriate programmes to ease the transition to full-time third-level education;
- make special arrangements for students to be assigned to mentors who can advise and support them on a regular basis during their first year.

The various institutional responses comprise of access programmes and access courses. A number of the institutions have focused on a community-based approach and forged links with communities and schools. These initiatives are predominately community-driven, while the access programmes and courses reflect an institutional approach.

The response of the third-level institutions recognises that while the primary access barrier for those from a socio-economically disadvantaged background is economic, social and cultural barriers are of considerable significance as are education-specific constraints (Lynch & O'Riordain, 1998).

Against this background most of the institutions have appointed access officers or nominated an individual with specific responsibility for access issues. Most of the third-level institutions have also introduced measures to create entry routes for these students in the form of direct entry or ex-quota places.

Access programmes

The access programmes are driven by a commitment to equality of educational access for all. The programmes aim to address the financial, social, cultural and educational barriers facing students from socio-economically disadvantaged areas from accessing third-level education. The programmes are generally targeted programmes which are school-based.

Links can be established on an ongoing basis with the school population and various initiatives can be introduced at different stages of the school cycle. The programmes are informed by the principle of subsidiarity - of working in partnership with parents, schools, area-based partnerships, community groups, guidance counsellors and home-school-liaison officers and the staff, students and graduates of the institution along with other third-level institutions. The aim is to supplement rather than supplant.

The programmes generally comprise of a range of pre-entry activities with the targeted schools. An integral element of the programmes is the post-entry supports provided for the undergraduate students by the access officer.

The key elements of access programmes at pre-entry include:
- visits to the third -level institution;
- summer schools;
- award schemes;
- shadowing days;
- school visits / outreach school programmes;
- transition year projects;
- study skills seminars;
- supervised study programmes;

- mentoring programmes;
- programmes for parents.

At the post-entry stage, students from the targeted initiatives have access to all the student services of the institution as well as the additional support of the access officer. The students also participate in a range of further undergraduate supports:
- summer orientation course;
- scholarships / studentships;
- tutorial and academic support;
- mentoring / peer support;
- personal tutor system.

Access courses

More recently some third-level institutions have responded by providing access courses for students from socio-economically disadvantaged areas. The courses are designed for young people who completed the Leaving Certificate who have a particular academic strength or interest but who would require an additional year of education to prepare them for a third-level course. It is envisaged to offer an alternate pathway to third-level education for young adults whose social, economic and cultural experiences have prevented them from realising their educational potential. A repetition of the Leaving Certificate is not a realistic nor viable option for these students. The course is intended to ease the transition from school to an independent learning environment.

Schools and/or community organisations nominate the applicants on the basis of socio-economic disadvantage or the students may have attended a school linked to the third-level institution. Applicants are selected on the basis of an interview. Participants who successfully complete the access course are eligible for direct entry to a full-time undergraduate course. The criteria for successful completion of the access course involve adequate attendance and satisfactory performance in all elements of the course.

On-going support is offered to these students, this includes meetings with the access officer, financial support and a personal tutor system. The course content comprises of core modules and elective specialist modules.

Community-based initiatives

The community-based initiatives were established with the specific intention of attempting to have an educational impact on severely marginalised communities.

The aim is to create a small yet increasing critical group of educational achievers to act as role models in the community. The interventions, both financial and cultural, aim to increase educational aspirations, not only in the local schools but also in the wider community. Community-based projects also forge links with a local third-level institution and in some cases with more than one.

Developments, issues and outcomes

Funding and resources

All of the literature supports the view that financial aid given to students from lower socio-economic groups gives them a greater chance of completing their courses (Olivas, 1986; Stampen & Cabrera, 1986; Nora, 1990; St. John, Kirshstein & Noell, 1991). If students knew in the first place that a certain amount of grant aid was available it would encourage more to participate and give greater freedom in the selection of course and college. The feedback from students contained in studies by Kennedy and Fleming (1999) and Lynch & O'Riordain (1996) suggests that finance is a major issue for students in Ireland. There are problems not only with the amount of grant aid available, but also with the method of application. Students often apply late for their grants which results in late payments in the crucial first year in college. It is generally accepted that the grant aid is completely inadequate.

In terms of resources, it is clear that increased funding should be made available to all third-level institutions for direct entry programmes supporting students on access programmes. Currently, top-up scholarship finance is raised privately by individual institutions and as such is not guaranteed. Increased funding should be invested in student supports for institutions who run college-based access programmes. For example, to provide crèche facilities for lone parents, to cover transport costs in the case of rural students, and for the provision of study skills training, academic tuition, peer mentoring programmes and in-college counselling. Resources should also be targeted at extra guidance and information services for disadvantaged groups/areas for both second-level students and mature students if they are to be adequately prepared for third-level.

Research

It has become clear that there is a need for more research on retention rates within third-level. The Commission on the Points System attempted to access data on students' examination results and ran into difficulties: 'systems for recording data are not synchronised across the colleges, even when data is held in electronic format' (1998: p84). It is clear that tracking systems also need to be implemented to gather data on how students entering third-level via an access route fare, and where students go when they drop out or complete their courses.

National strategy and institutional co-operation

While pilot schemes and targeted access initiatives are an important first step, it is becoming increasingly apparent that the problem needs to be tackled on a national level. There is much valuable work being done at the level of building links between institutions and their local communities, however in the long-term, consideration needs to be given to a national co-ordinated access strategy. At present, given the nature of the access initiatives in place, co-operation across institutions is difficult to implement. For example, there is no common set of agreed criteria for the selection of students or schools; students from schools participating in targeted direct entry programmes have a limited choice in that they can only access courses on offer in the institutions linked to their schools. School-based targeting has many limitations in that many individuals in an area are not catered for if they chose to attend non-participating schools.

Third-level institutions while providing some support to students they have identified on their own programmes, have no way of catering for other students equally in need of support. The fragmented nature of current access activity in Ireland mitigates against real equality of choice, support and mobility for students. In real terms students need to be fortunate enough to live in a target area, attend a designated school linked to an access programme, and want to pursue a course on offer in that particular institution. An integrated national strategy needs to be developed in order to allow students the broadest choice, with strong pre- and post-entry support.

Limitations/class issues/the role of the state

The state operates as a mediator between students and their educational choices by specifying a range of educational, cultural and economic conditions within which choices are framed. The state controls the organisation of schooling in terms of curricula, examinations, teacher appointments and the relationship between schools and higher education institutions. It is only at state level that real change can occur.

In their recent research, Lynch & O'Riordain (1998), explore how the prevailing ideologies of liberalism perpetuate class-based inequalities. Class is a taboo subject in Ireland. There is a resistance to an open debate on the dynamics of existing class structures and their inherent inequalities. Current access initiatives focus on distributing inequalities across society and not on eliminating inequality. The concentration on the few *successful* individuals serves to perpetuate the myth that the *success of the few becomes the pattern for the many*.

The 'gatekeepers' of the education system preserve the status quo by adhering to traditional and standard entrance systems, thus maintaining the educational, social and cultural barriers facing working-class students. Working-class students do not give up on the education system, they negotiate and inhabit it with an eye to the opportunities which are open and those which are not.

Current access policy and practice does not address the challenge of eliminating class-based inequality. This can only be achieved by a series of challenges, which must be initiated at several different levels within the education and state system. Otherwise, the 'fat cats' of the Celtic Tiger will continue to skim the cream.

References

Clancy, P. (1982) *Participation in Higher Education*. Dublin, Higher Education Authority.

Clancy, P. (1988) *Who Goes to College?* Dublin, Higher Education Authority

Clancy, P (1995) *Access to College: Patterns of Continuity and Change*. Dublin, Higher Education Authority.

Commission on the Points System (1998) *Background Document*. Dublin, Government Publications Office.

Coolahan, J. (ed) (1994) *Report on National Education Convention*. Dublin, Government Publications Office.

Department of Education (1995) *Charting Our Education Future, White Paper on Education*. Dublin, Government Publications Office.

Department of Education (1998) *Adult Education in an Era of Lifelong Learning, Green Paper on Adult Education*. Dublin, Government Publications Office.

Hyland, A. (1998) '*Challenges and Opportunities in Higher Education*' in Access and Diversity, Proceedings of the Sixth Biennial Conference of the Confederation of Student Services in Ireland, Tuffery, A. (ed), Dublin, C.S.S.I.

Kelleghan, T., Weir, S., O'Hallachan, S. and Morgan, M. (1995) *Educational Disadvantage in Ireland*. Dublin, Department of Education and Combat Poverty Agency.

Kennedy, O. and Fleming, B. (1999) *Young People, Living in a Severely Disadvantaged Area, and Their Experience of Third Level Education.* Dublin (Unpublished).

Lynch, K. and O'Riordan, C. (1996) *Social Class, Inequality and Higher Education: Barriers to Equality of Access and Participation Among School Leavers.* Dublin, Higher Education Authority.

Lynch, K. and O' Riordan, C. (1998) *Inequality in Higher Education: A Study of Class Barriers.* Dublin, Equality Studies Centre, University College Dublin.

Nora, A. (1987) 'Determinants of Retention Among Chicano College Students: A Structural Model' in *Research in Higher Education,* 26:31-59.

Olivas, M.A. (1986) 'Financial and Aid and Self Reports by Disadvantaged Students: The Importance of Being Earnest' in *Research in Higher Education,* 25:245-252.

St. John, E.P., Kirshstein, R.J. and Noell, J. (1991) 'The Effects of Student Financial Aid on Persistence. A Sequential Analysis' in *The Review of Higher Education,* 14:383-406.

Stampen, J.O. and Cabrera, A.F. (1986) 'Exploring the Affects of Student Aid on Attrition' in *The Journal of Student Financial* Aid, 16:28-40.

10. Social inclusion: a national example of good practice

Amos Carmeli

Introduction

This chapter examines a national tutoring and mentoring project in Israel, which both supports and encourages underprivileged pupils in schools to aspire to higher education, and reduces the burden of cost to some less well off university students. In a Utopian state all citizens would be able to enjoy, free of charge, those basic services most countries aim to provide their citizens with, for example: internal and external security, health, employment, housing and education. Unfortunately, no country in today's world can supply all of these services free of charge. Everyone has to pay for them, either directly, or indirectly via taxation. As someone who has been involved in the funding of education throughout most of my life, I do envy countries such as France, Germany or Holland where a university education is free. Unfortunately, Israel does not enjoy that privilege and the cost of university studies is quite high. The diverse cultural and socio-economic backgrounds of the population of the modern state of Israel pose a major challenge: how to provide equal education opportunities for all of its citizens.

According to my belief there is a great difference between 'education'- that is the acquiring of basic knowledge, which every citizen in a modern world must have - and 'higher education' - that is the acquiring of a profession. This raises an important question: why should a country pay for the higher education of students, most of whom come from the middle-classes and upper stratas of society, who in many cases study professions which are not needed? (I know, academic freedom and the powers of the free market, but these are slow to react and in the meantime the public pays for thousands of needless lawyers, dentists, architects and others).

Poor students - those who do not have the financial means to study in higher education – are the ones who should get the help and support of their country, and this is what the state of Israel is doing. The government and many different public and private organisations offer scholarships to students in need, so that they may have an equal opportunity and start, to acquire a profession, like their better-off peers.

Background

On October 26th 1998 a large-scale strike started in Israel, involving 150,000 men and women. The issue – as always – was money. The government, their rival, said 'no'. The sums demanded were impossible and the national budget was already stretched to its limits. It was a fierce strike, which involved the closing of roads and junctions, tyre burning, police intervention, force, TV coverage, and thousands of words in newspaper editorials and commentary columns. The public was in favour of the strikers. Negotiations began and lasted long days and nights, involving key figures including even the prime minister himself. The treasury held firm - more money will be given on one condition - more work. On December 6th, after six long weeks of struggle, the strikers gave up. The battle was lost.

The strikers, as you probably realised, were the university and college students of Israel. What they asked for was a reduction in the sums they have to pay as tuition fees (which are quite high in Israel). They lost the strike, and came out with one significant gain - it is called PERACH, a tutorial project.

'There is no free lunch' is a slogan that we have learned from the richest country in the world. There is a price for everything. Those who enjoy public funds, should in return give something back to the public. Let's give students in need scholarships, but put them to work serving the community in return. PERACH was established 25 years ago to work out these ideas. PERACH means 'flower' in Hebrew, but it is also an acronym for a 'tutorial project'.

The PERACH tutorial project

PERACH was created to ensure that as many Israeli youngsters as possible – from kindergarten to graduate school – fulfil their potential. University students volunteer to spend a few hours each week, tutoring, helping and motivating underprivileged children. In return, they receive a scholarship covering approximately half of their university tuition. PERACH has grown over the years to become the largest programme of its kind in the world, and about 20% of all Israeli students and 45,000 children are involved, as well as hundreds of staff members. Today it is a role model for many universities and countries. The goals of PERACH are to:

- give every child an opportunity to fulfil his/her potential;
- reduce social and educational differences between children in Israel;

- provide enrichment programmes for needy children in the schools, community and recreation centres;
- help university students meet the rising cost of tuition; and
- make university students more aware of the social problems of the country by fostering close relationships between themselves and disadvantaged families and children.

Children from disadvantaged homes receive educational stimulation and support through individualised or small group tutoring from a caring young adult who is a potential role model. Tutor-mentors are selected carefully and guided by co-ordinators in PERACH's eight regional offices, based in Israeli universities throughout the country. The tutors and their co-ordinators work closely with the children's families, schools and relevant social service programmes in an integrated approach to develop the child's self-esteem and academic potential. There are also special cultural and other events for the children and their tutor-mentors under the auspices of the regional and national centres.

Tutoring and mentoring takes place primarily on a one-to-one basis (85%), although some group sessions are run by one or two university students for school pupils (15%). Two-hour tutorial sessions take place twice a week for the entire academic year (34 weeks). The sessions take place mostly during the afternoons, either at the tutee's or the tutor's home, or take the form of a trip out.

Following the success of the one-to-one programmes, PERACH developed group programmes to enable tutors with special skills and interests to work with children in their chosen fields, such as science, health, art and nature. There are now eleven special programmes.

The PERACH project is financed by a number of partners: the Council for Higher Education, the Ministry of Education and Culture, universities and colleges, local municipalities, public funds and foundations and private donors. The operation of the project accounts for 86% of the costs of the programme – this includes scholarships and enrichment activities. 14% of costs are administration – travel expenses and salaries.

Benefits of PERACH

The success of PERACH is largely based on its simplicity of operation, the selection of interested and motivated people, the allocation of money and other compensations and co-operation between all the parties involved. Disadvantaged children receiving intensive individualised attention from a student who serves as a role model are more likely to fulfil their potential. The tutor-mentor also benefits by being reimbursed with a partial scholarship at college or university-level, and/or with academic credits within a facilitated training programme. Many tutors come from low or medium-class backgrounds and would not be able to attend university without PERACH's financial assistance. Tutors receive accreditation for the training course, and travel expenses are reimbursed. It should also be emphasised that tutors are also rewarded indirectly, not with money, but with the satisfaction derived from improving the life of young people, although the reward is not unconditional, but requires sustained input by the tutor. Society is rewarded with motivated individuals learning civic responsibility.

The high success rate of the PERACH programme for Israeli children at risk offers society a better rate of return compared to the alternative of large numbers of 'drop-outs' or socially excluded people, and increased crime. Evaluation research shows that as a result of the PERACH programme:

- tutees are 46% less likely to start using drugs and alcohol;
- tutees are 32% less likely to hit someone;
- there is a 50% improvement in school attendance and performance, and attitudes towards completing school work; and
- there is an improvement in peer and family relationships.

The evaluation, based on anonymous questionnaires given to a sample of school counsellors, tutors and co-ordinators found overwhelming support for the scheme from both schools and tutors.

School Counsellors

Tutors' contribution to the academic achievements of the children (%)
High 55   Medium 40   Low 5

Tutors' contribution to the academic motivation of the children (%)
High 63   Medium 34   Low 3

Tutors' contribution to the self-image of the children (%)
High 82   Medium 16   Low 2

Tutors' contribution to improving the children's social adjustment (%)
High 75   Medium 22   Low 3

Number of children who have benefited from the tutoring (%)
Most 93   Half 6   Few 1

Tutors

Contribution of tutoring to the academic achievements of the children (%)

High 49   Medium 33   Low 18

Contribution of tutoring to the self-image of the children (%)

High 78   Medium 19   Low 4

Enrichment from tutoring of general knowledge of the children (%)

High 77   Medium 19   Low 4

Would recommend friends to join PERACH (%)

Yes 87   No 13

Co-ordinators

Satisfaction from their tutors' work (%)

Very satisfied 91   Satisfied 9   Not satisfied 0

From these statistics it can be seen that both schools and tutors feel that PERACH makes a difference to the lives of the children it is intended to benefit. Furthermore, the voluntary nature of the scheme, the recruitment process and the extensive support system result in a low drop-out rate during the year-long work at PERACH, and co-ordinators are largely very satisfied with tutors, and none are dissatisfied.

Conclusion

Tutoring and mentoring is gaining momentum, and may become the next millennium's largest serious, profound and positive students' revolution. There are many young, talented people who just need the leadership and guidance to help them flourish. It is our task to show them the way. It is my belief that a PERACH-like scheme should and could be developed in every country to encompass millions of students and children around the globe. It certainly can develop into a social and educational programme that no nation has known before, in numbers, depth and impact. A programme in which there are no losers, just winners.

11. Approaches to widening access to higher education in Malta

Paul Heywood

Introduction

This chapter examines ways of widening access to higher education in Malta. Firstly, through measures taken at the interface between the post-secondary[1] sector and the University of Malta (UM), which constitutes higher education (HE) in Malta, and secondly, by tracing different routes to HE. The government is currently investigating strategies for expanding HE, especially to those who have pursued a vocational rather than an academic route. Attendance at the EAN conference at Cork in 1997 served as a think tank for such an exercise. Meetings were also held with heads or assistants heads of a number of schools in the post-secondary sector.

Malta has achieved diversity in HE, but it is far from a mass system. A few terms need clarification at the outset. Quality has traditionally been measured in terms of students completing their course with good examination grades. A recent development is to combine such quantitative measurements, with the recognition of the responsibilities of higher education towards society at large in contributing to social and economic wellbeing. Quality in this sense involves adopting a holistic approach. Pauline Perry says:

'Quality in this broader sense cannot be measured only quantitatively against one or two isolated performance indicators, but requires qualitative criteria, which enable institutions to identify their strengths and weaknesses and to enhance their performance over their activities as a whole. For example, in relation to their students, higher education institutions would demonstrate how their needs are being met in the widest possible sense, including their personal, academic and learning needs, as well as their long-term need to find fulfilment in contributing to their society...not only in the narrow economic sense, but in the wider sense of society's aspirations for itself.'

(Perry, 1991; quoted in Woodrow, 1996: p6).

Such a grasp of 'quality' involves looking into the interplay between the curriculum, the student intake and the student output. It is with such a conception of quality that the access project in Malta has operated.

The term 'higher' education obviously includes non-university higher education institutions. And it should be borne in mind that most advanced continental systems have binary systems of education. Germany opted for such a system, with universities and Fachhochschulen (universities of applied sciences) because the latter are far cheaper to run (Mönikes, 1997). The UK, on the other hand, has officially plumped for a unitary system, with former polytechnics being upgraded to the status of universities. In addition to the enduring divide between Oxbridge and other old universities, and subsequently between these and the former polytechnics, a new binary system seems to be springing up. This takes the form of partnerships between universities and further education institutions, such as the one between the University of Central Lancashire and further education institutions in the area, where the mutual aim of both the colleges and the university is to provide access to education for the local community. The partnership is formalised so that the colleges are 'associated' or 'licensed colleges' of the university with associated colleges working with the university exclusively in the development of their higher education provision whereas licensed colleges deliver university courses at the foundation and first-year level.

Still, for reasons dictated by size, when talking of widening access to higher education in Malta, it needs to be made clear whether a unitary or binary system is intended. This policy decision will be revisited later.

There are important issues in relation to the concepts of equality of opportunities and equity and their relation to quality and access. Not to get caught up in a lengthy, albeit central, philosophical discussion, the project group adopted a distinctive interpretation of 'access', which sets the framework of the project:

- greater participation in good quality higher education;
- the extension of participation to include currently under-represented groups;
- recognition that participation extends beyond entry to successful completion.

Quality and equality are deemed complementary and pose no threat to standards. 'Equality of opportunity comprises an integral part of quality, both within the institution itself and in respect of its contribution to the wider community outside' (Woodrow, 1996: p7).

In a period of mass higher education in most European countries participation rates hovering around 30% may be viewed as poor. Although Malta between 1987 and 1997 succeeded in raising the access rate from 6% to 17%, there is no room for complacency. Every effort should be made at least to double the rate in the next five years, to promote convergence with other European countries. Furthermore, it can be argued that a high correlation exists between widening access to higher education and socio-economic progress (see section 2.1 Draft Recommendation on Access to Higher Education (DECS-HE 97/40).

Alternative routes into higher education

Increasing participation in quality HE depends to a very large extent on the articulation between secondary and higher education. One of the basic problems is how to widen access to higher education for students who have taken a secondary and post-secondary technical and vocational educational route.

> 'The relationship between intellectual and manual labour, between the work of the hand and the work of the mind, between vocational learning traditions and academic learning traditions, has been the underlying concern in all school reforms in Norway since the Second World War...Vocational education and apprenticeship originate in the guild system, where learning for one's working life took place in the midst of work. The learning tradition of the gymnasium has its roots in the old Latin school, with its more conceptual and theoretical traditions, based outside the world of work.'
> (Mjelde, 1994: pp87-88)

Should the theory-to-practice route continue to dominate higher education to the virtual exclusion of the practice-to-theory approach? Each, of course, is coloured by distinct cultural values, born to a large extent of the prevailing educational system, which has so far favoured sixth-form students with their essentially academic A level qualifications. The students from other institutions in the post-secondary sector, such as technical institutes like M. Sapiano Technical Institute and the Fellenberg Centre for Industrial Electronics, are given only partial acknowledgement of their certificates for the purpose of access to higher education. Thus, the Ordinary Technician Diploma (OTD) awarded by the City and Guilds of London Institute has been declared equivalent to one pass at A level at Grade C, while the Higher Technician Diploma (HTD) is equivalent to two A level passes at Grade A for the purpose of access to BEng courses. This approach seems arbitrary: why should an HTD not be given an equivalence to three A levels at Grade C instead of two at Grade A? This would have given the technical institute graduates access to UM.

The Matriculation and Secondary Education Certificate (MATSEC) system has now been brought closer to that of the International Baccalaureate, rendering programmes of study leading to access more interdisciplinary. But the situation for technical students with vocational qualifications has not improved. The objection to admitting these students on the strength merely of their vocational qualifications is that they lack theoretical knowledge and the ability to think creatively as they have been bred on the practical application of schemata unquestionably entertained. Even if this were true, the articulation between secondary and higher education could be managed in a way that would make up for such a shortcoming.

This could be accomplished by the setting up of different routes to higher education from different post-secondary bases and strengthening access through pre-access and access courses run at the post-secondary base, reinforcing all access with developmental education in order to ensure retention and completion of courses.

At the interface between post-secondary and UM, promoting equal participation in higher education in fact involves consideration of the following:

a) the matriculation examination and the whole MATSEC set-up;

b) the various professional qualifications awarded by vocational/technical institutions in the post-secondary sector and the weighting to be assigned to them for the purpose of access to higher education;

c) exploring the possibility of forging links between UM and certain post-secondary institutions on the lines of the partnership model used by the University of Central Lancashire.

a) One obvious approach to widening access consists in recasting the Matriculation Examination to give greater scope for skills such as practical thinking, manual dexterity and teamwork, talents that very often characterise groups at present under-represented in higher education. If the education system is seen to value such talents, their very refinement and promotion will inevitably lead on to academic interest, enquiry and attainment. This was one of the reasons for the introduction of project work in the Systems of Knowledge syllabus at Intermediate Level (IM),[2] especially the artistic and technological projects. But reaping the benefit of such an approach is only possible if project work were to form an integral part of the curriculum from the early years of the secondary sector. Implementing such a system, however, is no easy matter. It calls for trained staff, administrative backing and material resources. These have been sadly lacking in carrying through the Systems of Knowledge project so far.

Academic levels of attainment could and should be maintained. This, however, should not imply a need to hold on to our present overloaded syllabuses. For example, most of the syllabuses for subjects taken at Intermediate Level are, in fact, overloaded, thereby creating panic among teachers in their endeavour to cover them in time, and frenzy among students to learn by rote. Little space is allowed for thoughtful assimilation through discussion and questioning. This is one of the main shortcomings of our examination-ridden system. There is hardly any room at all for teaching that is interactive, experiential and student-centred. As a first step, it is suggested that one of the Intermediate Level requirements, other than Systems of Knowledge, in the Matriculation Certificate examination should be dropped. Students would still be called upon to obtain passes amounting to three A level passes. Indeed, since IM syllabuses amount, in point of fact, to more than a third of the content of an A level subject, our students are still being made to clear far higher hurdles, on average, than their UK counterparts in order to make it to university.

b) Courses run by Mikielang Sapiano Technical Institute, Fellenberg Training Centre for Industrial Electronics, Hannibal Scicluna Secretarial School, Guze Micallef College for Agriculture, Art and Design Centre and other institutions in the post-secondary sector should be given clear and unequivocal recognition by HE, not merely for the admission of mature students. What is called for is an objective assessment of the relevance of the certificates awarded by these schools to specific HE routes. The route from Mother Theresa Pre-Vocational School for nurses and paramedics to the Institute of Health Care at the University of Malta is an excellent pioneering example of good practice in widening access to HE and promoting upward social mobility among the so-called disadvantaged. All admissions to HE may, where necessary, be reinforced in a similar way through access courses and development education.

According to Dennis Kallen (Kallen, 1995), there are in fact a number of measures being adopted in vocational and technical education that aid such a process:
(i) A larger place is given to general subjects in the curricula, often a dominant and sometimes even a quasi-monopolistic place in the first one or two years of longer programmes;
(ii) at the same time, priority is given to training in broad-skill areas and in broad or 'generic' skills that lay the foundation for later (possibly post-school) training in job-related skills;
(iii) the number of specialisations is strongly reduced in connection with (ii)

above but also in accordance with the development of the labour market; strongly reduced, often from several hundred to a few dozen. (p29).

Moreover there is a movement in the UK through the National Council for Vocational Qualifications (NCVQ) to define correspondences between purely academic qualifications and essentially vocational ones. It is now accepted by some UK universities that an Advanced General National Vocational Qualification (AGNVQ) is equivalent to two A levels and it grants access to undergraduate courses at university. An AGNVQ in turn, is comparable to a National Vocational Qualification (NVQ) level 3, while a GCSE (Grades A-C) is comparable to an Intermediate GNVQ, which in turn is comparable to NVQ level 2.

Australia is carrying out a similar exercise. The Australian Qualification Framework (AQF), introduced in 1995, recognises that the school sector, the vocational and training sector and higher education have different industry and institutional linkages. It attempts to connect them in a comprehensive, nationally consistent, yet flexible, framework for all qualifications in post-compulsory education and training. What is interesting in the Australian approach is the policy to have curricula and programmes of studies drawn up in terms of skills and competencies. There is a move to develop a national tertiary system with increased links between HE, vocational education and the school sector. It is an approach that could be adapted for application in Malta.

If definite credit value could be assigned to each of the vocational certificates in the post-secondary sector, it would be possible to fashion apposite pre-access and access courses for the various routes to HE. These access courses need not necessarily be run at UM. They could be held at the post-secondary institution with the aid of UM, through a UM partnership office set up on the lines suggested by the University of Central Lancashire initiative.

In an attempt to widen access to under-represented groups, UM has broached the idea of the hub model, with each post-secondary institution negotiating with UM its specific access route (see Figure 1).

This is one way of making progress towards equity by affording chances of access to HE to persons with technical skills not traditionally associated with higher education, which if developed could be immediately relevant to national economic and social strategies. This could, in the long-term, help change the balance of the student population to reflect more closely the composition of society as a whole (see section 2.2 Draft Recommendation on Access to Higher Education (DECS-HE 97/40).

Figure 1: UM hub model: negotiated access routes

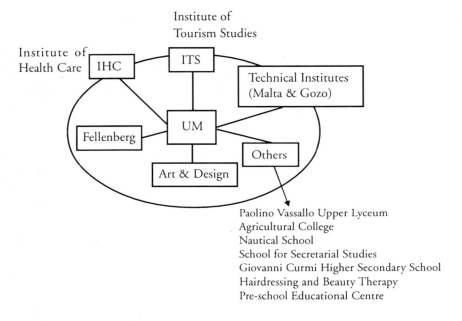

'The university should not act as a gatekeeper or a ticket-puncher checking examination grades in a rigid entry policy, but be an integral part of an education continuum dedicated to widening access.'[3] The university with its involvement in MATSEC is ideally placed for working hand-in-hand with the post-secondary sector in a way that favours not just traditional sixth-form, but also the post-secondary technical and vocational institutions. This is what governments and higher education institutions are recommended to do in terms of section 4.2 of the Draft Recommendation on Access to Higher Education (DECS-HE 97/40).

'The range of access routes should be widened by extending admissions criteria to include alternatives to the conventional 18+ school-leaving certificate. In particular:
• high-level vocational qualifications should be accepted as appropriate preparation for higher education;

- appropriate credit should be given to experiential learning;
- applicants who are generally well-qualified but suffer from specific educational gaps should have opportunities to follow preparatory or access courses provided by higher or further education.'

Apart from the pre-vocational school (health care) already mentioned, the Institute of Tourism Studies is another example of good practice in widening access to HE in a way that does not involve a lowering of standards. Both examples are worth considering; the education strategies they exemplify should be applied to other areas of the post-secondary sector.

c) The model mentioned in (b) above can be made to operate on the lines followed by the University of Central Lancashire initiative (see above). One suggested modification to the hub model is the possibility of setting up a polytechnic by gradually merging Paolino Vassallo Upper Secondary School, Mikielang Sapiano Technical Institute and the Fellenberg Institute of Industrial Electronics. This could be accomplished in the Finnish way. It would take at least five years of definite annual targets being budgeted for, and the results assessed.

But this, of course, brings one back to the broader issue of the overall strategy to be adopted for widening access to HE. If it is agreed that our participation rate in HE should be boosted from a meagre 17% to at least double that figure and beyond, a central question is: should our HE system comprise just the University of Malta or should we go for a binary system as most continental European countries have done? Setting up a non-university system of HE should be given serious thought. Most continental European countries have such a system. Fachhochschulen in Germany, Ammattikorkeakoulut in Finland, Grandes Ecoles in France and so on; even the UK has a disguised binary system. The location of a polytechnic at the Paola complex offering certificate, diploma and first degrees could contribute to widening access in the south of the island and diversifying the two main industries in the area.

As for student stipends, Malta should take a long-term view. Never before, perhaps, has money been more soundly invested. Stipends have helped raise the participation rate from 6 to 17 per cent. It is fair to assume that most degree holders find their way into well-paid jobs. This means more income-tax revenue for the state.

Widening participation: links to other parts of the education system

Widening participation involves action not simply at the interface between post-secondary and HE but right through the educational mainstream. There is a danger of widening access and increasing the mature student intake but continuing to ignore the social, cultural and political distribution of knowledge and skills.

In fact, it might be prudent to consider issues related to widening access at age three in kindergarten. Here it might be more useful to ask questions than make statements.

1. What attitudes and values should one try to mediate in kindergarten to make up for a poor hidden curriculum?
2. What attitudes and values are today's kindergarten assistants planting and fostering in their charges?
3. What kind of in-service training courses are being laid on for kindergarten staff?
4. Should the present model of recruiting kindergarten assistants be reviewed?

This chapter has already touched upon mainstream education. However, a development especially in the secondary sector, brought on by modern technology, especially computers, needs highlighting. Perhaps the greatest challenge to secondary education in modern society derives from the development of the labour market: '...many jobs involve more work with information than they used to...There is an increasing use of computer numerical control in production processes. Other occupations appear to have become more 'theoretical' or 'scientific' or require better grasp of theory and abstraction than when they relied more on practical know-how; this is the case in agriculture just as much as in some service occupations such as health care' (Squires, 1989).

This argues for eventually discarding the vocational-academic divide and working towards doing away with trade schools in their present form altogether. The old divide between the abstract world of academic education, unaffected by practical reality, and the concrete world of vocational education, with its roots in practical work is being whittled down by modern technology. The need for integration between vocational and general studies in mainstream education is urged upon educators by the labour market. Hence a more relevant education mainstream system is called for. In recasting the curriculum, however, special attention should be paid to the transmission of genuine ethical norms and a sense of values. '...there is a growing demand for interpersonal skills and social skills also for things such as training for citizenship, for consumership, for leisure behaviour and, perhaps equally significant, for transmitting ethical norms and a sense of values. Access is an ethical, not merely an administrative initiative' (Kallen, 1995).

Access to HE is fundamental to the achievement of equality of educational opportunities and empowerment, and here adults and lifelong education should play a vital role. The Adult Education Unit, in conjunction with the network of Non-governmental Organisations (NGOs) can do a lot to promote access to HE among groups that are socially and economically marginalised. An outreach policy is called for, not only to reinforce established NGOs, but also to support and guide non-formal community-based groups in enabling access to HE. It is here, at the community level, that the project for doing away with trade schools in their present form should start.

'At the core of the debate on social justice in post-modern society is the question of access to knowledge as the key to empowerment and democratic participation...The access deficit for working-class people is one of the biggest challenges facing Irish education at the end of the twentieth century'. (Powell, 1997)

Participation involves successful completion

In Malta the drop-out rate is approximately 6 to 8 per cent. It must be borne in mind that there are no firm statistics or a clear definition or classification of the different types of failure to complete courses. Accepting this figure, there is no room for complacency even if the drop-out rate of around 70% in Italy might prompt one to shelve the issue. If Malta is to embark on a definite policy of widening access (which it may have to do if it accepts the Council of Europe Recommendation on Access to HE) it should take up the drop-out problem and adopt appropriate measures to contain it. This position is supported by most people in the field of access, as Dwinell and Higbee note:

'The researchers agree that retention is a by-product of improving students' experiences in college, and it is not an end in itself' (Kinnick & Ricks, 1993). Educators need to develop intervention programmes early in students' academic careers to help them focus on the personal, social and academic factors that impact their lives. These programmes may include orientation courses (Salter & Noblet, 1994; Starke, 1994) or pre-college orientation courses (Pascarella, Terenzini &Wolfe, 1986). Such orientation programmes can establish a bridge between students' needs and available campus resources. They can help students develop the necessary study strategies and time management techniques proven essential for college survival. 'The implementation of orientation programmes needs to be unique to each institution's strategic plan, mission statement, goals and curriculum.' (Dwinell & Highee, 1995, p,16)

The profile of students who drop out of courses varies from country to country, with social class being a recurrent element. 'Drop-out may be caused by individual or institutional factors, by socio-economic factors or by inter-related factors. A major factor is that HE has expanded but the systems have not adapted to the needs of the new groups who are entering education. The curriculum and assessment systems have not been adapted to reflect the diversity of students, which has led to increased drop-out (Egan, 1996).'

Conclusion

Malta's HE system compares well with other countries in terms of rates or participation by gender, age, ethnic origin, religion, political creed or physical disability. However, steps must be taken to expand access. The UM will need to adjust, reinforcing its guidance and counselling services and providing development education programmes. It will have to reverse its decision to do away with the Foundation Course for Maltese students. In fact, it might have to extend and diversify such access courses, and pre-access programmes.

The running of pre-access, access and first-year UM courses in certain post-secondary institutions on the lines adopted by the University of Central Lancashire might help smooth the transfer to university for certain disadvantaged groups. Merging institutions in the post-secondary sector into polytechnics over a period of years in the Finnish style could also help.

It is useful to highlight a central problem in the Maltese public mainstream education system: the medium of instruction. Empowerment of the individual implies above all imparting the necessary language skills. The private sector will continue to enjoy an advantage as long as we remain without a sound language policy. This would involve the introduction of language sections, with part of the curriculum being taught exclusively through Maltese and the rest exclusively through English.

References

Council of Europe (1997) *Draft Recommendation on Access to Higher Education.* Council of Europe DECS-HE 97/40.

Dwinell, P.L. & Higbee, J.L. (eds) *(1995) Enhancing Student Retention.* National Association for Development Education.

Egan, O. Paper presented at the convention of the European Access Network 1996, Amsterdam.

Kallen, D. (1995) *Articulation between Secondary and Higher Education.* Council of Europe.

Mjelde, L. (1994) 'Will the Twain Meet?' in Heywood, P., Wain, K., and Calleja, J. (eds*)* *Research into Secondary School Curricula.* Swets and Zeitlinger.

Mönikes, W. (1997) Plenary 6th EAN Conference, Cork.

Perry, P. (1991) 'Quality in Higher Education' in Schuller, T (ed) *The Future of Higher Education.* Buckingham, Open University Press.

Powell, F. (1997) *Adult Education, Cultural Empowerment and Social Equality.* Paper presented at the 6th convention of the European Access Network.

Squires, G. (1989) *Pathways to Learning.* Council of Europe, 1989.

Woodrow, M. *(1996) Quality/Equality, Project on Access to Higher Education in Europe.* Working report, Council of Europe DECS-HE 96/35, 1996.

Note

[1] The term 'post-secondary' in the Maltese education system refers to education after the fifth year of secondary school, i.e. from the age of 16 onwards.

[2] Intermediate Level exams are similar to the English Advanced Supplementaries. However, the subject content instead of being half that of an Advanced Level is only one third.

[3] Cork RTC handout at the 6th convention of the European Access Network in 1997.

Part Four

Institutional Responses to Promote Inclusion

12. Restructuring to broaden access: a comparative study including Australia, Bulgaria, South Africa and the UK

Julia Preece, Bill Blunt, Margaret Heagney and Nikolay Popov

Introduction

Higher Education Institutions (HEIs) interpret access and equity policies differentially in the context of their country's wider agendas. Moreover it is hypothesised that the perceived nature of inequities of the past defines notions of disadvantage for each country or state. All four countries cited in this chapter, South Africa, Bulgaria, Australia and the UK, have experienced varying degrees of higher education (HE) reform in the context of substantial political change. They are chosen to demonstrate the global nature of HE reform and corresponding interest in who participates in HE. The countries offer an opportunity to compare and contrast two countries undergoing political and economic transformation with two which have relatively long-standing political systems, but with recent changes of political parties. Whilst there are similarities of response to global demands of increased competitiveness and national concerns for equity, there are also very different legislative and institutional contexts within which this happens. In South Africa, for instance, universities have consisted of provision whose participation was divided mostly on racial grounds. In Bulgaria a major transition has been from state control to institutional autonomy. In Australia and the UK largely autonomous institutions are now subject to increasing state influence over perceived equity concerns regarding who participates in HE. Access priorities for each country are contextualised by their current and recent political histories, but implementation is still controlled by the attitudes of individual institutions.

Space limits the opportunity to describe the institutions in detail. The focus here is on strategies to address access and participation within the wider national circumstances. The chapter introduces a preliminary comparison of some of the base-line national circumstances in the four countries and how one university in each country is addressing, or not, the underlying issues for widening participation. Each university is then briefly described according to size, national status, participation rates in relation to national populations and present strategies for encouraging wider participation. The conclusion suggests that individual universities often position themselves in their responses to national equity policies according to vested internal interests which are balanced against the perceived political gain of change for that institution.

South Africa

South Africa's reforms are predicated on a designated apartheid system of segregated and unequal education according to racial background. The reforms have developed in a context of uneven and divergent levels of economic growth. With a population of a little over 40 million, of which 53% are urbanised, it has an unemployment rate of 34%. Port Elizabeth is situated in a region (the Eastern Cape) for which approximately three-quarters of the households survive below the bread line, and large numbers of people live in shanty towns constructed of make-shift materials. In 1994 the country experienced its first democratic election where the black majority were entitled to vote and the African National Congress (ANC) was elected to government. Educational reform addressed the previously segregated education system at all levels.

The post apartheid HE Act (1996) united all HEIs under one national ministry, thus eliminating all special provisions of apartheid. The Act provides for governance, funding, institutional registration, quality assurance, and repeal of 'certain laws'. A main feature of reform was the South African Qualifications Authority (SAQA, Act No. 58 of 1995), set up to institute fundamental curriculum reform and develop a National Qualifications Framework (NQF). The SAQA vision included pressurising institutions to strip their curricula of the features of knowledge control endemic to apartheid institutions. The SAQA criteria for accreditation of university programmes were that the curriculum should enhance the learner's employability, provide social and economic benefits, redress legacies of inequity, and promote progression in education and training (SAQA, 1997).

University of Port Elizabeth (UPE)

UPE positioned its responses to this legislation in terms of its relatively low national profile as a research university and in the context of a newly appointed Vice Chancellor. UPE was established in the 1960s and caters for approximately 6000 undergraduate students. Most of its students were drawn from privileged 'white' schools, whose educational culture was similar in character. Little learner support was needed and little given, apart from a careers counsellor and a Dean of Students. After the elections in 1994, students arriving from the historically disadvantaged 'black' schools posed a new challenge, and the university undertook to respond directly to their needs. It now has a majority of 'black' students, many of them from historically disadvantaged schools.

UPE is one of very few 'historically white' institutions of HE to be spared student riots in the years following the democratic elections. This is attributed largely to its commitment to involving the widest range of stakeholders in negotiating the institution's transformation (Havenga, 1995). However, it also undertook to respond directly to the needs of its more diverse range of students in several ways.

Strategies of support

Strategies to assist the participation of students include the modularisation of degree programmes and multiple entry and exit points within programmes, allowing students to register when they can afford to. Marketing of programmes was extended to historically disadvantaged schools to provide guidance with respect to the available degrees, bursaries and state–sponsored loan schemes. Coupled with the marketing strategy, the university substantially increased its access courses and student development strategies within the university curriculum.

The first strategy was Supplemental Instruction (SI). Originating in the University of Missouri Kansas City (UMKC), SI uses peer collaborative groupwork to improve the quality of learning in courses which have high failure rates (Clark, 1995). SI sessions are voluntary and facilitated by a 'near peer', who is trained to help students discuss anything in the course about which they are concerned (Clark, 1998). SI creates a feedback loop for students' input to the curriculum, and has thereby been instrumental in changing both curriculum structures and the teaching culture.

Some faculties have introduced a semester module entitled Introduction to University Practice (Snyders, 1998). The module is compulsory to avoid discrimination, and includes sections on university education, using campus resources, oral presentation, problem-solving, decision-making, goal-setting, time management, research, essay writing, stress management, relationship building, conflict resolution, assertiveness, and several seminars on coping in the broader social context. The module is taught in small groups by trained facilitators, some of them tenured lecturers. The facilitators of this programme, together with those in the SI programme, and a group of 'peer helpers' trained by the Student Counselling Unit, provide a broad capacity for mentoring across the institution. In addition to a module in English for Academic Purposes, the university also provides accredited foundation modules in mathematics, statistics, and end-user computing.

Australia

Like South Africa, Australia has indigenous black populations and vast areas of remote desertland as well as urban centres. Its majority population, however, is white and the inequities of racial divides were less overtly legislated for in terms of the country's economic strategies. Australia's HE system has increased between 1983 and 1996 by approximately 80% – one of the highest growth rates of any OECD country. Its response to creating national equity legislation within this system consequently emerged at a faster rate than most European countries and is relatively prescriptive.

The 1990 national equity plan *A Fair Chance for All* identified the following disadvantaged groups as needing support and special programmes to increase their participation in HE:
•   Aboriginal and Torres Strait islander people;
•   people from Non-English-speaking backgrounds;
•   people from rural and isolated backgrounds;
•   people with disabilities;
•   women in non-traditional areas and in higher degrees by research;
•   people from low socio-economic backgrounds (postcode of home address is used as a proxy for students' socio-economic status. A new method based on index of parents' occupations, income and level of education is being trialed in 1999).
Equity performance indicators were introduced in 1995. This enables funding from the HE Equity Programme to be tied to performance. However, since 1997 universities have been able to charge full cost tuition fees to both domestic and overseas students.

While the number of students from equity backgrounds entering HE has increased, their share of the total number of new entrants, relative to those of other students has not (West, 1998). Recent research demonstrates that the main barriers to participation of these groups are financial ones. Furthermore, many students experience double disadvantage, that is they have membership of more than one designated equity group. There are 82% of students from low socio-economic backgrounds, for instance, and 62% of rural and isolated students who have multiple membership of equity groups (Dobson, Sharma & Ramsey, 1998).

Monash University

Monash University is amongst the high profile research sector and one of Australia's largest with a student population of 40,000. There are six Monash campuses in Victoria, a campus in Malaysia and offshore arrangements in several Asian countries. Compared with universities of similar research status, a relatively high proportion, more than 50%, of the student population belong to one or more of the university's designated equity groups. However, compared with some neighbouring teaching universities the curriculum does not reflect this international presence, although working parties have been established to develop university-wide guidelines and policy on this issue. This would suggest that where equity has political currency the context for institutional reform can be shifted.

The university has a well resourced Disability Liaison Unit which provides a great deal of support both pre- and post-enrolment. It also researches new approaches to many disability issues such as alternative arrangements for assessment and peer group learning.

Strategies of support

Strategies being implemented to assist the participation of disadvantaged students at Monash University include:

- establishing Student Equity Officers in faculties to assist with equity planning and provision of equity services at local level;
- establishment of a Transition Scheme to facilitate the successful transfer of all students from secondary to tertiary education;
- reviewing scholarships including proposed equity scholarships which would assist low-income students by providing a stipend and discounted place in Halls of Residence on campus;
- reviewing the Special Access Scheme to increase the number of students from disadvantaged schools coming to the university;
- reviewing pathways to university from colleges of Technical and Further Education (TAFE) in the Vocational Education and Training sector.

The current HE climate in Australia is a challenging one for equity officers. The increasing tendency to shift education costs to students makes it difficult to improve access and participation for disadvantaged students. This is exacerbated by a widening gap between advantaged and disadvantaged groups in the community and by increasing levels of poverty in the student population. In addition educational disadvantage presents in more complex configurations than in the past. A case in point is mature age students who are first in their family to attend university, are from disadvantaged backgrounds and live in rural areas.

Although these difficulties are very real, the current political climate does offer equity officers some opportunities. For example, the current Federal government continues to express concerns about the poor access and participation rates of students from low socio-economic and rural backgrounds and the high costs of student failure to students themselves and to HEIs. These concerns help to motivate equity officers to untangle the web of disadvantage. Similarly the push to internationalisation and global competition helps to bring the issues around dealing with diversity to the forefront of institutions' consciousness. It is perhaps this latter point which has enabled the development of economic rationales for equity agendas at national policy levels.

The United Kingdom

In many respects Australia's economic picture reflects that of the UK, whose policies for expansion have, at least partially, emulated those of Australia. In contrast to Australia, however, measures have been directed at a policy, rather than legislative, level. As with Australia, overall participation has increased since 1961 but the increase of undergraduates from semi-skilled and unskilled manual backgrounds is proportionately smaller. Disabled students are also significantly under-represented. The government's response to this problem is paradoxical. On the one hand they have introduced a student fee payment system as a means of off-setting the rising costs of HE. On the other hand, the HE Funding Council is providing financial incentives to encourage institutions to widen the participation profile of their students. The funding is in two forms. The first is an additional sum per enrolled undergraduate who is identified as 'working-class' or disabled. The second is in the form of a continuation of existing special project money to encourage institutions to undertake preparatory development work to raise expectations amongst communities, schools and colleges and to raise awareness and develop infrastructure support systems within HEIs. Institutions are now required to provide a statement of their initiatives to widen participation and demonstrate the support measures they have in place to monitor and facilitate student progression.

Surrey, an aspiring research-led university is situated in the country's most affluent county and has a vastly different student profile from that of UPE and Monash.

The University of Surrey (UniS)

Current participation statistics for UniS show its middle-class profile is 16% higher than the national average and 36% lower than the national average for students from the lowest social classes (HEFCE, 1998).

UniS is one of 115 universities and 69 HE colleges in the UK. Its undergraduate population consists of approximately 6,000 full-time students, with a separate, part-time programme of courses for 2,000 local adults. It has for some years run 'Compact' agreements between eight HEIs and 55 local organisations – schools, employers and government sponsored enterprise agencies (TECs). The Compact scheme allows students who are identified by their schools as likely to underachieve to develop a portfolio of evidence which can be included alongside their traditional admissions criteria of A level passes (achieved in school at age 18). In addition to this partnership between school pupil and HEI, the participating schools have access to the following awareness raising initiatives:

- ACE days (aim for college education) – entailing discussion workshops, talks and pupil visits to local institutions;
- INSET – (in-service training) where school staff attend one-day events to update themselves on relevant educational issues;
- Student tutoring – where university undergraduates help out in local primary and secondary schools with the aim of presenting themselves as role models and thereby raising the profile of university students. In return the students receive accreditation of the skills they develop – as part of their portfolio of achievement for future employers.

Responding to the new council funding incentives a new scheme 'ACCORD' aims to work more closely with partner HEIs across a wider area. The goal is to produce a consensus about the kind of admissions criteria which will be acceptable for students who may not have traditional A level qualifications. The argument is that they should be allowed other ways of proving their abilities, perhaps using the Compact idea of a portfolio of evidence.

Strategies of support

The above initiatives are generally marketing and admissions strategies to raise aspirations amongst all potential students, rather than targeted at specific groups. Once UniS students are in the system they are expected to utilise existing student support mechanisms, such as a student counselling service and the Special Needs Officer with responsibility for disabled students' needs. There is evidence, however, that students who overcome considerable difficulties in reaching HE often need additional support during their transition period (McGivney, 1996; Woodrow, 1998).

Bulgaria

Although in terms of size the UK landscape approximates more closely to Bulgaria than South Africa or Australia, Bulgaria's political and economic infrastructure is very different. Significantly, in its emergence from the state controlled communist system, the 1995 Bulgarian HE Act is explicitly anti-discriminatory and promotes curriculum reform on similar lines to the South African new democracy. However, whilst the Act specifies equity issues as one of its key features, Bulgarian HE cannot be examined outside the ongoing economic, social and demographic crisis which the country has been in for the last ten years. The free market economy, which replaced the former centralised economy, is not yet developed. Privatised industries face considerable difficulties on a daily basis.

Bulgaria signifies a number of differences from the three other countries in this chapter, although sharing some similarities to the South African economy. A significant feature of Bulgaria is that there is no middle-class. About 10% of the population are well off and rich; the other 90% live in penury. More than 65% of the people live under the subsistence minimum, and half live in awful poverty. It can be said that to be middle class in Bulgaria normally means to be poor. High death rates mean the population decreased from 9 million in 1989 to 8.2 million in 1998. Unemployment is 17%. It is higher among minorities who are much less educated or skilled. The largest minority groups are Turks (8.5%) and Romany (3%, however nobody knows what percent Romanies really are). In some rural and mountain areas unemployment reaches 90%!

In this extremely negative situation, HE has been one of the few sectors which have continued to develop. In contrast to the disincentives of fee costs for the UK and Australia, Bulgarian parents have preferred to starve in order to ensure HE opportunities for their children. Many people see HE as an investment to avoid unemployment and create a fairer chance of getting a decent job.

In the last few years there have been a number of developments in HE. The number of students in higher schools (universities) increased from 182,000 in 1991/2 to 255,000 in 1996/7. The main reasons for this increase were as follows:
- broadening of access by establishing many new faculties and programmes at state higher schools;
- introducing paid education (charging tuition fees) at state higher schools in addition to free of charge education;
- opening private higher schools;
- providing opportunities to college graduates to continue their education in short-term, part-time programmes at universities.

On the one hand, the free competition between higher schools brought about a raising of the quality of HE. Indeed Bulgaria now has signed international contracts with many European Union member countries regarding mutual equivalence of Bulgarian HE diplomas, certificates, degrees etc. On the other hand, the increasing staff : student ratio in the most attractive programmes (law, financing, economics) is seen as contributing to a fall in the quality of education in those programmes. Legislation has attempted to ensure Bulgarian HE is comparable to Western Europe. This was achieved principally through the new HE Act in 1995 (amended in 1998); establishing the National Evaluation and Accreditation Agency in 1997, creating a system of student loans and grants and paying special attention to the academic autonomy of universities.

There are 0.5% of students with disabilities in the HE system, even though 15% of 18-30 year olds have some form of disability. Also, students cannot be divided according to their family background. Such terms like 'working-class', 'manual and semi skilled social backgrounds' are extremely relative terms in today's Bulgarian society. Some of the worst-paid employees in Bulgaria are teachers, artists, university professors, doctors, and so on. Industrial and manual workers earn much more than the people in intellectual professions. University access policies are therefore formulated without explicit funding or political directives attributed to the other three countries above.

Current governing policy in the field of HE is contradictory. As a whole, government supports wide participation in HE. However, it must be said that the government is not financially independent and all its decisions and acts are supervised by the country's Currency Board which does not encourage investments in HE. Grants are given to the poorest students but only where they have excellent or very good examination scores in their study. Loans are available to all students but almost no-one uses them because no-one is confident that they will find a job after graduation. There are no special grants for disabled students. Furthermore, Sofia University's response to access is contextualised by its own highly prestigious position as the leading university in the country.

Sofia University (SU)

SU is not only the oldest and largest university in Bulgaria but it can also be considered as an embodiment of Bulgarian university education. It is not seen in the same way as the other 41 universities and 47 HE colleges in this country. SU comprises about 10% of the students and academic teaching staff in Bulgaria. 75% of the students are from places outside Sofia, 35% from small towns and villages. Students from all ethnic groups (Bulgarian, Turkish, Armenian, Jewish, etc.) are enrolled at SU. Some of the poorest students get grants from the state, Soros Foundation or other trusts.

Sofia University does not have a specific access policy and has to be seen in the country's overall context which is that:

1. there will not be quantitative widening of participation in HE. It is expected that the number of students will decrease mainly because of the decreasing number of 18-30 year olds;
2. there will be no state commitments to helping disadvantaged students nor for students with special needs.

Strategies of support

Nevertheless there are key actors in restructuring to broaden access among the other higher schools, especially the largest universities. The most active role in this process is played by the universities' faculty and department managing bodies. Strategies for broadening access across the education system include:

- making university admission and forms of study more flexible;
- offering programmes which are more practically orientated to the needs of society and students;
- decreasing the percentage of drop-out students in basic and secondary education;
- providing a better level of secondary education (some laws on the national curriculum and the levels of education are under preparation);
- involving students from all ethnic groups by ensuring equal access (this is a tradition in Bulgarian HE); Romanies are the only minority who do not participate in HE (with some exceptions);
- and providing opportunities for students to combine their study with work.

Conclusions

This chapter has only allowed an outline of how access is interpreted by institutions in relation to their national context. National access policies are influenced by the national economy, levels of poverty and unemployment, political histories and consequent international pressures for reform in the context of an increasing globalised market. South African laws bear some comparison to those of Bulgaria. That is, the goal was broad sweeping transformation of a system which had previously been seen as controlling the curriculum. As such, both countries have concentrated on systems of governance and standardisation of quality assurance. More specific initiatives to balance out underrepresentation would be left to individual institutions and their historical contexts. (Some South African universities, for instance, were historically black. Participation itself was less an issue than quality of provision). In the UK and Australia, legislative reform has been tackled differently. Australia has introduced legal equity requirements and identified specific groups who would be targeted for equity purposes. The UK has acknowledged such equity imbalances but preferred a funding incentive policy which allows institutions to independently adopt their own voluntary code of conduct in this respect. Within these different contexts, each institution re-articulates its own interpretation of those agendas according to its own perceived positioning in the field of HE. Indeed Lingard and Garrick (1997) suggest that a 'further rearticulation occurs at institutional policy-making stages', according to 'competing ideas and interests within the institution' (pp 162-163). They conclude that real institutional commitment to equity requires executive managerial influence if strategies are to have lasting effect. This perspective is reflected in UPE's transformation strategies which were initiated by their vice chancellor for instance (Kirsten, 1996).

On the other hand, countries are also engaging with different political histories and contemporary policies which struggle to balance a global agenda of economic competitiveness with the need to include those least able to pay. The goal of HE study, as Popov highlights, is to ensure greater prosperity and economic growth, yet only those who already partake in that economic prosperity have any real access to HE. The extent to which individual institutions overcome this paradox seems dependent on a mixture of external pressures, internal interests and rearticulation of policy. It is too early to say how all these different approaches to reform will affect participation after a generation of educational practices, but there are some signs of differential responses to political pressures and voluntarism. So UPE for instance is working within a context of higher profile participation changes, but without the higher institutional status of Sofia University. UniS still aspires to be a research-led university but does not come under the same legal pressures that Monash University is subject to. Taking student funding issues aside, there are indications of the need for a combination of both legislative pressures and institutional commitment to effect real equity reform. Furthermore institutional commitment to change may well be stronger if it does not already have the luxury of high national status for its current position. These hypotheses need to be examined in more detail at institutional policy-making level across a broad range of universities in all four countries. Such contrasting contexts provide an opportunity to consider the influences of different social and political variables in the drive for achievable equity policies.

References

Bulgaria Higher Education Act (1995), Chapter One, Article 4. Sofia.

Clark, C.M. (1995) Academic Development in Universities in the New South Africa: a Case Study of Supplemental Instruction in *Conference of the South African Studies Association and the Africa Institute.* Port Elizabeth, University of Port Elizabeth.

Clark, C.M. (1998) Supplemental Instruction as a Tool to Improve Student Success at South African Tertiary Institutions in *Conference of the South African Association for Academic Development.* Bloemfontein, University of the Free State.

Dobson, I. Sharma, R. and Ramsey, E. (1998) *Designated Equity Groups in Australian Universities: Performance of Commencing Undergraduates in Selected Course Types - 1996,* Australian Vice-Chancellors' Committee, Canberra, ACT.

Fast Facts (1999) Cape Town, South African Institute for Race Relations.

Havenga, A.J. (1995) 'Democratising a South African University: Negotiated Transformation as a Model for Strategic Change' in *Tertiary Education and Management,* 1(2):196-204.

Higher Education Funding Council for England (1998) *Basic Geodemographic Profiles for University of Surrey (0161).* Bristol, HEFCE.

Kirsten, J. (1996) 'Diversity, Governance and Institutional Transformation: a South African Perspective' in *Ford Foundation 6th Annual International Conference on Campus Diversity.* Seattle, Seattle University.

Lingard, B. and Garrick, B. (1997) 'Producing and Practicing Social Justice Policy in Education: a Policy Trajectory Study from Queensland Australia' in *International Studies in Sociology of Education,* 7(2):157-179.

McGivney, V. (1996) *Staying or Leaving g the Course: Non-completion and Retention of Mature Students in Further and Higher Education.* Leicester, NIACE.

National Committee of Inquiry into Higher Education (NCIHE) (1997) *Higher Education in the Learning Society.* London, NCIHE.

South African Qualifications Authority (1997) *Bulletin* 1(1), Cape Town, SAQA.

Snyders, S. M. (1998) (ed) *Higher Education Made Easier.* South Africa, Prentice-Hall.

Watson, A.S.R., Van Lingen, J.M. and De Jager, A.C. (1996) *Special Admission at the University of Port Elizabeth, 1993-1996.* Unit for Student Counselling. Port Elizabeth, University of Port Elizabeth.

Woodrow, M. (1998) *From Elitism to Inclusion: Good Practice in Widening Access to Higher Education.* London CVCP/HEFCE.

West, R. (1998) *Learning for Life - Review of Higher Education Financing and Policy.* Department of Education, Training and Youth Affairs. Canberra, ACT, Australian Government Publishing Service.

13. Horses for courses but whose courses?
Challenging élitism: the place of curriculum innovation

Jan Smith

Introduction

Over the past 10 years there have been major changes in the post-compulsory curriculum in the UK. At the root of these proposed changes has been the wish to increase the post-16 staying-on rate, improve vocational qualification levels and rationalise the qualifications system. Education and training in Britain has for a long time been blighted by an élitist education system, based on a division between the academic and the vocational. The mainstay of the post-16 academic route has been the General Certificate in Education Advanced Level examination (A Level), the so-called 'gold standard' which encourages early discipline-based specialisation for the minority who progress to higher education.

The new vocational qualifications framework proposed three ladders of progression: the vocational, the academic and the general vocational, with broad equivalencies in level, and the potential to transfer credit across the three routes. The purpose of this was to break down the academic/vocational divide and in so doing remove some of the barriers to progression so that, in theory at least, it would be possible to move into higher education through an entirely vocational route. The general vocational route, in the form of General National Vocational Qualifications (GNVQs) has succeeded to some extent in facilitating access to higher education. At the same time, there have been challenges to the higher education curriculum to respond to a wider range of learner needs and to the needs of the workplace.

Advantages of a vocational curriculum

Some of the arguments put forward in favour of the new 16-19 vocational curriculum are the emphasis on valuing the student experience, curriculum relevance to work and life, and support for diversity. The attempts to provide a ladder of opportunity for less academic students was intended to extend this support for diversity into higher education.

There have been particular features of the GNVQ curriculum design that have been identified as crucial to making it more widely accessible. First, a more open assessment system, based on competencies, is more transparent to the learner. Second, the curriculum encourages self-direction through the opportunity to negotiate projects and work independently, and third, the acquisition of key skills, including problem-solving, managing own learning, action-planning and evaluation prepares students well for future learning, both academic and work-based.

A second more recent policy shift affecting 16-19 curriculum was marked by the publication of the Tomlinson report on inclusive learning (FEFC,1996). Further education (FE) colleges have been major providers of learning opportunities for less able learners over the last ten years, to the point where unhelpful divisions were emerging between 'mainstream' and 'special needs' students. This influential report argued the case for a more inclusive approach to delivery, a focus on the needs of the individual learner, and a move away from the labelling and ghettoisation of special needs. One of the major challenges to further education has been to review curriculum delivery so that diversity in learning styles, preferences and capabilities are reflected in the classroom. As a consequence, there has been considerable interest in encouraging students to understand how they learn and for teachers to use a wider range of approaches to teaching. This is not just a matter of recognising difference, but about challenging notions of ability which are based on a narrow and traditional interpretation of learning.

In theory, GNVQs, with their emphasis on skill development, on learning through practical experience, opportunities for negotiation of content and context, and independent and group-based study can take account of different learning styles. This chapter will return to this later with reference to some of the research carried out at Sheffield Hallam University.

Some problems relating to a vocational curriculum

Critics of these curriculum trends have identified several problems. The first concerns the effect a competence-based curriculum has on motivation. The dominant approach to motivation in the vocational curriculum and beyond derives from performance management in industry, which is achievement-oriented, and involves target-setting, action planning and rewards for achieving personally negotiated targets. In the case of education, the reward is deferred until qualifications are received. This kind of extrinsic motivation depends on the external reward system remaining predictable. The uncertainty of the employment situation, however, makes this increasingly unreliable as a motivator.

A second criticism is about an unhelpful distinction between skills and knowledge in education, which reinforces élitism. Although reference is increasingly made to 'the knowledge economy' this is often in the context of higher paid work, and is not reflected in curriculum design. Government policy documents on education and training tend to focus on the need to up-skill and re-skill the workers and citizens of the future. For the design of the education and training curricula the world continues to be divided into those who need skills gained through low level training, and knowledge associated with higher level education.

This disadvantages the majority, as the connection between knowledge and power in societies is well recognised. Its implications for learning are explored in some detail by Williamson in his essays on lifelong learning:

'Within most bodies of expert knowledge, there are clear hierarchies of expertise. Entry into a particular domain, for example medicine or law, is governed by clearly specified rules and standards which themselves reflect, as is well known, the standard divisions of the wider society. Only those thought to possess the appropriate intellectual and social qualities, are allowed to enter the academy to study.' (Williamson, 1998)

In the 16-19 vocational curriculum, knowledge is given less prominence than competencies, which are applied skills, backed up by what is termed 'underpinning knowledge'. Even where knowledge is recognised as having a place in the vocational curriculum, if it is applied or practical knowledge, its status is reduced. This attitude, as Eraut (1997) has identified when writing about professional education, is a major barrier to rethinking the curriculum:

'This condescending, back-handed, denigration of applied knowledge is reminiscent of the old aristocratic/upper middle-class disdain for 'trade'. It symbolises the image of the curriculum as the last bastion of cultural and intellectual snobbery. What many educators choose to call a broad liberal curriculum appears to me as narrow and exclusive because it gives so little attention to any form of practical knowledge.'

He notes the irony of a curriculum discourse in the UK which puts the acquisition of general skills and qualities high on the agenda in major policy statements (Confederation of British Industry, 1989) and then demotes the vocational curriculum as narrow and illiberal. It is another example of the ambivalent thinking about the purpose of learning which gets in the way of any curriculum innovation. Although these divisions are most marked in the 16-19 curriculum, they have a knock-on effect in higher education at the point of transition. They help to reinforce an academic élitism which works against the interests of the majority of students.

The promotion of generic 'key' or 'core' skills has attempted to challenge this, but there persists a tendency to see them as necessary only for less able learners. This is one of the reasons why the introduction of key skills into A Levels has been resisted for years as a distraction from, and a dilution of, 'real' learning. The belief that truly able and academic students get where they need to without any special hand-holding may have been acceptable when only a very small number took these examinations and an even smaller number progressed to higher education, but it is unhelpful in the context of a mass higher education system.

A third criticism levelled at the new vocational curriculum is that competence-based assessment leads to a reductionist 'checklist' approach towards delivery, that by tightly defining the 'end-point' of learning, the potential for encouraging student autonomy or of developing intrinsic motivation, is considerably reduced. The original concept behind National Vocational Qualifications (NVQs) developed before GNVQs, and outlined by Jessup (1991) did not intend this to be the case and these criticisms were largely rebutted in his later writing (Jessup, 1995). Unfortunately, however, good design is not always realised in practice, as a number of studies indicate.

For example, in a study of the delivery of Advanced GNVQs carried out in 12 further education colleges in the UK, the researchers found that although GNVQs do develop independent work habits, this does not amount to the autonomy of academic enquiry (Knight, Helsby & Saunders, 1998). Academic work should involve questioning frameworks and disciplinary structures, and in this respect GNVQs fail to prepare students adequately for higher education. The authors place some blame for the failure to deliver the kind of independent and autonomous learning which the curriculum planners intended on the inherent ambivalence in ideas about vocational education. On the one hand it tries to respond to the immediate dictates of the workplace and on the other to engender skills, qualities and concepts which go beyond this. They contrast post-Fordist rhetoric (emphasising 'fuzzy' achievements like independence) with delivery through a plethora of learning outcomes, and the employers' wish for workers to be self-motivating, self-managing, flexible and good at problem-solving with the view that vocational education is about behaviour within prescribed contexts.

Similar arguments can, and have, been levelled at other curriculum developments in post-compulsory education intended to promote student autonomy. Modularisation is one example. It increases choice but weights formal assessment over learning development time. Computer assisted learning increases student access to information and can offer tutors the opportunity for a greater degree of learner support. In practice, however, these changes may restrict choice over ways of learning and encourage dependence.

The study by Knight *et al* (*ibid*) identified a problem with GNVQs which is not simply about curriculum design, but about the mismatch between intention and reality. This has been noted in other studies and attributed to a variety of factors. Bloomer and Morgan (1993), for example, when writing about the experience of A Level and Business and Technician Education Council (BTEC) students, commented on the tendency for new curricula to be overloaded, and for quantity to be emphasised at the expense of quality. The current obsession in the UK with standards at every level of education is certainly fuelling this tendency, and leaves less and less room in any curriculum for the student to develop their individual learning potential.

Research at Sheffield Hallam University

Some of the findings from two studies into the experience of GNVQ qualified students in higher education are particularly relevant to earlier points made in this chapter and are briefly described here. Both were small-scale, qualitative studies and used questionnaires in combination with follow-up group discussions. The first was carried out in 1997 as the first groups of GNVQ qualified students entered higher education. This was intended by the government to offer a significant new route for non-academic students to enter university, and it was the 'new' universities, such as Sheffield Hallam, already providing a wide range of professional and vocational courses, which tended to recruit these students.

The research was based on a 10% sample (40) of second-year Advanced GNVQ students from five local further education colleges, and a 17% sample (20) of GNVQ qualified students in their first year at the university. The purpose was to find out from the students' perspective whether this curriculum innovation was, in reality, opening doors and breaking down barriers.

It was very encouraging that some of the early prejudices against GNVQs were not realised. The expectation that GNVQ qualified students entering higher education would find it difficult to adapt to the academic teaching environment was not borne out.

Students found the workload manageable, and adapted well to the style of teaching in higher education. They had less formal teaching time and less individual contact with their teachers, but did not see it as significantly different in other ways. In fact, as a result of their GNVQ course experience, they felt more confident with some teaching methods, such as group work and presentations, than their peers.

On the other hand some other innovative aspects of the course design which should have promoted independent learning did not appear to have influenced the students' approach in any significant way. Students on GNVQ courses are expected to develop the core skill of managing their own learning through the systematic use of specific techniques such as action planning and self-evaluation. Findings from the research suggested that students did not internalise their experiences of 'core' skills because the relevance was not apparent to them. In spite of the fact that the skills of action planning and evaluation were formally assessed, students saw them as hoops to jump through for assessment purposes. For example, many had difficulty in linking the written evaluation carried out at the end of each assignment with real life evaluation and improvement. In other words, they did not recognise the transferable value of that skill. Furthermore, there were signs that the bureaucracy of the assessment procedure, requiring students to produce evidence against an enormous number of competencies, may have reinforced rather than reduced dependency on the teacher (Smith, 1998).

This research highlighted areas worth further exploration, in particular, how far the 'rhetoric' of the new vocational curriculum is changing the way students choose to learn, and the relationship between motivation, expectations and student 'ability'. Further research in 1998 looked at students' approach to study and learning and whether this appeared to be influenced by prior curriculum experience (in this case, Advanced GNVQs and A levels). It looked in particular at the relationship between students' learning styles and previous course experience.

A sample of 51 students from three types of course, discipline-based, thematic/vocational and vocational/professional (based on categories developed by Breenan & McGeevor, 1988) were asked to complete a questionnaire designed to identify their preferred learning style. Twenty-nine of these students then took part in small group discussions about their experience of study and prior learning. Just under half of each group had A levels as their main entry qualification, the rest had Advanced GNVQs. The purpose of the questionnaire was twofold: to explore the correlation between previous course experience and preferred learning style, and to provide a stimulus for the discussion. The questionnaire was based on the inventory of learning styles developed by Kolb (1984) and linked to the experiential learning cycle of experience, observation, conceptualising and action. It was developed by Honey and Mumford (FEDA, 1995) for use with post-16 students to help them identify their own preferred learning styles, which they labelled activist, reflector, theorist and pragmatist. As with many self-administered and decontextualised questionnaires of this kind, the generisability of the findings can be questioned, as can their theoretical basis. Its use with a number of groups of adult learners does suggest however is that it has some validity in testing student preferences.

Responses to the 'learning styles' questionnaire indicated that the majority of the students had a preference for active learning over other modes of learning, but that this bias was more marked in the students who had followed the GNVQ curriculum prior to university entry. There was a slight preference for some of the students following academic courses to be theorists. The majority of students showed some preference for learning through reflection, regardless of prior curriculum experience. Only a small proportion of each group of students showed a very low preference for any learning style. The expectation that GNVQ students would draw on a range of learning styles, would show some preference for active learning and far less for learning through theory, was to some extent met, but there was no marked difference between the academic and the vocational group. Perhaps a more significant finding was that few students showed a very uneven profile in their learning styles. In other words, although some strong preferences did emerge, most students could operate in all four styles, were 'well-rounded' learners, and were not disadvantaged in that respect.

As the GNVQ curriculum should encourage students to think, plan and reflect on their learning experiences, it was expected that they might show a greater awareness than the A Level students of how they learn. In the follow-up discussions, however, there was little difference between the perceptions of the vocational and the academic students. None made direct reference to their prior curriculum experiences, and when asked how they knew when they had learned something, their responses tended to fall into predictable categories of memorising, reproducing knowledge, understanding and application. Application for quite a few was about preparation for assessment rather than application to life or work. 'You understand points and can pass the assignment' was a typical response. In fact, the notion of transferring learning did not signify in any of the responses and this bears out Eraut's observations that we give too little attention to the transfer of knowledge and skills in the design and delivery of the curriculum (Eraut, *ibid*). There were clear signs that many of the students recognised learning in higher education as being about integration of knowledge, about making meaning for themselves out of information and ideas presented to them, but there were hardly any references to skills. There were no apparent differences between the students with vocational and academic backgrounds.

Asking students to explain what they understand by learning is expecting a great deal. We all do it and do not normally think about it. The point here is not that the students were particularly unaware or inarticulate – they were not – but that the GNVQ curriculum had failed to raise their level of understanding in any significant way about how they learned. Their lack of reference to skills and the emphasis on knowledge suggested that they did not consider these particularly important. This in turn indicates a mismatch between their further and higher education experience, a reinforcement of the academic and vocational divide, and bad news for lifelong and inclusive learning.

The way forward?

So far this chapter has argued that the new vocational curriculum has helped to encourage students from a non-academic background to enter university, but that the design of the curriculum does not develop autonomous learning or higher level generic skills in the way intended. There are several reasons for this: one is the curriculum design itself, another is the failure to deliver the curriculum as planned, and a third is the mismatch between the further and higher education curricula.

Current discussion around lifelong learning, its meaning and implications for the curriculum, make the need to resolve some of these issues more urgent. Attempts to define lifelong learning identify two key issues relevant to inclusion: one is the problem of an approach to education which is individualistic and market-driven, putting responsibility on the individual to anticipate and respond to changes in the labour market while the source of the problem remains unresolved. Another is the need for curricula which are empowering and inclusive, addressing community as well as individual need (Coffield, 1999). Longworth, (Vice President of the European Lifelong Learning Initiative) in attempting to summarise the implications of different models for Europe, described the holistic approach favoured by the United Nations Educational, Scientific and Cultural Organisation (UNESCO) as one which 'focuses on giving learners the tools by which they can learn according to their own learning styles and needs' and which 'excludes no-one and pro-actively creates the conditions in which learning develops creativity, confidence and enjoyment at each stage of life' (Longworth, 1998). Clearly, the more humanistic and developmental vision of lifelong learning is the one which best supports inclusion.

There is a need to move the discussion of skills beyond the mechanistic and compensatory, and to bridge the gap between knowledge and skills in curriculum design and delivery. Eraut (1997) believes one reason for the failure to innovate is that educators have ignored the problem of knowledge transfer to contexts outside educational institutions. He argues that transfer cannot be taken for granted but is an important learning process in its own right. More inclusive definitions of knowledge are needed which extend beyond propositional knowledge made available through books and databases to include the learner's perspective and experience. He argues for curriculum models which make interaction between theory and practice their main focus and against curricula which focus on skills while ignoring the key issue of transfer of learning.

The dilemma extends beyond this particular 16-19 curriculum. A policy discussion paper produced some years ago by NIACE (1993) envisaged a curriculum framework for higher education which would embrace:

- mechanisms to negotiate individual learning routes;
- support for lifelong development of personal transferable skills;
- support for the development of skills for autonomous learning;
- specialist knowledge and skills;
- opportunities to participate in research;
- issues which underpin a plural, tolerant and learning society.

The core curriculum would include diversity in teaching and learning and 'teaching strategies which will help learners to understand and develop their repertoire of learning styles'. Although this referred to a curriculum for adults, it might equally apply to young adults entering university, and is consistent with a broad vision of lifelong learning, with the best intentions behind vocational curriculum reforms, and with an inclusive approach. Why is it taking so long?

References

Bloomer, M. and Morgan, D.(1993) 'It is planned, therefore it happens – or does it?' in *JFHE* 17(1):23-37.

Breenan, J. and McGeevor, P. (1988) *Graduates at Work: Degree Courses And The Labour Market.* London, Jessica Kingsley.

Coffield,F. (1999) Inaugural professorial lecture, *Breaking the Concensus: Lifelong learning as Social Control.* Newcastle, University of Newcastle.

Confederation of British Industry (1989) *Towards a Skills Revolution*. CBI.

Eraut,M. (1997) 'Curriculum Frameworks and Assumptions in 14-19 Education' in *Research in Post Compulsory Education*, 2 (3):281-297.

FEDA (1995) *Learning styles*. London, Further Education Development Agency.

Further Education Funding Council (1996) *Inclusive Learning*. Coventry, FEFC.

Jessup, G. (1991) *NVQs and the emerging model of education and training*. London, Falmer.

Jessup, G. (1995) 'Outcome based qualifications and the implications for learning' in Burke, J. (ed) *Outcomes, Learning and the Curriculum*. London, Falmer.

Kolb, D. A.(1984) *Experiential learning: experience as a source of learning and development*. New York, Prentice Hall.

Knight, P. Helsby, G. and Saunders, M. (1998) 'Independence and prescription in learning: researching the paradox of Advanced GNVQs' in *British Journal of Educational Studies*, 46 (1):54-67.

Longworth, N. (1998) *Lifelong Learning – Europe's Future. A Brief Guide for the Busy Person*. European Lifelong Learning Initiative, unpublished paper.

NIACE (1993) *An Adult Higher Education: a Vision*. Leicester, NIACE.

Smith, J.(1996) *Bridge or Barrier*. Sheffield, Sheffield Hallam University.

Smith, J. (1998) 'Beyond the rhetoric: are General National Vocational Qualifications (GNVQs) doing students any good' in *Journal of Vocational Education and training*, 50 (4):537-548.

Williamson, B. (1998) *Lifeworlds and Learning*. Leicester, NIACE.

14. Flexible delivery and inclusivity: pedagogical and logistical perspectives

Glen Postle, James Taylor, Janet Taylor and John Clarke

Introduction

There is little doubt that few, if any, universities in Australia have escaped the influences and pressures on higher education unleashed in the Dawkins' era (Dawkins, 1988) and pursued relentlessly by successive federal governments. Influences of particular relevance for this chapter and largely responsible for significant change in the 'culture' of higher education were:

- the growing legitimacy of flexible pathways for university entry;
- the expansion of teaching strategies available, particularly through flexible delivery initiatives; and
- the shrinking financial support from government and increasing trends towards 'user pays'.

In just over two decades, beginning in the Labor Government's Whitlam era, there has been a substantial increase in numbers of students accessing university education and a substantial change in the student profile of those entering universities. Supported by such changes as those contained in *A Fair Chance for All* (1990), a government initiative to increase access, participation, retention and success in university programmes for a number of targeted disadvantaged groups, universities have opened their doors to a more diverse student group. Such widening of access has resulted from universities themselves legitimating flexible pathways for university entry.

The emergence of student diversity has placed increasing demands on the university sector (demands found difficult in some of the more traditional universities), to find ways to address the equity issues which arise from having to meet the educational needs of a more diverse student body. In many universities, particularly the newer, more innovative ones, this focus on such equity issues has positioned equity as a central and strategic concern for teaching and learning within the institutions. Such strategic concerns in some institutions have resulted in the adoption of teaching-learning models such as those based on distance education.

In a recent paper, Taylor (1995) provides a useful framework for understanding the rationale behind the expansion of teaching strategies available through distance education initiatives, particularly those involving technology.

The delivery 'generations' described by Taylor are not necessarily linear, exclusive or discrete. Some universities, particularly those which by design or circumstances began to provide opportunities for non-traditional students, adopted distance education well before governments began to focus on access and equity initiatives. In such cases, they often operate across all four generations or across more than one generation at any given time. They are also in a much better position to be able to apply technology to teaching and learning in a manner that acknowledges the influences of such variables as 'the type of subject matter, the specific objectives of the course ... and not the least, the student target audience' (Taylor, 1995). Their initial involvement in distance education has much to do with responding to changing student populations and an increasing demand for lifelong learning opportunities. This claim is supported by Hall when he argues that:

> '... with the growing number of non-traditional students on and off campus and the parallel developments in learning theory ... learner centred approaches to education [have increased]. For the most part these continue to be confined to the non-traditional institutions and programmes for adults and distance learners.' (Hall, 1996: p31)

Unfortunately these developments in flexible delivery have been accompanied by shrinking government financial support for higher education. This has led to unsubstantiated claims such as those that argue that the emergence of flexible delivery initiatives is a budgetary driven response by university administrators. Such claims have often been based upon analyses that lack any empirical evidence. For example, the Barlow and de Lacey study of 1998 where they reviewed the literature concerning the use of flexible delivery approaches in higher education and have inferred possible impacts on equity groups. However, their arguments lack any quantitative cost-benefit analysis to support such conclusions. The general absence of studies based on quantitative assessments make it difficult to argue conclusively one way or the other and unfortunately hinder the further development of initiatives aimed at linking flexible delivery and inclusivity.

Flexible delivery and inclusive teaching-learning practices: a case study
The quote by Hall (1996) cited earlier provides support for the claim that many of the 'non-traditional institutions' (the newer universities) have made most of the running in

Table 1: Flexible delivery technologies – a conceptual framework

Models of Distance Education and Associated Flexible Delivery Technologies	Characteristics of Flexible Delivery Technologies				
	Flexibility			Highly Refined Materials	Advanced Interactive Delivery
	Time	Place	Pace		
First Generation – **The Correspondence Model**					
• Print	Yes	Yes	Yes	Yes	No
Second Generation – **The Multi-media Model**					
• Print	Yes	Yes	Yes	Yes	No
• Audiotape	Yes	Yes	Yes	Yes	No
• Videotape	Yes	Yes	Yes	Yes	No
• Computer-based learning (eg CML/CAL)	Yes	Yes	Yes	Yes	Yes
• Interactive video (disk and tape)	Yes	Yes	Yes	Yes	Yes
Third Generation – **The Telelearning Model**					
• Audio teleconferencing	No	No	No	**No**	Yes
• Videoconferencing	No	No	No	**No**	Yes
• Audiographic Communication	No	No	No	Yes	Yes
• Broadcast TV/Radio and Audio teleconferencing	No	No	No	Yes	Yes
Fourth Generation – **The Flexible Learning Model**					
• Interactive multimedia (IMM)	Yes	Yes	Yes	Yes	Yes
• Internet-based access to WWW resources	Yes	Yes	Yes	Yes	Yes
• Computer mediated communication	Yes	Yes	Yes	No	Yes

providing leadership in both distance education and inclusivity in university teaching and learning.

Since commencing its involvement in distance education in 1977, and following successful efforts in establishing niche markets, the University of Southern Queensland's (USQ) major strength has become the development and delivery of distance education programmes at both undergraduate and graduate levels. USQ's leadership in the area of distance education, is recognised both nationally and internationally. Consequently, USQ currently enrols over 21,000 students with more than two-thirds of these students studying in accredited degree programmes offered by distance education.

Prior to 1996, the university's distance education degree programmes were delivered almost exclusively via print using audio-visual, computer mediated communication (CMC) and teletutorial support. Since 1996, the university has moved increasingly to on-line delivery for its graduate programmes. However, at this point USQ does not aspire to be an open university. It is a dual-mode institution.

There is a sense in which USQ's pedagogical tradition was built upon an evolving 'rejection of the classical tradition of passing on knowledge in the form of unchangeable ideas', and the acceptance of 'the active engagement of the learner in the formation of their ideas' (Laurillard, 1993: p15). The university attempts to 'situate knowledge' in real world activity. USQ has always recognised that the classical tradition of imparting decontextualised knowledge was inappropriate. In this sense, many of the issues arising from the explosion of information and the information technology revolution, as well as the changing student population, have been more easily understood by USQ than by traditional universities.

The move from more traditional distance education to flexible delivery models has done nothing to damage the reputation of the University of Southern Queensland. A jury of international higher education experts has judged the university the best university in the world for its global initiatives and expertise in providing flexible learning opportunities to the world (1999 International Council for Open and Distance Education, Prize of Excellence, (ICDE)).

The Executive Committee of the ICDE, based in Oslo Norway, awarded its top two Prizes of Excellence for 1999 to The University of Southern Queensland based in Toowoomba. The ICDE has membership in 130 countries and is officially recognised by the United Nations as the global non-governmental organisation responsible for the field of open and distance learning, and is affiliated with the United Nations through UNESCO.

Theoretical framework for the case study

In order to explain USQ's transition from 'face-to-face' teaching-learning to its more recent adoption of flexible delivery initiatives, a theoretical framework developed by Imershein (1976) has been used. Imershein details a theoretical framework which he suggests can be used to study organisational change. This framework seems to be eminently suitable to explain change in the fields of social sciences and education, particularly where knowledge in institutional settings is the major focus.

Imershein extended Kuhn's (1970) ideas about progress in science for ways of offering explanations for change and progress in organisational settings. His basic thesis is that organisational change can be thought of in much the same way as Kuhn explains progress in science. Kuhn argues that membership of a paradigm in science implies an adherence to particular ways of 'doing' science. Imershein believes that membership of organisations can be explained in much the same way. Just as Kuhn points out that advances in science occur because scientists as a group perceive a need for a paradigm shift, Imershein believes that organisational change requires shifts in the 'world views' of those involved in change.

Imershein claims that exemplars provide the basis for shared understandings among members of an organisation. A critical element of exemplars he defines as 'a shared knowledge of ways of undertaking organisational tasks and procedures' (in this instance we are referring to pedagogical techniques). Paulsen's (1995) ideas concerning pedagogical settings for Computer Mediated Communication (CMC) in electronic environments have been used to define a range of teaching-learning techniques. It is considered legitimate to use these settings in contexts other than electronic since the techniques defined are not context-specific. Paulsen provides the following settings:

- One-alone;
- One-to-one;
- One-to-many; and
- Many-to-many.

Another critical element of Imershein's exemplar is defined as 'an understanding of roles appropriate to different group members' and is essentially the 'roles and responsibilities' of key stakeholders in undertaking the 'organisational tasks and procedures'. Thus the two elements that constitute an exemplar in an organisational setting such as a university would be its teaching-learning approaches (organisational tasks and procedures) and its policies, procedures and guidelines defining its members' roles and responsibilities in undertaking any aspect of teaching-learning.

Another central element to Imershein's framework is his reference to anomalies. He indicates that paradigms are more easily identified where participants perceive anomalies and respond to these anomalies. In this chapter it is argued that the presence of anomalous conditions is more likely to have been precipitated when the institution is confronted with significant pressures or influences to change. In the case of USQ, two major points in its history have been located where such pressures and influences have led to 'changed conditions'. These were when it embraced 'distance education' and became a 'mixed mode' institution and then when it moved to flexible delivery. If these are accepted as critical points in its history, then, as far as models of teaching-learning are concerned, it may be possible to identify three periods, each of which might represent different paradigms.

Paradigm shifts or 'reinterpretation of dominant paradigm'?

During the initial phase of USQ's history, it was involved solely in face-to-face teaching and learning. This has been defined as the 'Classroom-based Model'. Using Paulsen's framework, aspects of the dominant teaching-learning approaches may be described thus:

Techniques		Typical Activities
• One alone	–	Library research/reading and writing tasks
• One-to-one	–	Counselling/Pastoral care
• One-to-many	–	Lectures
• Many-to-many	–	Tutorials/Seminars/Forums

The typical roles of those involved in teaching-learning tasks and procedures were essentially framed in a 'person culture'. This means that individuals, particularly academics, were left to their own devices as far as preparing and presenting teaching materials were concerned. As long as timetables provided rooms and times for teaching and learning pursuits, academics were not required to work closely with other people. Nevertheless, an administrative rationale was dominant inasmuch as it set the scene for length of courses, numbers of lectures and tutorials and assessment times. Time was very much a controlling variable. It is also possible to indicate that at this point in USQ's history, the main role of teachers was to prepare undergraduates for a range of professions.

During the mid 1970s there emerged a number of significant pressures and influences which resulted in the institution's adoption of what appeared to be at the time, quite different teaching-learning models and approaches. For example, during the 1970s, the expansions of higher education, began in the 1960s with the Martin Committee and continued with the work of the Karmel Committee under the Whitlam Labor Government, began to take hold.

In 1975, there were 148,000 students enrolled in 19 universities and college enrolments were up to 125,000. By 1985, this had increased to 175,000 students in universities and 192,000 in colleges - a total of 367,000 in the sector - this represented a more than 14 fold increase in 40 years (DEET, 1993). This level of growth provided almost unlimited scope for the increasing diversification of the student body. However, while some studies (Anderson & Vervoorn, 1983) concluded that little had changed in respect to the student makeup in the sector generally (universities tended to remain socially élite institutions) institutions such as USQ (still a College of Advanced Education at this time) recorded a significant increase in 'non-traditional' students, particularly students from rural and isolated areas and those from low socio-economic backgrounds. In addition to this growth in student numbers, equity had been advanced in several areas of education during the 1970s and 1980s. For example, apart from school-level initiatives such as the Disadvantaged Schools Programme, the National Policy for the Education of Girls in Australian Schools and the National Aboriginal and Torres Strait Islander Education Policy, the early part of the Hawke Labor Government saw several initiatives aimed at promoting educational equity considerations in the higher education sector. These included the Higher Education Equity Programme (HEEP), a programme of growth in funded places which favoured institutions likely to attract under-represented groups, and moves to encourage young people to stay on in the education system.

Accompanying changes in the numbers and profiles of students accessing higher education, developments in educational technologies provided opportunities for tertiary education providers to offer innovative teaching-learning opportunities for such a potentially diverse student body. Taylor's (1995) first, second and third generation models of distance education provide insights into the range and function of such technologies.

USQ responded to these pressures and influences by adopting distance education as a major education platform. This second phase of development at USQ has been labelled the 'Mixed Mode Model'. USQ academics were required to provide 'face-to-face' teaching on campus as well as design and deliver a range of distance education materials.

Using Paulsen's framework again, typical teaching-learning tasks during this period can be described in the following manner:

Techniques	Typical Activities
• One alone	– Accessing information through books of readings, study materials, library research.
• One-to-one	– Counselling/Pastoral care on campus; outreach programmes - telephone contact
• One-to-many	– Lectures - print-based, audio and video presentations, face-to-face
• Many-to-many	– Tutorials - telephone, face-to-face

The typical roles of those involved in teaching-learning tasks and procedures were changed but only minimally. The 'person culture' remained a strong feature although the production of distance education materials (study materials, books of readings, audiotapes, videotapes) required that academics work in unit teams with instructional designers. Other players such as graphic artists and audio-video specialists were consulted only after the design was formulated. There remained a heavy emphasis on the administrative rationale for providing 'order' in both face-to-face and distance education contexts. Other role changes resulted from an increasing number of postgraduate students, but the major teaching-learning emphasis was still in undergraduate programmes.

While this phase no doubt brought about changes to teaching-learning within the institution, they are more changes of emphasis than changes of kind. The teaching-learning activities associated with distance education were designed to 'fit into' existing structures. The 'lecture' and 'tutorial' were still dominant features, in fact the writers of the distance education materials were required to detail the lecture/tutorial elements of units of study through common requirements detailed in a document known as 'Unit Specifications'. Perhaps the most noticeable effect the introduction of distance education had on the academic community was the more 'visible' design of teaching-learning materials, a factor which elevated the status of teaching and learning within the institution.

The next significant chapter in the history of USQ began with the government White Paper *Higher Education: A Policy Statement* (Dawkins, 1988). This statement guided the dismantling of the binary system of universities and colleges and the development of the Unified National System of higher education. Equity was stated as a central pillar of this new national system. It saw increased levels of education for more people as the starting point of a restructured economy and viewed equity in terms of the fulfilment of the potential available to society and to its contribution to creating a more diverse and dynamic skilled workforce.

In 1990 the Department of Employment, Education and Training, in consultation with the higher education sector, developed the policy statement '*A Fair Chance for All: Higher Education That's Within Everyone's Reach*' (DEET, 1990). It placed the goals of equity in measurable terms by stating that:

'The overall objective for equity in higher education is to ensure that Australians from all groups in society have the opportunity to participate successfully in higher education. This will be achieved by changing the balance of the student population to reflect more closely the composition of society as a whole.'
(DEET, 1990: p2)

Much has changed in the higher education environment since the introduction of the national framework for educational equity in 1990. The sector has grown very significantly and become more entrepreneurial and competitive, particularly with regard to expansion in fee-paying postgraduate courses. More specifically:

- enrolments in the sector have grown considerably - 485,000 to 604,000 from 1990 to 1995 (rate of growth has declined really);
- significant growth has occurred in postgraduate areas - 47,000 Equivalent Full-time Student Unit (EFTSU) - 74,000 EFTSU from 1990 - 1995;
- very dramatic growth has occurred in fee-paying postgraduate courses, following increasing deregulation in the early 1990s and greater pressure for universities to raise non-government sources of revenue;
- international education has developed rapidly - 18,000 in 1988 to over 52,000 in 1995;
- Australia has been experiencing a gradual move towards lifelong learning which is expected to become even more pronounced in the future. DEET (1995) predicted that the proportion of people in the workforce with higher education qualifications will rise from 22% in 1994 to 26% in 2005 with most of this increase coming from the upgrading of qualifications through a commitment to 'lifelong learning';
- increasing pressure for a user-pays environment in conjunction with a trend to increase non-government sources of funding and a declining level of government funding per student are placing pressure on the system to broaden fee-paying arrangements and to alter the nature of student income support. Such considerations have come to

fuller fruition under the federal coalition government in 1995; and

- governments have placed increasing pressure on the higher education sector to adapt to the challenges created by the need for universities to support economic development and workplace reform, to become increasingly entrepreneurial, increasingly efficient in their operations and hence to become increasingly competitive.

All universities have been forced to respond to these pressures and nowhere has this been more evident than in the core business of the sector – the provision of teaching and learning opportunities. In order to present itself as a 'university of the new millennium' USQ has responded to the challenges inherent in the various pressures and influences which are changing the way higher education is offered. This is epitomised in the following statement taken from the Vice Chancellor's Home Page on the university home page (www.usq.edu.au):

'The University of Southern Queensland is a leader in the flexible delivery of services to students and members of the general community. The University believes that flexible delivery is about giving people WHAT they want, WHERE they want it, WHEN they want it, IN their style, IN their place, IN their time. We are REGIONAL, FLEXIBLE and INTERNATIONAL.'

This has resulted in a third phase of teaching and learning at USQ labelled 'Flexible Delivery Model'. Using Paulsen's framework, some tentative teaching-learning tasks can be identified. However, it is much less clear than the first two phases since the institution is still in the process of generating what 'flexible delivery' might mean and how this might relate to previous models of teaching-learning. Nevertheless it can be tentatively described as follows:

Techniques		Typical Activities*
• One alone	–	Researching information - online databases, online journals, webliographies.
• One-to-one	–	Mentoring, counselling - email
• One-to-many	–	Lectures, symposiums - bulletin board, listserver
• Many-to-many	–	Tutorials - computer mediated communication.

* These activities are in addition to those mentioned earlier. These refer to activities derived from courses which are taught entirely online. Paulsen refers to one-to-one as 'Email paradigm', one-to-many as 'Bulletin board paradigm' and many-to-many as 'Conferencing paradigm'.

The change of roles of those involved in teaching-learning tasks and procedures is significant. However, it must be remembered that the 'Flexible Delivery' model is still in its early stages of implementation and many of the roles of those involved in teaching-learning tasks and procedures have placed the participants in an uncertain world, somewhere between the 'person culture' of the face-to-face model and the 'team culture' of the flexible delivery model. Whereas the teacher operating in a 'person culture' is a free agent within some limits, the teacher in a 'team culture' must accept that there are many involved in both the design and delivery of teaching-learning via the web.

As well as this, there is a need for the administrative rationale to play a more supportive role to the 'educational rationale' encapsulated in the Vice Chancellor's words of 'giving people what they want, where they want it, when they want it …'. Policies and procedures which are based on rigid systems and guidelines, however well intentioned, will not support a flexible delivery model.

As previously indicated, one cannot conclude that USQ has adopted fully the flexible delivery model. The members of the institution's community are still in the throes of developing a shared understanding of what it means and how it might relate to previous models. There are questions relating to how this model will provide access to higher education, for a more diverse student body, particularly those disadvantaged groups whose participation may be hindered through their inability to access the technologies, so very much a critical component of the flexible delivery model. There are suggestions that such technology will be available to a wider cross-section of the community as costs of equipment continue to decrease and telecommunications infrastructures continue to expand. However, there are limitations of access to technologies by some students as the following table indicates:

Table 2: Assumptions about student access to technologies at USQ

	Undergraduate		Postgraduate	
	On-Campus	Off-Campus	On-Campus	Off-Campus
• Print	RA	RA	RA	RA
• Audiotape	RA	RA	RA	RA
• Videotape	RA	RA	RA	RA
• Audiographic/ Powerpoint	RA	SCA	RA	SCA
• Tutorial/Teletut	RA	SCA	RA	SCA
• Computer Access	LA	?	LA	?
• IMM/CD-ROM	LA	?	LA	?
• Internet Access	LA	?	LA	?

Key: *RA* — *Ready Access* *LA* — *Limited Access*
SCA — *Study Centre Access* *?* — *Unknown*

There is also the issue of whether such an approach as flexible delivery is suitable for all students. Experience at USQ would suggest that postgraduate students work well under a flexible delivery model. This may have much to do with the fact that many, if not all, are equipped with independent learning skills, having already achieved in the higher education arena. It may also have something to do with the fact that most, if not all, have some knowledge and understanding of the world of work. This provides greater opportunities for constructivist approaches (situated learning, co-construction of knowledge, collaborative learning) to be utilised, approaches which are more easily accommodated in online teaching-learning environments. Moodie (1998) considers 'flexible delivery' to be much the same as 'guided independent learning' and thus assumes that learners placed in such teaching-learning contexts need to have advanced learning skills and be able to demonstrate some level of independence and autonomy over their own learning. These issues suggest that the 'flexible delivery' model is not so much a new way of teaching and learning for all but a valid model for some learners.

A teaching-learning framework for USQ: a proposal

USQ has established itself as a leader in distance and international education, a reputation which has recently been acknowledged by the Executive Committee of the ICDE. However, like other institutions of higher education, USQ is faced with shrinking financial support from government and increased competition for students in what is rapidly becoming a market-driven environment. Universities must streamline their use of resources in a cost-effective strategic manner if they are to survive and prosper in the current context created by the emergence of mass higher education and a political mindset apparently dominated by adherence to the principles of economic rationalism.

As has been demonstrated in the brief case study of USQ's transition from a single mode teaching-learning institution to a multi-modal teaching-learning institution, the critical phases of this transition have demonstrated not so much a number of paradigm shifts (using Imershein's framework) as a reinterpretation of existing and dominant frameworks. The flexible delivery model has been more problematic for it suggests a need for more significant change, particularly in respect to the roles of participants in the teaching-learning tasks and procedures and its appropriateness for a wide range of learners. In fact it may well be that the success of the flexible delivery model is a function of such variables as the student target audience.

Decisions about the optimal development of flexible delivery initiatives should be informed by the varying degrees to which student target audiences have access to different technologies (Table 2) and the varying degrees to which the learning needs of different target groups are currently not being met. Preliminary information suggests that undergraduate students, particularly those entering higher education carrying some form of educational disadvantage (low tertiary entrance scores, content deficits in subjects such as mathematics and students lacking in appropriate study and learning skills) would not benefit from exposure to flexible delivery teaching-learning contexts.

The authors believe that flexible delivery should be driven primarily by pedagogical considerations, tempered by the constraints imposed by limited resources. One of the challenges to the university is deciding how to distribute limited resources equitably to flexible delivery initiatives, especially since not all technologies are readily accessible by different groups of students. With this backdrop the authors have proposed the following teaching-learning framework:

1. Reaffirm the current policy of concentrating resources for the development of 4th generation technologies on full fee paying postgraduate courses, while supporting (wherever possible) the efforts of enthusiastic individuals at the unit team level, irrespective of student target audience.

2. In courses based on the application of 4th generation technologies, treat postgraduate students both on and off campus as a single cohort, with intensive interface support in the initial stages, but with an emphasis on pedagogical approaches aimed at engendering independent learning.

3. Apart from the aforementioned support for individual enthusiasts, limit undergraduate courses to the appropriate use of the current hybrid combinations of 1st, 2nd and 3rd generation technologies.

4. In the first year of undergraduate studies, ensure that the best available teachers work initially in a relatively structured teaching-learning framework which might include a diversity of approaches designed to suit the student needs, experience and access. Traditional lectures and some components of 4th generation technologies could both be considered if they were blended into this structured environment. Further, provide commencing undergraduates with *enhanced learning support* as an integral part of their first year experience to facilitate the effective transition to tertiary study.

5. In the second year a less structured more mixed mode approach, providing reduced access to learning support, with a view to engendering independent learning.

6. In the third and fourth years, emphasise independent learning approaches. Such an initiative might well mean that some units with relatively small enrolments are available only via the distance education mode.

Conclusion

This chapter set out to explore how flexible delivery initiatives might be used to provide enhanced levels of inclusivity in university teaching-learning contexts. Supporters of flexible delivery initiatives claim that its emphasis on flexibility encourages teaching-learning practices that do not exclude individuals and groups from accessing higher education and is an essential element of student-focused learning. Others argue that, by virtue of the varying degrees to which students have the necessary prerequisite learning skills and access to different technologies, flexible delivery effectively excludes different groups of students. Using a case study analysis of a university's transition from single mode (face-to-face) to multi-mode (Taylor's four generations) the authors argued that the various teaching-learning models adopted at critical points in its development by the institution were more about changes in emphasis than changes in kind. It is argued that the different models presented all have a role to play in university teaching-learning contexts but their successful implementation appears to be a function of the nature of the student target audience. In order to understand this relationship between models of teaching and learning and student target audience, the authors recommend the development of teaching-learning frameworks at the institutional level to guide the selection and adoption of such models.

References

Anderson, D. S. and Vervoorn, A. E. (1983) *Access to Privilege: Patterns of Participation in Australian Post-Secondary Education.* Canberra, ANU Press.

Barlow, A. R. and de Lacey, P. (1998) 'Issues in Introducing Technology into Equity Groups', unpublished paper presented at the 3rd National Equity and Access Conference, Yeppoon, Queensland.

Dawkins, J.S. (1988) *Higher Education: A Policy Statement* ('Higher Education White Paper'). Canberra, AGPS.

Department of Employment, Education & Training (DEET) (1995) *Selected Higher Education Student Statistics.*Canberra, AGPS.

Department of Employment, Education and Training (DEET) (1990) *A Fair Chance for All: Higher Education That's Within Everyone's Reach.* Canberra, DEET.

Department of Employment, Education and Training (DEET) (1993) *National Report on Australia's Higher Education Sector.* Canberra, AGPS.

Hall, J. (1996) 'The educational paradigm shift: Implications for ICDE and the distance learning community' in *Open Praxis,* 2: 27-36.

Imershein, A. W. (1976) 'The Epistemological Bases of Social Order: Toward Ethnoparadigm Analysis' in D. Heise (ed) *Sociological Methodology.* San Francisco, Jossey Bass.

Kuhn, T. S. (1970) *The Structure of Scientific Revolutions,* (2nd edn.). Chicago, University of Chicago Press.

Laurillard, D. (1993) *Rethinking University Teaching: A Framework for the Effective Use of Educational Technology.* London, Routledge.

Moodie, G. (1998) 'Virtual University: Real Hype' in Hart, G. (ed) *Online-Ed,* August, 1998.

Paulsen, M. F. (1995) *The Online Report on Pedagogical Techniques for Computer-Mediated Communication.* Report presented at the ICDE-95 Online World Conference in Distance Education, Birmingham, England.

Taylor, J. C. (1995) 'Distance Education Technologies: The Fourth Generation' in *Australian Journal of Educational Technology,* 11(2):1-7.

15. Creating a culturally diverse and inclusive higher education: an Australian example

Jarlath Ronayne

Introduction

As one of the most culturally diverse societies in the world, the creation of an inclusive and culturally diverse higher education system in Australia is both an economic and social imperative. Only Israel has a more diverse ethnic and recent migration mix than Australia (McConnochie *et al,* 1988: p175). This, combined with the impact of the joint forces of massification of higher education and globalisation, has underpinned policy development at the level of both government and individual universities. The transformation of higher education requires changes to curricula to respond to the needs of increasingly diverse student populations, which will at the same time meet broader social and economic policy objectives. Higher education thus plays a critical role in the nation building process because:

- an inclusive and culturally diverse tertiary education system is a precondition for the creation of a shared culture, one which incorporates and promotes diversity, while at the same time being unified around the importance of tolerance and shared dialogue;
- of the need for a highly skilled and flexible workforce, able to compete in an increasingly internationally oriented economy, which has a particular focus on strengthening relationships with neighbouring countries in Asia;
- a post-school qualification is the passport *all* Australians need for full participation in society, particularly in the labour market.

Massification of higher education has produced two post-school education sectors in Australia: the higher education (HE) sector, and the vocational education and training sector. While they have been historically divided into universities and Technical and Further Education (TAFE) institutes, in some parts of Australia the two sectors are becoming increasingly integrated within the one institutional framework. There are 10 dual-sector universities in Australia, and in the state of Victoria five of the eight universities contain both a HE and a TAFE component, with 40% of all TAFE provision in Victoria being offered through universities (*Victoria University of Technology* 1998 Section 1:1).

Victoria University is a large dual sector university, with 50,000 students spanning HE and TAFE divisions.

This chapter describes the way Victoria University has attempted to create a culturally inclusive university. The first section identifies the national context for Victoria University's activities. The second profiles the western region of Melbourne, the students who attend the university, and our dual sector nature in the context of national policies. The third part describes two early initiatives from our predecessor institutions that contributed to the formulation of the university's Personalised Access and Study policy (PAS). The final section describes two PAS-initiated activities which typify our approach to an inclusive and culturally diverse higher education.

The Australian context

The key defining feature of Australia is its ethnic, cultural and linguistic diversity. McConnochie *et al* (1988: p169) point out that everyone 'not of Aboriginal descent is an immigrant of relatively recent origins.' Forty-four per cent of Australia's population were either born overseas, or had one parent who was born overseas (Australian Bureau of Statistics [ABS] 1998). The population of Australia '... almost doubled between 1946 and 1986 with immigration responsible for 40 per cent of the total increase' (McConnochie *et al,* 1988). Not only is Australia a country of immigrants, but the intake of immigrants underwent tremendous diversification after the Second World War, and particularly from the 1970s. In 1947, 81% of those born overseas were from English-speaking countries, reflecting Australia's origins as a British colony and its explicit 'White Australia Policy'. Australia began looking for immigrants in Europe after the Second World War, and when the White Australia Policy was officially disbanded in 1972 the immigrant composition changed dramatically. In 1997, English-speaking immigrants constituted only 39% (ABS, 1998) of those born overseas. The proportion of arrivals from Asia rose from 15% in 1977 to 51% in 1991-92, before declining to 37% in 1996-97 (ABS, 1998). The changes in the migration mix to Australia in the last three decades have been underpinned by social policy that has moved from a rigorous, institutionalised assimilationist approach *vis-à-vis* its indigenous and immigrant communities, to a country that has embraced multiculturalism (Collins & Jamrozik *et al,* 1995).

Australia's cultural and social diversity is reflected in the composition of its social institutions—and increasingly in the institutions comprising its tertiary sector. As the social composition of Australian society has transformed as a result of mass migration from the 1950s, successive Australian governments have sought to shape the system in the context of gradual globalisation, and (correspondingly) the need to produce a highly skilled work force able to compete internationally. Initiatives have varied, but have focused largely on increasing participation in post-secondary schooling for all Australians. In general, the combined policies have had a long-term impact, with Australia experiencing one of the fastest growth rates of student enrolments in Organisation for Economic Co-operation and Development countries (OECD, 1997: p4). In Australia in 1970, 175,358 students were enrolled in higher education and 387,812 in TAFE (Marginson, 1997: p140). In 1997 there were 658,827 students in higher education and 1,458,600 students enrolled in Vocational Education and Training courses (mainly in TAFE colleges)[1] leading to a vocational award (ABS, 1998). It is estimated that 45 per cent of Australian teenagers today will at some time enter higher education, while 45 per cent are likely to enter vocational education and training (West, 1998: p71).

The dramatic national increase in participation in higher education has not occurred evenly across all social groups, or across all universities. Government policies at both the state and federal levels over the past decade have focused on increasing participation rates in tertiary education (particularly in HE, as participation in TAFE has always tended to be more representative of the Australian community) for students from under-represented groups through the use of 'profile targets' and regular reporting at the institutional level. As a consequence, participation rates in HE for women, students from non-English speaking backgrounds, and indigenous students have improved, though students from low-socio economic backgrounds and rural and isolated students remain under-represented (DETYA, 1998: pp12-3). For example, students defined as coming from low socio-economic backgrounds constitute less than 15% of all higher education enrolments, and 17% of commencing undergraduate students, but constitute 25% of the population overall (Dobson & Birrell, 1998: p4).

Similarly, some tertiary institutions have higher numbers of students from under-represented groups than others. For example, in 1996 Central Queensland University had 36%, Victoria University 24%, and the University of Newcastle 26% of students coming from low socio-economic backgrounds, while the University of Canberra had 5%, Macquarie University 5% and Monash University 7% of students coming from this background (DETYA, 1998: column 85). The uneven distribution of students from such groups across the nation's 37 universities demonstrates that challenges facing individual institutions differ. These challenges range from assisting students to acquire skills to participate in tertiary education, as they are often the first in their families to do so, to ensuring that curricula are culturally inclusive, with students receiving support attuned to their specific learning needs. This is particularly so for Victoria University which has a greater percentage of students from such groups.

The western region of Melbourne and Victoria University

The challenges facing Victoria University in both meeting the learning needs of its student population and increasing participation for under-represented groups arise from the nature of the population in our surrounding region. The western region of Melbourne, where the university's 14 campuses are largely located, has a higher than average proportion of its population from immigrant non-English speaking backgrounds—with large concentrations of specific groups such as Vietnamese-speakers and recent refugees. While the percentage of Australians born overseas was 23% in 1997 (ABS, 1998), in the western region it was 33% in 1996.[2] Of those in the western region born overseas, 84% were born in non-English speaking countries (Grace & Shield, 1998). In 1996, approximately 36% of the region's population spoke a language other than English at home—double the national average (Grace & Shield, 1998).

As in other OECD countries, immigration is associated with economic and social disadvantage, and Melbourne's western region tends to have lower income levels and lower levels of participation in post-school education than does the rest of the state of Victoria and, correspondingly, more of its population in lower earning occupational groupings (Grace & Shield, 1998).

The social, cultural, ethnic and economic diversity of the area is regarded as a source of strength and pride by many of those who live and work in the region. In 1997 all the mayors from the region's ten municipalities joined together to condemn racism and intolerance, and to celebrate the region's diversity. Victoria University, as the provider of post-school education in the region, and one of its largest employers, has consistently and publicly condemned racism and promoted diversity. There is a strong belief among the municipalities and employers, and shared by the university, that the diversity of the region helps to create a tolerant and inclusive society. Moreover, such diversity is seen to have direct economic benefits that will be increasingly realised as the Australian economy becomes more internationalised, with employers who recruit graduates from diverse backgrounds gaining a competitive edge. Central to this is that the numbers gaining post-school qualifications in the region is undergoing tremendous expansion, and will continue to do so as post-school qualifications become a basic prerequisite for participation in the labour market (Grace & Shield, 1998).

Victoria University's student profile largely reflects the region's social structure, as well as national trends in the social profiles of the nation's TAFE and HE components. Victoria University has, like other dual-sector universities, a more diverse student population than higher education-only institutions. Approximately half of the university's funded student load is in TAFE and students in this sector broadly reflect Australian socio-economic structure. Unlike many other institutions, the university's HE division has attained participation rates of more than 24% for students from low socio-economic backgrounds—close to the 25% of the population from this background. 41% of the university's HE students and 63% of its TAFE students come from the western region. 29% of the University's TAFE students were born overseas, while 15% of our HE students are defined by government as coming from non-English speaking backgrounds. It is difficult to make direct comparisons between TAFE and higher education in defining the proportion in each sector who come from non-English speaking backgrounds, as the government requires the university to count students in each sector according to different criteria. But, however they are counted, students at Victoria University are often the first in their families to enter tertiary education, and often work part-time. 31% of our TAFE students and 38% of our HE students speak a language other than English at home. In addition, students at Victoria University have combinations of such attributes.

Victoria University's dual sector composition thus accommodates the region's cultural and social diversity, building on its existing educational infrastructure to produce curricula truly reflective of and reactive to the needs of the student population and the region. While the university is relatively young by Australian standards, it has always focused on developing multi-faceted policy approaches which meet the needs of its diverse student population. This multi-faceted policy approach has been directed at meeting the needs of discrete target groups, as well as meeting the needs of individual students from diverse backgrounds. We believe that a policy approach to institutional arrangements and curriculum based on meeting the needs both of *groups* traditionally excluded from tertiary education and of *individuals* from a range of backgrounds benefits *all* students, including those from backgrounds which have a tradition of participation in tertiary education. This is because the policy focus is on improving the quality of student learning *per se*, as exemplified in our Personalised Access and Study policy.

Beginning the partnership approach: individuals and groups

The evolution of Personalised Access and Study began with early initiatives to meet the region's educational demands by the university's predecessor institutions, the Footscray Institute of Technology and the Western Institute.[3] The university, and its predecessor institutions, consciously sought to support students from non-traditional backgrounds in tertiary education with two distinct but related strategies. The first strategy supports students as individuals, as they present in programmes of study. The second strategy seeks to stimulate involvement by groups who have been traditionally excluded, by involving them in university programmes on the basis of their group membership. Simply put, the university has sought to build partnerships with individuals and with groups. A range of initiatives attempts either to meet the needs of students as they present in learning programmes, or to stimulate involvement by groups in the community in educational processes.

The Educational Development Department (EDD) formed in 1982 at Footscray Institute of Technology, for example, gradually changed its programme orientation from mature-age students as a target group, to non-English speaking background (NESB) students. In parallel, learning support provision shifted from individual consultations to programme-based provision – largely in response to increasing numbers of students in programmes. During this period, EDD programmes, although supported by federally-funded grants aimed at increasing retention rates of targeted groups, were also increasingly funded through institution sources, as the need for assistance for students increased as the student profile became more diverse. At the Western Institute, learning support provision focused on the learning needs of students from a non-English speaking background, and from its beginning support provided concurrently with mainstream classes was a feature of its educational provision. The primary mechanism was individual consultations with additional on-demand parallel or group sessions. The Student Learning Unit (SLU), formed in 1995, has seen a further shift in learning support provision towards a curriculum-based model with greater emphasis on embedding learning support mechanisms in subject and course design and delivery systems.

In addition to programmes or structural arrangements that were essentially reactive to student needs once enrolled, the university has a history of stimulating participation of discrete groups in the educational process, for example Melbourne's Maltese community. This group is concentrated in the western suburbs of Melbourne and were largely excluded from higher education institutions for a variety of reasons. In

1989 a research team from the Faculty of Arts worked closely with the Maltese Community Council of Victoria on a government-funded project investigating why many Maltese-background students were not continuing on to higher education, and why there was an apparent lack of interest in the Maltese language among these students. The team's report (Terry *et al*, 1993) signalled the kind of relationship which the university was keen to establish with its various constituent communities. It is a relationship based on partnership and mutual support. In relation to the Maltese community, the partnership has been distinguished both by its strength and by its diversity – with public lectures, seminars and symposia drawing on visiting Maltese scholars and public figures, community use of university facilities for such events as the annual Manoel de Vilhena Awards, provision of scholarships, a close liaison with local schools and community organisations, encouragement of post-graduate study, and university publication of books, pamphlets and CDs relevant to the Maltese community. All of these initiatives have been complemented by an active staff and student Exchange Agreement with the University of Malta, built on, and at the same time, extending the firm foundation established with the local Maltese-background community. The synergy between the community partnerships and international links was demonstrated last year, when Maurice Cauchi returned to Victoria University as a Visiting Professor under the Agreement with the University of Malta and organised a Community Forum on Maltese Background Youth, the proceedings of which the university published earlier this year with financial support from local Maltese businesses.

The university's partnership with the Maltese community brought important benefits to both, while laying the foundation for the development of a model the university would subsequently use to initiate partnerships with other communities. These partnerships have become fundamental to the way in which the university defines itself, with its emerging links with the various ethnic communities in the region influencing global exchange links. Agreements have been negotiated with universities in Italy, Ireland, Greece, Albania and Macedonia, for example, reflecting the composition of the region in which the university is located, and should be viewed as a natural extension of the university's longstanding involvement in the transplanted ethnic communities from which so many students are drawn and whose interests we are committed to serve. This international orientation creates a further sense of location for the diverse peoples of the western region, and at the same time helps to promote multiculturalism as the fundamental underpinning of local citizenship.

In essence, the Maltese project provided a model for working strategically with communities in the western region when the university's Personalised Access and Study policy was adopted. Implementation of the policy has intensified the community development/education nexus by seeking to tailor curriculum as a result of a targeted pro-active strategy to involve more of the region's communities in the university.

Personalised Access and Study (PAS) policy: groups and individuals

The Personalised Access and Study policy attempts to build on existing institutional practices and processes, as outlined above, whilst simultaneously extending and developing them in response to national (education) policy and regional (population and economic) trends. PAS comprises a complex set of processes focused around the inter-related issues of access (creating alternative mechanisms for students to enter the institution) and study (assisting them to stay in the institution once they arrive).

The 'access' component, in its initial stage in 1998, concentrated on establishing alternative entrance arrangements to the Tertiary Entrance Ranking (TER), an exit-secondary schooling score traditionally used by Australian universities for student selection. As with all aggregated score models, students from higher socio-economic status backgrounds are known to be over-represented in the higher scoring bands (Pascoe *et al*, 1997; Andrich & Mercer, 1997). Student interviews are a primary means of assessment of individual student point-of-entry learning needs, and a personal Student Compact sets out how the institution will attempt to meet those needs. Simultaneously, the 'study' elements of the policy have been addressed through a re-working and enhancement of institutional policies relating to the design and delivery of the curriculum: student progress procedures, study pathways between the TAFE and HE components, and student learning support at course and subject levels. In addition to working with individual students at point of entry, institution initiatives in 1998 also focused on tailoring alternative-entry processes and curricula in targeted subjects and courses to meet the needs of specific communities in the region.

For example, extensive consultation with the region's recently arrived communities from the Horn of Africa resulted in the design and delivery of culturally-sensitive curricula in a range of TAFE and HE courses provided specifically for these communities. Negotiations, largely conducted by a cultural support worker whose role is to liaise between the communities on one hand and the teaching staff on the other, resulted in some course components taught in one of the mother tongues (in this case

Amharic), English language support integrated at all levels, and content areas re-contextualised to take account of African cultural mores, beliefs and practices. Components of the course were also taught, where possible, by leaders from the communities. The existing curriculum was thus reworked in consultation with, and partially team-taught by, community leaders.

The partnership between Horn of Africa communities and the university has resulted, among other outcomes, in the establishment of a University-African Community Advisory Committee. This is used as a forum to discuss and negotiate the education, training and employment needs of the African communities, and has been extended to include other partners, including Federal, State and local government departments. It will, in the future, include local employers. A recent example of the partnership in action is the agreement entered into between the African communities, the university, the Electrical Trade Union and a Group Training Company employing apprentices. The university and the African communities collaborate to provide a pre-apprenticeship programme for African young people, while the Group Training Company and the Electrical Trade Union guarantee to provide students with apprenticeships upon successful completion of the programme.

This initiative in the university's TAFE Division parallels developments in the HE Division. For example, refugees from the Horn of Africa have taken advantage of the university's Recognition of Prior Learning (RPL) provisions to access a range of courses in several disciplines. Targeted bridging programmes have helped articulate such students into programmes such as the Community Development degree course, where students from refugee backgrounds are able to use their experience of working in refugee camps in the course.

In 1999 Victoria University used its partnership approach to respond to the educational needs of Kosovar refugees who were provided with a 'safe haven' in Australia. The Kosovars' lives were severely disrupted and they were faced with the huge task of rebuilding their lives. Education is one of the concrete and practical activities ideally suited to helping with the general healing process and restoring hope and continuity between a shattered past and a purposeful and productive future. Soon after the settlement of refugees in Victoria, a meeting was held between senior university staff and a delegation of fifteen Kosovar academics from the refugee community at the safe haven of Puckapunyal, just to the north of Melbourne, to devise a strategic plan for those Kosovars whose education and training had been disrupted by the war.

At the local level, these initiatives are supported by the local Albanian community, with whom the university has been working closely for the past year through the Centre for Commencing Students. At the international level, credit transfer arrangements were explored with the University of Tirana and the Polytechnic University of Tirana, with whom Exchange Agreements were signed last year, so that Kosovar refugees can be linked with academic study on their return to the Balkans. The University has also had contact with counterparts from Prishtina University, who are working with and through the two Tirana universities, so that the Kosovar studying in Australia might readily be fitted into educational programmes on their return home.

In all of these initiatives, the university's approach to meeting individual student learning needs focuses on the establishment of learning pathways that are negotiated at point-of-entry and are designed to cater to the needs of individual learners, regardless of cultural, socio-economic or linguistic background. These arrangements are monitored in the Student Compact, which details the student's vocational aspirations, any specific learning needs, and how the university and the student will work together to ensure that the student's goals are met. At the end of the programme of study each student in the university will have his or her own individualised learning portfolio, encapsulated in the Student Compact.

Student Compacts nominate learning pathways, which can articulate between accredited courses in both the university's TAFE and HE sectors via credit transfer arrangements—providing students with ways of constructing learning over time and across sectors at pre-degree, degree and post-degree stages of tertiary education within designated fields of study. Students who wish to enter a particular course, but who do not yet meet the entry requirements for that course, are offered a learning pathway which reserves a place for them in their desired course provided they meet all the conditions of the agreed pathway. Through the Student Compact and learning pathways, the university is able to individualise its relationship with all its students, and focus more clearly on understanding individual student needs.

The full effects of negotiated curriculum as a result of learning pathways are still to be seen, but indications are that the process will have the effect of more thoroughly embedding curriculum-based learning support processes at the course level in both of the university's sectors.

Conclusion

Curriculum development and design responsive to the needs of the diverse student population at Victoria University is a complex set of tasks being undertaken within the PAS policy framework. At present there are two broad programmes: the development of strategies to stimulate participation of specific socio-cultural groups, and the accommodation of large numbers of students from a variety of linguistic, cultural and socio-economic groups. Both of these approaches have raised challenges that need to be met at a number of levels of the organisation if PAS is to achieve its full potential to provide curricula that are responsive to and appropriate for the needs of diverse individuals and groups.

The immediate dilemma for the 'group' strategy is in finding ways to meet the demand that the success with the African communities has generated in other community groups—such as Kurdish, Turkish and Indian. In addition to needing cultural support workers for each group, there is the need to continue to tailor appropriate content and teaching methods for each community effectively and efficiently according to demand. As such successes mobilise communities, the university will be increasingly involved—in partnership with communities—in strategic planning for those communities' educational provision through such bodies as the University-African Community Advisory Committee. Such enterprises are highly desirable, but require careful planning and co-ordination of resources. The level of resources required to develop such partnerships and provide communities with the support they need is not included in the government funding provided to institutions.

The dilemma for the 'pathways' strategy is no less complex. It implies review and evaluation of accredited courses on a regular basis so that adjustments to content and teaching methods can be made in the light of the (changing) needs of students. It implies the adoption of a student-centred approach to the development of curriculum, both content and delivery. Although the PAS policy endorsed principles for learning and teaching which are, in effect, a commitment to a student-centred learning approach at the institutional level, more is required to monitor and evaluate learning programmes according to how well they meet the learning needs of students. The co-ordination of effort across a number of areas of the university will be crucial in the maintenance and continuing development of pathways.

Culturally inclusive teaching has profound implications for the curriculum. It is not a matter of bringing students from diverse backgrounds and asking them to shed their previous culture in favour of a new one, based on Anglo-Celtic traditions. Rather, it involves drawing on an understanding of the way in which cultural diversity is itself constitutive of the social relations within the teaching environment (cf. Rizvi & Walsh, 1998). Learning, if it is to be effective, must value and draw on the culture, values and traditions students bring with them. Different cultures cannot be 'added' to the 'mainstream' curriculum. Rather, the curriculum needs to draw broadly on the experiences of all students. This approach helps *all* students meet their individual learning needs and, perhaps more importantly, equips them to assume their place as full citizens in a multicultural society. As the Kosovar initiative demonstrates, by virtue of the unique and crucial position that education occupies in all societies, a partnership approach enables universities to contribute to building relationships, ranging from the local to the global, in a culturally diverse world.

Acknowledgement

I wish to record my indebtedness to Professor Ron Adams, Deputy Director of Victoria Unversity's Europe-Australia Institute for his key input to the content of this chapter and the technical detail embodied in its presentation.

References

Andrich, D. and Mercer, A., (1997), *International Perspectives on Selection Methods of Entry into Higher Education*. National Board of Employment, Education and Training, Higher Education Council, Canberra, AGPS.

Australian Bureau of Statistics (ABS), (1998), *Australia Now – A Statistical Profile*, http://www.abs.gov.au.websitedbs/

Collins, J. (1975) 'The Political Economy of Post-War Migration', in Wheelwright, E. L. and Buckley, K., *Essays in the Political Economy of Australian Capitalism*, Vol 1. Sydney, Australia and New Zealand Book Company.

Department of Education, Training and Youth Affairs (DETYA) (1998) *The Characteristics and Performance of Higher Education Institutions*. Occasional Paper Series, Higher Education Division, Canberra, Department of Education, Training and Youth Affairs.

Dobson, I. R. and Birrell, B. (1998) 'Equity and university entrance: a 1997 update' in *People and Place*, 6(3).

Grace, M. and Shield, L. (1998) *The Western Region Social Profile*. Melbourne, Outer Urban research and Policy Unit, Victoria University of Technology.

Jamrozik, A., Boland, C. and Urquhart, C. (1995) *Social Change and Cultural Transformation in Australia*. Cambridge, Cambridge University Press.

Marginson, S. (1997) *Educating Australia: Government, Economy and Citizen since 1960*. Melbourne, Cambridge University Press.

McConnochie, K., Hollinsworth, D. and Pettman, J. (1988) *Race and Racism in Australia*. Wentworth Falls, Social Science Press.

Organisation for Economic Co-operation and Development (OECD), (1997) *Thematic Review of the First years of Tertiary Education Australia*. Paris, Directorate for Education, Employment, Labour and Social Affairs.

Pascoe, R., McClelland and McGaw, B. (1997) *Perspectives on Selection Methods for Entry into Higher Education in Australia*. Commissioned Report No. 58, Higher Education Council and National Board of Employment, Education and Training, Canberra. AGPS.

Rizvi, F. and Walsh, L. (1998) 'Difference, globalisation and the internationalisation of curriculum' in *Australian Universities Review*, 41(2).

Terry, L., Borland, H. and Adams, R. (1993) *'To learn more than I have ...' The Educational Aspirations and Experiences of the Maltese in Melbourne*. St Albans, Victoria University of Technology.

Victoria University of Technology (1998) *Higher Education Division Education Profile for the 1999-2001 Triennium*.

West, R. (1998) *Learning for Life: Final Report: Review of Higher Education Financing and Policy*. Canberra, Department of Employment, Education, Training and Youth Affairs.

Note

[1] The Vocational Education and Training (VET) sector includes providers other than TAFE colleges, including private providers. However, TAFE is overwhelmingly the largest provider of VET training in Australia.

[2] If the children of the 23% born overseas are included, then more than 40% of the Australian population were either born overseas or had one parent born overseas. If the off-spring of the western region of Melbourne's 33% born overseas are included, the

numbers in the western region born overseas or with one parent born overseas would be close to half the overall population of the region.

[3] The university was created in 1991 through a merger between the Western Institute (formed in 1985) and the Footscray Institute of Technology (formed in 1919). In July 1998 the university incorporated the Western Melbourne Institute of TAFE, to become the only provider of post-school education in Melbourne's western region.

16. Inclusivity workshops for first-year engineering students

Vivien Hope and Andi Sebastian

Introduction

The University of Adelaide has a conservative culture, which neither easily nor quickly responds to initiatives designed to make it more inclusive and welcoming of individuals and groups outside a selective norm. It is the third oldest university in Australia and the first established in South Australia, and it has an excellent research reputation.

The Faculty of Engineering includes Schools of Chemical Engineering, Civil and Environmental, Computer Science, Electrical and Electronic and Mechanical Engineering. Approximately 18% of the Engineering students are female, and there are nearly 20 different nationalities represented in the Faculty. 17% of all students in the Faculty are international students. Additionally, 22% of the local students are from families where English is not the main language of communication. 0.5% of students are known to have a disability of some form and many others are likely to have not disclosed a disability to the Faculty. 0.07% of students are Indigenous Australians which is much lower than their representation in the general population (approximately 1.4%).

Over the past four years, the Faculty has participated with the university's Equal Opportunity Office in six collaborative projects on aspects of gender and diversity. These have resulted in a much greater awareness within the Faculty of the critical impact of these issues on the social and learning environment. Specific outcomes include alterations to curriculum and teaching methodology, the production of a campaign designed to encourage female school students to consider engineering as a career and seminars on equity and diversity as part of a communications subject for 3rd and 4th year Mechanical Engineering students in 1996-1997.

Other initiatives in working towards the development of an inclusive culture within the Faculty have been increasingly important in the past few years. Many international students arrive in Australia for the first time at first-year level, and sometimes as a cohort from a partner institute in Malaysia at second or third-year level. Recognising their particular needs, orientation and peer programmes have been implemented through the university's International Programmes Office. These programmes have focused on introducing international students to the local environment and culture. Some local students volunteered to participate in cultural awareness training and they elected to act as mentors to the newly arrived international students. They formed peer groups to facilitate social contact, resource location and for reassurance.

The arrival in 1998 of an established cohort of 85 students from the university's partner programme at the Sepang Institute of Technology in Malaysia highlighted the need for Faculty staff to receive some information about cultural communication and awareness issues. Accordingly, the Faculty organised three one-hour sessions for administrative staff, technical staff and academics. The three sessions were tailored to those staff groupings, with the session for academics concentrating on cultural differences in learning, teaching and communicating. A three-hour training session was held for senior academics, administrators and technicians in the Faculty.

One of the classic dilemmas facing workplaces in which women are a minority is the management of sexual harassment issues. The Faculty of Engineering has been no exception in this. In collaboration with a group of senior female students, the Equal Opportunity Office and Deans of Schools, a series of three seminars was designed and conducted for academic staff in Civil and Environmental Engineering in 1998 which focused on issues of gender and sexual harassment. Simultaneously, a workshop on Equity in the Workplace was conducted for all 4th year Engineering students in 1998 and has in 1999 been expanded to include 2nd and 3rd year students.

Thus, the Faculty of Engineering has been pro-active in attempting to deal in a variety of ways, over a period of time, with a range of issues associated with creating an inclusive culture. The result of much of this work has been to highlight clearly the existence of a culture within the Faculty that is exclusive and alienating to many of its members. In 1999, the Faculty implemented a pilot programme, which has the capacity to interrupt this pattern and to raise the value of behaviours that are respectful and inclusive of the multi-cultural and diverse reality of the communities of Australia, the University of Adelaide and the Faculty of Engineering.

A description of the Inclusivity Workshops

Ten workshops were conducted for 1st year Engineering students in the first week of semester one. The workshops were advertised in the Engineering Student Information Newsletter and preliminary lecture folders, but it was compulsory for students to attend. Out of approximately 330 students, 80% (265) attended.

The goal of these sessions was to introduce ideas of inclusivity and diversity in the first week of university. It was decided to focus on first-year students as they enter the university. This provides them with an immediate opportunity to engage with the issues of difference, rather than waiting until they have been exposed to the prevailing culture, which tends currently to be based around alcohol and partying.

The term 'inclusivity' was chosen to express the intention that students, regardless of their racial, cultural, lifestyle background, gender or disability, would feel included in the training process and learn about behaviours which are inclusive of others (Hutchison, 1997: pp1-3). The framework for much of the training was skills development in small group work and team participation. These had previously been identified as lacking among many of the older students despite being critical for professional success. The programme was developed and co-ordinated by an Equity Consultant from the Equal Opportunity Office in close collaboration with the Outreach and Liaison Manager in the Faculty of Engineering and the Head of International Support Services. Two key elements of the training were established. These were particularly that the training be conducted by a diverse team of trainers and that there was a minimum time-frame which would allow some engagement with participation. Trainers were not prepared to deliver in a lecture format as had previously been done with the programme for staff. The reasons for this include:

- the risk of alienating participants;
- the de-humanising of an intensely human subject and experience; and
- an analysis that this style of presentation with engineering staff (February 1998, see above) was unsatisfactory.

Students attending the seminars were divided in two groups for an hour and twenty minutes, with a short break at the change over. One group raised the complexity of diversity issues in the framework of group work skills, while the second focused on the importance of cross-cultural respect and communication in successful professional lives. Each of the two groups was facilitated by an experienced trainer who was in turn accompanied by 'student trainers' who completed spectrums of diversity in the training team.

The composition of the training team was another of the key elements of the programme referred to earlier. The authors are not alone in believing that inclusivity programmes, diversity training and cross-cultural awareness and communication programmes are best delivered by people who have some personal experience of the issues involved and who have the capacity to respond to a range of diversity issues and challenges (Westwood *et al*, 1996: p20; Howard, 1995). Of the two lead trainers, one was from the mainstream Australian Celtic culture and the other a migrant Australian of Chinese Malaysian background.

The belief in the value of a visibly diverse training team who would model respect and the valuing of difference was seen to be particularly important given the nature of many first-year engineering undergraduates. In the main, students would be school leavers and might not have had much exposure to openly gay people, people with a disability, people of other cultures and people clear in their commitment to feminism and the equal rights of women and men. It was further thought that first-year students might particularly value learning with older students. Peer models of training have been utilised to great effect in a variety of settings as diverse as public health education and sport, and aspects of this methodology were utilised in this programme (Pintos-Lopes, 1990: pp13-16). Thus, a diverse team of trainers was put together drawing strongly from the student body.

The final programme consisted of a range of activities in each group designed to be complementary and to serve the overall goals of the programme. A brief outline of these activities follows. In the group covering a range of diversity issues including gender, disability and sexuality, the activities were:

- An **introduction** by the trainers who explained their interest in diversity issues. In the case of the young trainers this was based around personal disclosure. There was usually a total of three or four trainers present in this group.
- A **bingo game** designed to introduce the participants to each other and raise issues of similarity and difference.
- A **brainstorm** of all the issues which make humans conscious of their difference despite their genetic similarity.
- A **brainstorm** focusing on what constitutes a successful team or group and the skills necessary to achieve this.

A **group work** component where participants were placed in groups of six and given an example of the kind of problem set for engineering students at this level. Additionally, they were given detailed descriptions of six characters making up the team in this fictional exercise. Through the stories of the various characters, issues of sexuality, gender, religion and disability arose, which had to be negotiated and accommodated in order for the group to undertake the set exercise. All the emphasis of the activity was on achieving focus on the common goal through the setting of agreements and the negotiation of differences.

The group which focused on issues of culture and race and cross-cultural communication undertook a similar array of activities:

- A **cultural IQ test** where participants worked individually to choose from multiple choice answers. This provided participants with an opportunity to absorb new information and privately gauge how aware they may or may not have been about a range of accessible cross-cultural information.
- A **presentation** on theories of cultural difference which was replaced after adverse feedback from students and trainers by the following two components.
- A **cultural work-sheet** requiring participants to work in small groups to decide how they might deal with a range of cultural situations experienced by engineers working overseas or with indigenous Australian communities.
- A **cultural bag component** where participants had to define culture and realised it is something everyone has. They were then encouraged to relate the findings of their work-sheet to this and see how some people feel more comfortable in various settings than others. Other information about adjustment and responses to cultural stress was given.
- A **communication component** where lessons of cross-cultural communication and the various aspects of communication were learnt. Participants worked in pairs with one having a piece of paper and a pen. The other, facing the board, could see a projected image which they had to describe to their partner who then attempted to draw what was described. No eye contact or gesture was allowed. The message was conveyed by words alone.

Both groups emphasised the use of experiential learning in small groups as a way to achieve the following:
- facilitating introductions between students;
- providing opportunities for meaningful discussion and sharing of information and ideas;
- development of group work and communication skills; and
- greater exposure to diverse ideas and experiences.

In the groups of approximately 30 participants, at least half of each session was spent in groups of six or in pairs.

Student impressions of the Inclusivity Workshops

Evaluation to determine the overall value of the programme will be conducted later in the year, but the trainers sought some immediate feedback from participants. All participants were asked to complete an evaluation form before leaving. This form aimed to establish some key value positions in relation to the training (first three questions) and assessments of individual activities. A total of 265 students attended at least one session. Some left during the break. All 227 students present in the second session filled out the evaluation form.

From this form we know that of the 227 students, 165 were local male students, 45 were local females, 15 were international males, one was female and international, one was indigenous and male and one did not indicate gender. See Figure 1.

Figure 1: Evaluation of workshop components

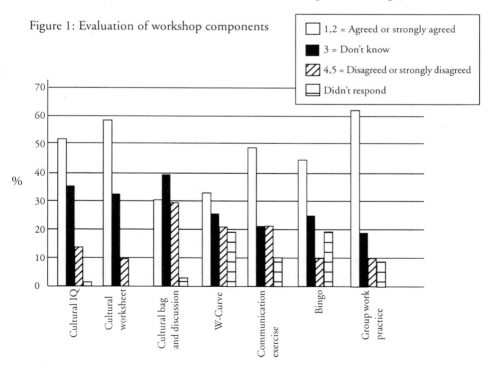

Participants were asked to score each activity from the 10 sessions, held over four days. 80% of participants gave each activity a score of 1, 2, or 3 where 1 represented the highest value and 5 the least; this is shown in Figure 1.

Both on the basis of the participant feedback and on the critical reflection of the group of trainers, we were able to make a range of observations about the relative value of each component.

The *introduction* by the trainers was not an activity which was evaluated on the form, but the impact on the participants was noticeable and worth comment. As each of the student trainers explained their interest in diversity issues and described the personal circumstances that led to their involvement, participants were attentive. For many in the group, it was clear that they had never before been introduced to someone who described themselves as indigenous, gay, having a disability or as being committed to gender equality. The impact of these introductions was enhanced by the respect between all members of the training team. This modelling seemed to be immediately accepted by the group as an appropriate response.

The *bingo exercise* worked best for the participants who attended this session first. In this context it served to introduce participants, raise a variety of equal opportunity issues and emphasise both similarities and differences. On a number of occasions when the participants attended this group as a second session, the lead trainer decided to leave it out. This explains the comparatively high level of non-responses in relation to this exercise.

The *brainstorms* generated lists of factors that make humans conscious of their difference; elements of a successful team or group and the skills necessary to achieve this. This exercise was also not put to the participants for evaluating as it was quite quick and served as a bridging function. However, it provided a baseline of information, which was useful in the debriefing of the following exercise. It was particularly interesting that although participants were easily able to nominate the factors contributing to a successful team, they struggled to put these into practice.

The emphasis of the *group work component* was on achieving focus on the common goal through the setting of agreements and negotiation of difference. This component was extremely popular and this is reflected both in the ratings where it achieved the highest score and in the additional comments made by participants. Factors which made it popular include:

- the sense that it provided skills development which would be immediately relevant;
- the novel way of being introduced to sometimes difficult conceptual issues;

- the reality of discrimination and harassment was made patent through such questions as to the preferred location for the group work. One member wanted the 'pub', which, as a venue for the consumption of alcohol, was inaccessible to Muslim members of the group and an uncertain venue for the female and gay members;
- the significance of learning in this exercise through the interaction of the group members and the input of the student trainers; and
- the opportunity for participants to interact closely with the student trainers.

In the second group, a *Cultural IQ test* was given to participants as a first activity. Participants rated this exercise very highly, giving it the third highest score. Impromptu comments from participants indicated that most people valued the opportunity to privately assess their level of cross-cultural knowledge.

After the first two sessions, when the theoretical presentation had clearly not worked well with the participants, a *work-sheet* was developed to make the information more accessible and more obviously relevant to immediate and future needs. Trainers speculated that the lack of enthusiasm demonstrated in response to the theoretical presentation was not a reflection of lack of interest in the subject, but was rather about the style of delivery. This first week of university tends to have an enormously high information content and many first-year students find it overwhelming. In this environment, it is not surprising that something that may not appear directly relevant, yet requires concentration may be less than appealing. This speculation was borne out. The same information, presented through small group interaction and focusing on challenging cultural situations that might form part of their future professional work, engaged their attention fully. This exercise was the second most highly-rated by the students.

The *cultural bag component* was adapted from one developed by Gary Howard (1998) from the Respecting Ethnic and Cultural Heritage (REACH) Centre. It was a technique designed to assist participants to define culture and to realise that culture is a common denominator. The exercise had the effect of reducing the alienation some members of the dominant culture felt when exposed to arguments for inclusivity. Participants were encouraged to define elements of personal (viz. Australian) culture and then elements of the cultures of international students, and to examine the overlap. This exercise worked particularly well in conjunction with the work-sheet, as participants were encouraged to relate the findings of their work-sheet to the definitions of culture, and to assess how comfortable various groups of people might feel in particular settings.

Other information about adjustment and responses to cultural stress were given through an instrument we called the *W-curve*. These tools have worked extremely well with other groups in the university and particularly with the senior academics, administrators and technicians who attended the three-hour cultural awareness workshop a year before. It may be, though, that the very nature of these techniques is based on a degree of life experience which is of necessity limited for first-year university students, the vast majority of whom are school leavers. Whatever the reason, it was the case that these exercises attracted the highest 'don't know' and 'disagreed/strongly disagreed' scores. It is interesting that the 'don't know' score was the highest given to this exercise and suggests some confusion about the intended message.

Finally, the *communication component* was quite highly rated. This again is a REACH initiative and is both enjoyable and instructive.

Evaluation of the Inclusivity Workshops

The evaluation forms included three value-based statements which attempted to gauge an attitudinal starting point for these young people. The results are striking, and are shown in Figure 2.

- 78% of participants either 'strongly agreed' or 'agreed' with the proposition that *I learned some new and interesting things.*
- 97% of participants either 'strongly agreed' or 'agreed' with the proposition that *I think learning to get on well with lots of different kinds of people will help make me a more successful engineer.* This statement may be slightly biased as it links an interest in diversity and inclusivity to a vested interest. Nevertheless, it suggests that there is a recognition among these young people that successful professionals are not people who have mastered technical skills alone. Significantly, many made the unsolicited remark, either on the forms or verbally to the trainers, that they hoped this work would be built on and that they would have the opportunity to further explore issues of diversity and what is involved in creating an inclusive culture.
- 75% of participants either 'strongly agreed' or 'agreed' with the proposition that *I found it interesting meeting the different trainers and hearing something about their lives.* An unsolicited remark made by many of the participants who disagreed with this statement was that they felt they had not had enough opportunity to fully engage with and learn from the student trainers.

Figure 2: Evaluation Responses

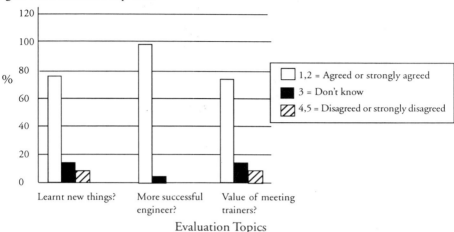

Evaluation Topics

Additionally of course, participants provided constructive feedback about the possibility for improvement. Where possible, sessions were altered to take feedback into account, and some comments have been noted for future sessions and indeed form the basis for the recommendations the training team have conveyed to the Faculty.

Conclusion

This initiative has been an exciting venture into the complex business of building an inclusive culture. The processes of having a diverse training team and using peer trainers allowed this process of learning to be in itself inclusive and attentive to many aspects of diversity. The pilot however occurred in an uncertain context. There is as yet, no Faculty commitment that these sessions will be built on or integrated into the curriculum. This is critical if the Faculty is to achieve their goal of interrupting an existing exclusive culture and building an inclusive one.

The real value of a pilot programme like this depends on its further development and integration into the life of the Faculty. Recommendations have been submitted to the Dean of the Faculty suggesting that this initiative be expanded through the integration of diversity issues, team work and communications training at all year levels and in a range of core Faculty activities. A particular focus on each of the key diversity issues (gender, race, disability, sexuality and culture) is required to develop fully the initial exercises in sensitisation.

Should these be accepted, the authors consider the Faculty well positioned to develop its culture in ways that are inclusive and which thrives on respect for difference. The competitive advantage to the Faculty is likely to be demonstrated in employer satisfaction with graduates who are skilled in interpersonal and cross-cultural communications, work well in teams and are able to respond quickly to a variety of challenges posed by location, community requirements and multi-cultural team constructions.

Should the Faculty not proceed with this programme in a formal manner, it remains true that almost all the first-year intake this year have been exposed to a new set of ideas and experiences to which they have responded enthusiastically and in the main, sensitively. The comment on many evaluation forms that 'I hope these sessions will be followed up', may yet articulate a consumer-driven need for new core components in the education of an engineer. The 97% who agreed with the proposition that 'I think learning to get on well with lots of different people will help make me a more successful engineer', are forecasting clearly that the universities of the future cannot restrict their core business to the development of technical skills. Equal opportunity and cultural diversity are moving from the margins of university life to the heart of the curriculum and have been identified as specific challenges for education (Pallotta-Chiarolli, 1999: pp53-57).

References

Ballard, B (1991) *Helping students from Non-English Speaking Background to Learn More Effectively.* Occasional Paper 91.1 Melbourne, Educational Research & Development Unit, RMIT.

Gunn, J (1992) *Aboriginal and Torres Strait Islander Cross-cultural Awareness Training Package.* Department of Employment & Training, Canberra, ACT, Australia.

Gunn, M (1991) *Project first-hand: the power of HIV infected educators in AIDS prevention.* AIDS Health Promotion Exchange 1:5-7.

Henes, R (1994) *Creating Gender Equity in your Teaching.* College of Engineering, University of California.

Howard, G (1998) *Leadership and Teaching for Diversity: Achieving Equity in the University Setting.* Workshop presented to the University of Adelaide. REACH Center for Multicultural Education, Seattle, Washington, USA.

Http://www.daniladilba.org.au/ahwrole.html *The role of aboriginal health workers at Danila Dilba* Last updated 25 July 1997.

Hutchison, K. (1997) *Inclusive Curriculum: An Annotated Bibliography*. Melbourne, Victoria University of Technology.

Hutchison, K. (1997) *Inclusive Curriculum: Project Report*. Melbourne, Victoria University of Technology.

Pallotta-Chiarolli, M. (1996) *'A Rainbow in my Heart': Interweaving Ethnicity and Sexuality Studies*. In L. Laskey & C. Beavis (eds), *Schooling and Sexualities* (pp.53-67). Geelong, Victoria, Deaking Centre for Education and Change.

Pallotta-Chiarolli, M. (1993) *Interweaving: Culture and Gender Inclusive Resource material: Annotated Bibliography*. Adelaide, SA: MARIA Professional Development Group for Women for Non-English Speaking Background in Education.

Pintos-Lopes, H. (1990) *Two Perspectives:* Hernan Pintos-Lopez conducts interviews with Jeanette Baldwin and Brent Mackie. National AIDS Bulletin, 4, 3, April 1990: 13-16.

Rothman, S and Nightingale, P. (1990, July 6-9*). Gender Race and Class Equity Issues in the University Curriculum*. Paper presented at the 13th Annual HERDSA Conference.

Samovar, L and Porter, R. (1995) *Communication Between Cultures (2nd edition)*. Belmont, California, Wadsworth.

Westwood, Marvin J., Mak A., Barker M., and Ishiyama I. (1996). *The ExcelL© Program: Developing Sociocultural Competencies for Success: Trainer's Manual*. Vancouver, Department of Counselling & Psychology, University of British Columbia.

Part Five

Targeting Specific Groups

17. Higher education in the context of social exclusion: community collaboration at all levels

Colin Trotman and Heather Pudner

Introduction

This chapter addresses the role that higher education institutions (HEIs) can play in relation to combating social exclusion and under representation of particular social groups in the British university sector. Whilst the political rhetoric of 'mass higher education' has been to the fore in recent years and the publication of the Dearing (1997) and Kennedy (1997) reports have placed this issue 'centre stage', the reality is that the class profile of the students in the university system has barely changed. In fact, some authors describe social class participation as 'the final frontier' in relation to widening participation objectives (Woodrow, 1998).

The most recent figures for HEIs in Wales show the social class distribution of applications to be dominated by the wealthiest social classes. Social classes 1 and 2 account for 53.10% of all student applications, whilst classes 3N – 5 share 38.78% of all applications. This percentage imbalance is not the only issue here. Social classes 3N – 5 are actually made up of four social groups (3 non-manual, 3 manual, 4 and 5). As we descend this scale, the less participation there is in higher education. This is however not the whole story. Firstly, if the classification 3N – 5 were disaggregated it would expose even worse participation rates for individual social classes, which are lost by aggregating all classes from 3N – 5. It has been estimated that applications from young people, in social class 5, for 1998 only amounted to 2% of all applications (Association of University Teachers, 1999). Moreover, applications to higher education as a percentage of all applications mean nothing. A focus on acceptances reveals a worse picture, and again the system favours applicants from social classes 1 and 2; 53.33% as opposed to 36.51% for social classes 3N – 5 (Higher Education Statistics Agency, 1999).

Thus, it is evident that a class bias exists and works against a more equitable and open higher education system (Woodrow, 1998). However, in the context of this discussion we must consider the double, and treble disadvantage that some groups encounter. To illustrate the case we shall draw upon our experience of working and teaching in a community education development project. The following description of the Penderry Project is not simply another 'community adult education' saga. It is more to do with a realistic acceptance of the barriers to participation in higher education that exist for socio-economically disadvantaged people and describes an ethos and a particular approach to constructing new learning opportunities by using the higher education system to combat some elements of social exclusion.

Community development

The Penderry Project focuses on one of the poorest wards in South Wales and its primary objectives are to combat the effects of social exclusion on participation in higher education. Amongst its aims perhaps the most important and most difficult to secure are those of increasing community confidence in education *per se* and the creation of a climate of learning through partnerships in the community. Whilst the barriers to participation for people affected by social exclusion can be formidable and include physical isolation, economic exclusion, social isolation and alienation from education in any form, the project was based on the belief that there are opportunities for change. Individuals and groups can be worked with to instil a more positive acceptance of the potential, strategic role that education can have in their lives. Even where groups of adults have all the appearance of being totally disaffected and alienated from education in all its guises, it is still possible to invigorate them educationally. What matters to them, is the education of their children. We can reach them as adult students through their concerns for their children, through the abilities, skills, and resources that they apply on a daily basis, to counter social and economic deprivation (Trotman & Pudner, 1998). The ethos and practice of the Penderry project is to create a new inclusive learning environment to build towards a learning community.

There are, of course, a variety of informal learning activities in all communities, most of which are not recognised as learning activities. These learning situations are equally observable in communities where participation in formal learning activities is low and in communities where participation is relatively high. Nevertheless there is a real and wide disparity between the two types of communities. Communities with relative wealth and high employment will have higher levels of participation in both formal and informal learning. Recent evidence from the Welsh Office also suggests that in addition to low participation in poorer areas, over 90% of adults do not participate in continuing education generally (Welsh Office, 1998). The Penderry ward is no exception to this trend. Only 0.7% of adults (out of a population of 12,000) have qualifications at degree level, compared with 5.8% in the whole of the City and County of Swansea and 7.2% in Wales. Thus, the aim of the Penderry work is to collaborate at all educational levels to produce a holistic approach to individual members of the community and to address overall community needs, where they are identified.

Parents' concerns for their children's education and more particularly their anguish in relation to supporting them, is one such 'need' that was incorporated into this community/agency wide collaboration. During the first years of the project it became abundantly clear that literacy and numeracy skills in the ward were well below the national average (Basic Skills Agency, 1995). In addition to this survey of community skills, the Penderry Project educational guidance workers also identified a number of people who were not fluent writers and had little confidence in their own numerical ability. A minority of these students was confident enough to be referred to further education colleges in the area. For a majority of people this was not possible, as their general confidence was extremely low. More importantly, for this initiative to be successful, new learning opportunities would have to be delivered in known, friendly and supportive community centres in the locality. This was not just a question of confidence. The other barriers to participation included the availability of affordable, quality childcare provision, plus the fact that public transport costs are high.

In order to progress this initiative it was necessary to connect parents' educational concerns for their children to the local schools. Due to the type of concerns that were expressed a partnership was developed with local primary schools and basic education services in the local education authority. Many of these parents were unsure how to contact their children's school and not clear about what was required of them as parents by the school. In addition to this, the dire circumstances that low literacy and numeracy skills produce in terms of self-confidence, employability and the potential hopelessness of the existing situation speak for themselves.

Primary schools emerged as one of the social settings where parents, particularly young parents, were willing to participate. Schools are now inspected by the Office for Standards in Education (OFSTED) in relation to community links and parental involvement and are consequently keen to become involved in work that strengthens links between family and school. This constructs an almost 'Illich-esque' notion of schools as a community resource, serving not just the needs of primary school pupils but reaching out to the wider 'parental/adult student' population and was used to structure a series of parent learning groups. As a 'bridge to somewhere' (Illich, 1971) these groups gave purpose to participants because they were seen as a worthwhile investment on behalf of their children. As Illich suggested (1971 p94) 'schools are difficult to sell as temples'. In this particular case, whilst the parents were not entirely sold on the proposition of re-entering the school gates, neither were the schools entirely happy with handing themselves over as a community resource. In essence, these mutually compatible entities, whilst favourable to the idea of a parent learning group, retained the suspicion born of previous, less than satisfactory experience of the state education system. On the one hand, members of the community, as parents and adults, quite obviously had a range of talents and skills to offer this learning initiative. The schools on the other hand, whilst they had most of the desired teaching resources – computers, telephones, library – were restricted by an image of themselves linked to their professional outlook and were limited by a nationally enforced curriculum. Communication between the school system, parents and the surrounding community was limited to minimal contact, with no funding in the schools to enable them to fulfil a truly pastoral role in their communities. Thus, using the schools as a community resource is, as might be expected, problematic. However, it is the aim of this initiative to contribute funding and ideas to help to make schools something more than a mere depository for children and to function as a wider community education resource.

The 'uselessness' of education

In addition to the schools' awareness of their need to provide evidence of their community connections, the project workers had to bear in mind the state of resourcing in primary and secondary schools and the morale of staff. Tight budget restraints and the introduction of a completely new and rigorous inspection regime have left the state school sector exhausted and demoralised. The attitudes of teachers in settings where social exclusion is high in a climate where achievement levels are compared is often a defensive one. They feel as if they are being asked to take on more tasks with tight timetabling and low resource levels, and are not being given credit for their efforts. In these circumstances it is not possible to ask very much of schools, especially where social conditions determine and produce high numbers of children who are difficult to teach. If they can be made to feel they are being helped in their task of delivering the National Curriculum and fulfilling the performance criteria set by OFSTED it is then much easier to develop a partnership. In the Penderry ward 69.5% of children have free school dinners because their parents' income is at the minimum state benefit level. The average free school dinner figure for the whole of Wales is 25%. These communities are amongst the poorest in Wales. As a result of poverty, in circumstances such as these, schools have multiple social tasks, and staff can feel overwhelmed by the daily responsibilities of delivering a basic educational service. Clearly, groups of adult students are easier to organise in communities where parents have time and resources to give to learning and social activities. New educational provision is also probably easier to introduce in communities where education has evidently proved to be useful and where personal records of achievement and attachment to continuing education are more visible. This was not the case in Penderry and project workers were aware from the beginning that there were large numbers of parents who did not feel ownership of, or a connection with, the education system.

To initiate a switch in people's perceptions of education and school from 'useless' to 'useful' has been a difficult process. For some adult students memories of school are full of feelings of alienation and estrangement. Overall, in the majority of students involved in the family learning programme there was an awareness of a previously attached label of 'failure'. However, a part of the process of learning has been to turn this proscribed identification on its head by questioning who actually failed whom? Failures in the system or failed by the system? This reconceptualisation is only possible as the result of an increase in confidence through participation in continuing education, which was supported by study skills, information technology and educational guidance provision. Thus, an initial commitment and interest in their children's education was in fact converted into a personal development programme for groups of parents and individual students. In the academic year 1998-99 there was a comprehensive range of adult courses on offer for parents (as students) and several courses that were structured as family learning (e.g. Learning Through Play, Maths and English for Parents). This particular initiative within the wider Penderry Project has been very successful. It has run for the past three years and has delivered 19,547 student contact hours to over 1,000 students across eleven academic subject categories. As the project enters its fourth and final year of funding (October 1999 – July 2000), previous students of this non-award bearing non-accredited community based continuing education initiative will be able to progress to study at undergraduate level, as students on a part-time degree course located in the same community. Thus, the Penderry Project has effected some change in the community, and this is now evidenced by student participation at all levels of higher education delivery: on non-accredited courses, foundation/access and part-time degrees. However, the point must be made that this is the direct outcome of widespread collaboration and partnership with community-based groups and statutory agencies. The curriculum has been developed in a user-manner. Moreover, it is deliberately parent and adult student friendly. It has offered and delivered a range of new learning opportunities in the community. However, the catalyst has been that of parents' concerns for their children's education.

Whilst it can be claimed that through collaboration and partnership, higher education can impact upon social exclusion and its effect upon participation, the success of using schools in the community as centres for community learning is more complex than it may appear here. It has been possible to connect the concerns of primary school teachers and those of parents, but we have not attained a position of equitable input over the educational process or affected change in relation to how schools should move towards becoming a community educational resource. This is an ongoing process that will only experience a radical shift in perception through governmental directives and funding. Within the Penderry Ward there are primary schools who are increasingly confronted by the threat of falling pupil rolls and a threat of closure. To suggest a movement towards establishing themselves as a community resource is patently obvious and not new. As Illich (1971: p94), identified, schools are facing the problems previously encountered by churches, 'the defection of the faithful', and he suggested that they should be given over to the people of the community. However, it is plausible to suggest that matters need not go that far. As was stated earlier, schools must not be seen as mere depositories for children. They are far more important than this. There is an opportunity to not only link the concerns of parents and teachers in relation to children's education, but to link the statutory sectors of Primary, Secondary, Further and Higher Education in a community education development project that delivers needs-based programmes for all participants. The traditional void that exists between the differing levels of educational provision has been reduced somewhat (Woodrow, 1998) but it would appear ludicrous as we approach the new millennium to accept a state of non-collaboration between most of the providers in what should be seen as one lifelong learning process. All providers at all levels of delivery must collaborate if we are to achieve a more open, fair and sensibly structured learning society. Community schools could be the hub for such radical programmes of educational change.

Conclusion

Community work had made a mark on continuing education in Wales even before the 1997 change of government and consequent policy changes that have had radical implications for the nation. The legislative changes mean that a democratically elected Welsh Assembly in Cardiff has taken over the administration of educational funding in Wales from the previously Westminster-directed Welsh Office. This body will direct the policy of, and take advice from, the Higher Education Funding Council Wales (HEFCW). There has been government-inspired support from HEFCW for initiatives that encourage options aimed at widening participation by previously under represented groups. One of these has been 'community universities' (Francis & Humphreys, 1995), which deliver higher education programmes in communities devoid of easy access to campus-based provision and build progression routes to the institution.

The vision of a 'community university', as it has emerged in the voluntary community organisations of South West Wales, is, that there is not a prescription that should be followed unquestioningly as a model for development. An effective model is one that allows students access to education and gives them scope to flourish in a locally delivered system, allowing a unique identity to be imprinted on each community arrangement. This approach has produced a variety of programmes and partnerships. The majority are delivered with crèche facilities and study times to match school hours and bus timetables. Curriculum developments have also been individually connected to access courses matched to the interests of the groups of learners. The initiative for these flexible programmes of learning is via a 'community development' approach, which maintains pressure upon the statutory education sector to become more responsive to local needs through local partnership and negotiation. This type of approach is a key component in the Penderry Project development work.

If there is to be integrity and honesty attached to initiatives to widen access and increase participation, then it will only be achieved through initiatives of this kind. Academic capability is a much flaunted requirement attached to priorities such as 'quality of undergraduates', which is used as a smokescreen by those who wish to maintain the status quo. Quite clearly, for the largest number of non-participants an opportunity to participate in a flexible, negotiable programme of learning is far more relevant. HEIs can occupy this role through adopting a far more fluid concept of lifelong learning in the community, built upon education as a two-way process. This relationship will never be entirely an equal one because even in situations of a negotiated curriculum, power will reside with the institution. However, the essential issue here is one of institutional commitment to increase access for under represented groups through collaboration with voluntary and community based organisations. All communities are 'learning communities' that quite obviously contain a diverse range of skills and resources. The role of providers is to unlock and support these attributes towards the goal of widening participation. This is more than simply adopting the role of honest broker. Higher education has the distinct advantages of being comparatively powerful in relation to matched funding, research and a history of expertise in adult liberal education. However, it has little credence amongst the population generally. It is largely 'unknown' and barely thought of other than as a distant ivory tower which has little relevance in relation to the lives that people are compelled to live in areas of social and economic deprivation.

References

Education and Training Action Group for Wales, (1999) *An Education and Training Action Plan for Wales*. Cardiff, Cardiff Welsh Office.

Francis, H. and Humphreys, R. (1996) 'Communities, Valleys and Universities' in Elliott, J., Francis, H., Humphreys, R. and Instance, D. (eds) *Communities and their Universities*. London, Lawrence and Wishart Ltd.

Higher Education Statistics Agency (1998), *Higher Education Institutional Profiles*. HESA.

Illich I. (1971) *Deschooling Society*. New York, Harper Row.

Kennedy, H. (1997) *Learning Works: widening participation in further education*. Coventry, Further Education Funding Council.

La Bonte R. (1998) *Fields of Wellbeing*. Toronto, Communitas.

McNair S. (1998) *Non-Award Bearing Continuing Education. An evaluation of the HEFCE programme*. London, HEFCE.

National Committee of Inquiry into Higher Education (NCIHE) (1997) *Higher Education in the Learning Society*. London, NCIHE.

Pudner, H. and Trotman, C. (1998) 'What's the point – Questions that matter in community based projects designed to increase participation in continuing education' in Preece, J. (ed) *Beyond the Boundaries*. Leicester, NIACE.

Staunton, D. (1996) *Making Education Work on Cork's Northside*. Cork, University College Cork.

Thompson, J. (1997) *Words in Edgeways, Radical Learning for Social Change*. Leicester, NIACE.

Welsh Office (1998) *Learning is for Everyone* (LIFE), Green Paper.

Woodrow, M. (ed) (1998) *From Elitism to Inclusion – widening access to Higher Education*. London, CVCP.

18. Targeting, tutoring and tracking potential undergraduates from disadvantaged backgrounds

John Blicharski

Introduction

Recent research has confirmed that disadvantaged young people, particularly from working class backgrounds, are underrepresented in UK universities (Woodrow, 1998). Many institutions now wish to ensure that the composition of their undergraduate cohorts mirrors society more closely. If we wish to ensure that those most able to benefit from a university education are those selected for it, a targeted approach to attract disadvantaged young people is needed to redress the present imbalance. It is widely recognised that disadvantaged students may be held back by their circumstances (Garner, 1989; Paterson, 1991). They often lack many of the personal transferable skills required for survival within higher education (HE) (Murphy *et al*, 1997) and social/financial support structures available to better-off students. Consequently, individualised help, guidance and counselling are essential if these students are to succeed.

This chapter outlines how one model of targeting, tutoring and tracking disadvantaged young people has, over the last seven years, allowed over 450 disadvantaged young people to prepare and qualify for higher education from which they were previously virtually excluded. It describes how, through partnerships, the course has allowed a Scottish university to create a more inclusive and diverse educational environment and how tracking student progression has enabled the course to be improved and student outcomes monitored. It outlines components of this course, which was recently selected as an example of best practice in research commissioned by the Committee of Vice-Chancellors and Principals (CVCP). As such it represents a combination of potentially transferable strategies aimed at supporting wider access and progression which have been tried and tested in an area with both urban and rural deprivation.

Targeting

In the UK, schools, colleges, universities and the government have recently placed renewed emphasis on ensuring that all sections of society can benefit from further and higher education. That being the case, some ask why disadvantaged young people need to be specifically targeted if tertiary education is now available to all in this age of lifelong learning. The development of both the further and higher education sectors would seem to offer many attractive options.

The answer lies in comparing recent targets with reality. The UK government has indicated their desire to have a progression rate to HE of 50% by the year 2010. Whilst this requires relatively modest growth in some parts of Scotland, in other areas much larger developments (in some cases of the order of five-fold increases) will be needed to achieve this target. The government publication 'Opportunity Scotland' (1998) helpfully outlines the state of play. It comments that 'the government is committed to the principle that anyone who has the ability to benefit from further and higher education should have the opportunity to do so' but also admits that 'the participation rate for students from less advantaged parts of society is significantly lower (than average)'. In fact, school pupils with professional parents appear to be three times more likely to gain a degree than those from working-class backgrounds. Many students, particularly in disadvantaged parts of Scotland, feel that HE is simply not for them or not an option for them regardless of ability. Disadvantage, largely due to socio-economic factors, has reduced their level of academic achievement to the point where they are effectively excluded from HE, or unwittingly exclude themselves by undervaluing their ability for post-school study. The government document is upbeat, stating that 'the cynicism that comes with failure or fear of failure can be addressed and overcome in time.' However, the virtual replacement of student grants with student loans and the introduction of student fees appears to have added to concern amongst potential students, and a reluctance to commit several years to a course that will not guarantee a job but will guarantee an overdraft. Consequently, undergraduate cohorts do not reflect the composition of social groups present in the society that universities serve, and targeting disadvantaged young people can be an efficient way to redress the balance. Whilst Scotland has not yet followed the US towards positive discrimination, targeting at least helps level the playing field by welcoming all social classes in a more even-handed way. In addition, raising awareness is vital if we are to ensure that career choices are based on knowledge and not prejudice, and once again a targeted approach can be highly effective and efficient. The wide range of courses now available are of little value if disadvantaged young people do not see them as an option for themselves, but rather for someone else who has been prepared for degree-level study since primary school. That being the case how, in practice, do we target to ensure that true ability, and not ability skewed by socio-economic circumstances, determines who is admitted to undergraduate study?

Whilst there may be no 'correct way' to target, three models of targeting merit consideration. The first identifies students by where they live - the geographical 'pick postcodes' approach. This approach may have to rely on perishable data. For example, the last UK census, which is often used to identify disadvantaged locations, took place in 1991. For highly mobile disadvantaged young people, the geographical approach used in isolation can have serious shortcomings as focusing on only a snapshot survey, however detailed, can be misleading. It also can give rise to the 'wrong side of the street' issue where a young person on one side of a street qualifies for help but someone on the other side does not. This problem also makes promotional work seem somewhat unfair, with neighbours potentially being treated differently.

Others prefer a more financially orientated approach to identifying disadvantaged young people. This has merits, including the ease with which those already in receipt of benefits can be identified. A danger of financial selection, however, is that it misses any non-claimants. Once again, disadvantaged young people are highly mobile and stigma is attached to 'signing on' for benefits. Others are 'gap people' who do not register for benefits immediately, hoping that their circumstances may improve and so hold off from officialdom, using personal or family reserves for support. In addition, using a 'registered for benefits' net will not identify all forms of disadvantage, for example, potentially missing personal crisis at critical times. Family break-up or illness immediately before examinations happens all too frequently and may delay or prevent university entry. This may not be picked up by financial measures.

At the University of Dundee, we would like to think that we take a third option – a more even handed, ethical approach. Working closely with local councils, we have hybridised the geographical and financial approaches and added a few other categories to pick up as many forms of disadvantage as possible. The addition of the latter categories has been necessary as our research identified other groupings who might be missed by a narrower focus, such as those suffering from abuse, disrupted family life and ill health. Consequently, we adopted a client-centred approach that has been described as the 'Swiss army knife' approach to identifying and then helping disadvantaged young people. Whilst this approach is highly labour intensive it does ensure that we do not miss those we seek to help nor raise aspirations that we cannot help people achieve. Selected by ability despite adversity, students enter our Access Summer School, details of which follow. Our selection process has operated since 1993 and, indeed, has now been adopted by some other higher education institutions (HEIs). Thus our policy seeks to identify students who have HE ability but have not got HE entry qualifications 'through no fault of their own.' To achieve this, all applications to join the course must be accompanied by a nomination prepared by someone aware of the educational and personal circumstances of the applicant. Thus by outlining why the applicant needs to attend the course, course provision can be tailored to meet their needs. This referral system, which is followed up by individual interviews, relies on specific criteria we use for selection, namely:

1. little/no parental experience of HE;
2. limited family income;
3. unskilled, semi-skilled or unemployed parent(s);
4. living in circumstances not conducive to study;
5. educational progress blighted by specific events at critical times (e.g. bereavement, illness, separation or divorce);
6. other exceptionally adverse circumstances or factors specified by nominating institutions.

Typically, three criteria will apply to each student we select – the 'other' category is increasingly used by nominators to disclose domestic upset and abuse. Experience has shown that students facing five or six often struggle to make up lost ground in what is, after all, a very short course. That said, as part of our access admissions promise all those we cannot help are individually referred to other agencies. Our vertically integrated system aims to ensure that there are no losers and that once a young person has been in touch with us we will engage with their needs as rapidly and effectively as we can. Equally importantly, our Access Summer School is simply one facet of our desire to widen access. We have embarked on a number of projects to raise awareness of the value of education in both primary and secondary schools. We are currently raising awareness of post-school options with primary school pupils in the hope of giving them more targets to aim at (both employment and education orientated) at an early stage. Most recently, we have introduced two new intensive entry initiatives. The ASPIRE course has, since 1997, helped pupils qualify and prepare for HE study. In 1999 Discovering Degrees was introduced to provide pupils entering their final year of secondary school with a short, hands-on, insight into HE options. Together, these three courses comprise our intensive entry initiative (IEI) suite of courses. A book aimed at disadvantaged young people in Scotland has also been published by our university (Blicharski, 1999).

Tutoring

Tutoring is the second step in boosting confidence and supporting achievement. In a
culture of disappointment, developing confidence is vital and lies at the heart of our
Access Summer School. Students used to under-performing can be prone to accept failure
all too easily and see their futures as being beyond their own control. Our Access Summer
School provides disadvantaged young people with a mock-undergraduate experience lasting
eleven weeks. The course is designed to enable students to prove their ability to study for
a degree. It involves the university working closely with a large number of partners,
especially local councils. The course is a recognised 'New Deal Education and Training
Option', thus enabling students who have been unemployed for more than six months to
attend the course whilst continuing to receive unemployment benefits. The course includes
comprehensive support from across all sectors of our institution including our Centre for
Applied Language Studies (which provides 33 hours of Personal Transferable Skills
development work per student), the Special Needs Unit, the Student Advisory Service,
the Counselling Service and the Chaplaincy. All students matriculate and so have full
access to all university facilities – the library stays open for extra hours to allow them to
study there. During the course, students are guided by trained postgraduate and
undergraduate students who act as guidance and peer-support counsellors. Many of the
latter have completed the course themselves. Students study three undergraduate subjects
and complete a personal transferable skills course during the intensive, eleven-week
programme. Taught courses are delivered by academic staff with experience of working
with first-year classes and spans a wide range of learning opportunities, including practical
work. Students are assessed both continuously and by final exam, their aim being to earn
one of the guaranteed places reserved for them. Drop-out from the course is low, averaging
5%. Fuller details of the course appear elsewhere (Blicharski, 1998).

One of the most useful measures of the success of our tutoring phase involves
our annual analysis of student course evaluation forms. We ask all students who complete
the course to tell us about the benefits that they perceive the course has offered them.
Analysis of their responses provides an insight in both their starting point and the apparent
'value added' they derived from the course. For the 1998 cohort of seventy-six students:

- 100% said that the course had helped them to analyse themselves as potential
  undergraduates;
- 100% reported that the course gave them a clearer understanding of life as a university
  student;

- 100% said that the course had helped them to organise their studies;
- 100% said that the course had helped them strike a balance between their academic and other aspects of university life;
- 100% said that the course had helped them to decide which courses and subjects they might take at university;
- 97% said that the course had helped them to decide whether to continue in education (the other 3% had already decided!);
- 95% said that the course had helped them consider possible future career(s), despite the fact that this was not an explicit course aim.

Such high figures appear to demonstrate the gap in awareness that needs to be addressed whilst helping some disadvantaged young people access HE. Many start the course very unsure of which faculty, never mind which undergraduate course, they wish to enter. To reflect this, students sign up for undergraduate destinations at the end of the course, not at the beginning. Relatively few have applied through the formal University and Colleges Admission Service (UCAS) application process largely because they have little or no perspective on which to base course choice decisions. Consequently, a 'try before you buy' perspective on subjects is beneficial to both students and staff who report high satisfaction ratings as a result of this process.

Tracking

If targeting enables us to reach out and tutoring enables us to provide support, tracking allows us to gather evidence of how well our students and our course perform. In terms of justifying staff time and budgets, outcome feedback is vital in ensuring we know that what we do works and that improvements are effective.

To date, 399 students have attended our Access Summer School and ASPIRE courses with further cohorts being added each year. Detailed research following students who have attended the course since 1995 is ongoing, with preliminary findings reported here for the first time. Between 1995 and 1998 (inclusive) some 277 students have started the course with 262 (95%) going on to complete it. Of those completing the course, 191 (73%) used the course to enter our university whilst a further 40 (15%) used the course to access another HEI. Whilst pleased with a progression to HE rate of 88% for students who previously lacked university entrance qualifications, and were anticipated to be unlikely to obtain them due to their circumstances, an equally important measure of success is how these students have performed as undergraduates. To date, 75% of those who entered our university remain on track to earn a degree – (indeed several dozen have already graduated). 144 students, together with a further nine who have now moved to other HEIs, indicates a retention rate in HE of around 80%. This reflects retention values for students who have been with us for between one and four years yielding an average annual drop-out rate from HE of 5%. This suggests that students who have completed these courses are, in general, coping well. In an attempt to further increase our progression and retention figures, we are now focusing on the 38 students who have left our institution in the hope that any additional support requirements may be identified and deployed for future cohorts.

Conclusion

The trinity of targeting, tutoring and tracking underpin the rich and varied course that we have tried to create in Dundee. The vision of our many partners in this work has enabled us to make what we hope is a specific and meaningful impact on underachievement by local disadvantaged young people. Continuing tracking will, year by year, reveal how each cohort has coped. The real bonus, however, is that the consequence of applying our policy has been to see many more young people coming forward from schools which traditionally produce few HE applicants. With brothers, sisters, cousins and, indeed, parents now attracted to return to study and follow the trail blazed by these ambassadors for education, a real sense of 'opportunity for all' blossoms at each graduation. We share their pride.

Thanks

My thanks go to the entire Access Summer School Team, especially Michael Allardice, Researcher for the 'Learning Their Lessons: exploring barriers to HE' project funded by Neighbourhood Resources Department, Dundee City Council and the University of Dundee. I also wish to thank the CVCP for their support of my attendance at the 8th EAN Conference. Finally I wish to thank the students who make it all worthwhile.

References

Blicharski, J. R. D. (1998) 'Disadvantaged youngsters: raising awareness, aspiration and access through a summer school' in Preece J. (ed) *Beyond the boundaries.* Leicester, NIACE.

Blicharski, J. R. D. (1999) Chapters in S. Watt (ed) *Choose university, how to get in and get on - a guide for students living in Scotland, their parents and teachers.* Dundee, University of Dundee.

Garner, C. L. (1989) *Does deprivation damage?* A report on research funded by the John Watson's Trust. Centre for Educational Sociology, University of Edinburgh.

Murphy, R., Burke, P., Gillespie, J., Rainbow, R. and Wilmut, J. (1997) *The key skills of students entering higher education.* A report commissioned by the Department for Education and Employment. Nottingham, University of Nottingham.

Scottish Office (1998). *Opportunity Scotland*, Edinburgh, The Scottish Office.

Paterson, L. (1991) 'Social origins of underachievement among school leavers' in H. Maguiness (ed) *Educational opportunity: the challenge of underachievement & social deprivation.* Proceedings of conference on access to further and higher education, June 1991.

Woodrow, M. (1998) *From Elitism to Inclusion.* London, Committee of Vice-Chancellors and Principals.

19. An access summer school: improving participation by young women in technology-related education

Renate Kosuch

Introduction

Although the numbers are increasing, in Germany female students continue to be underrepresented in science and engineering. The two universities in Oldenburg, Germany, have developed successful 'encounter programmes' to encourage young women to enrol on technology-related courses. These include one-week summer schools for young women, who are in secondary school (11th through 13th grade). In Germany there are two types of universities with different access routes. In addition to traditional universities there are less well-known universities of applied sciences, which were founded only 28 years ago. They are mainly characterised by a short standard period of study (eight semesters) and a strong emphasis on practical training. During the four-year study period, students complete two semesters of profession-related internships. Up to now these universities can only offer PhD-programmes to their former students in cooperation with the traditional universities.

The importance of attracting girls and young women to science and engineering

The importance of sophisticated technology is still growing. Almost all fields of everyday life are influenced by technological changes. The significance of technology in the workplace is increasing and, at the same time, the ways of doing sciences and engineering are developing. Recognition of the importance of teamwork, management and language skills is growing, and consequently, more collaborative styles of work are evolving, replacing traditional hierarchical styles that have proved to be less suitable.

Society not only needs to get more young people into these professional fields, but there is also a need to attract students other than the traditional clients of engineering studies. Women tend to have more social skills and different ways of solving problems, because they are still treated differently from their brothers and male peers within their families and at school. We cannot allow so much of our nation's intellectual potential to be excluded and it is important to widen women's opportunities, by preparing them for careers with higher incomes than traditional 'female' professions. Therefore it is important to adequately prepare young women to excel in the field of science and engineering.

Two projects to bridge the gender gap in science and engineering
Between 1993 and 1999, Fachhochschule Oldenburg, the university of applied sciences, was involved in two projects to improve the participation of women in science and technology (see Figure 1).

'Encouraging Girls and Young Women to Choose a Technical Career' is a project started by the equal opportunity officers of four universities of applied sciences in the Northwest of Lower Saxony in 1993, Fachhochschule (FH) Oldenburg, FH Osnabrück, FH Ostfriesland and FH Wilhelmshaven (Modellvorhaben, 1996). The project was funded by the Ministry of Science and Culture in Lower Saxony. It was prolonged after the first three years until August 1999. The main goal was to motivate young women to enrol in sciences and engineering as well as to lower external barriers for women in this field. It involved:

- engaging in *awareness building* within the participating universities e.g. through lectures and workshops;
- offering *open houses* especially for young women at the universities of applied sciences (particularly active in developing this module: FH Wilhelmshaven);
- offering *career guidance classes* for groups of schoolgirls, held at the schools (11th to 13th grade), providing insights into professional life in science and engineering (particularly active in developing these classes: FH Osnabrück);
- establishing and supporting *women's networks of professionals* in multiple fields of engineering and business (particularly active in supporting networks: FH Oldenburg);
- arranging *further education* for female engineers who re-enter the workplace after maternity leave (particularly active in arranging programmes for women returnees: FH Ostfriesland);
- setting up a *collection of texts on women and technology*. 'Women – university – technologies' was started in collaboration with the library of FH Oldenburg. In addition to providing books, every semester the university arranges two lectures dealing with women studies in engineering (e.g. a study on the development of the typewriter from the user's point of view), or the status of women in science and technology (e.g. questioning the unwritten rule, that part-time work in the field of engineering is impossible to organise).

In 1997 the Vice-Presidents of Carl von Ossietzky University Oldenburg and Fachhochschule Oldenburg applied for additional funding, to support the ongoing cooperation between the two universities in Oldenburg. Further funding for activities which were not included in the project mentioned above was given for 18 months. During that time:

- two one-week *summer schools* in Oldenburg to enable young women to encounter natural sciences and engineering were organised;
- in addition *four 2-3 day courses on selected subjects*, in geoinformatics, physics, mathematics and environmental engineering were given during the spring and autumn vacations, with a total of 75 participants attending (Tendler, 1998b).

This broad approach mirrors the experience that each activity alone is not sufficient to attain the goal. In the context of this programme the summer school was developed, improved and implemented to give young women orientation in the sciences, especially in those fields where they are still underrepresented.

The science and engineering summer school for young women

The one-week summer school to enable girls aged 16 and above to encounter natural sciences and engineering became one of the central and most crucial activities in the project. Between 1995 and 1998 it ran 11 times with a total of about 620 students (Arbeitsgruppe Sommerhochschule, 1999).

Concept and schedule

In one of the last weeks before the summer holidays, between 30 and 100 summer students have the opportunity to encounter different courses of studies within the natural sciences and engineering departments of a university of applied sciences. If possible, they complete the programme by alternating between the two different kinds of universities. The date of the summer school – one to two weeks before the summer holidays – was chosen, so that participants would not miss too much at school. Students have to apply to their school to be excused, but obtaining permission from schools has never been a problem. Sceptical headteachers were convinced once they saw the challenging schedule (see Figure 2).

Figure 1: Two projects to get more women into science and engineering

	Project I	Project II
Title	Motivating Girls and Young Women to Choose a Technical Career	Summer Programme for Young Women
Participants *(place of business)*	FH Oldenburg FH Osnabrück FH Ostfriesland FH Wilhelmshaven (FH = universitiy of applied sciences)	FH Oldenburg Universität Oldenburg (Universität= university)
Duration	9/1993 - 8/1999	7/1997 – 11/1998
Financed by	Ministry of Science and Culture in Lower Saxony	Ministry of Science and Culture in Lower Saxony
Project modules	• Open houses • Summer school • Science fairs • Career guidance classes • Tutoring • Exhibition 'Engineering career' • Women's networks • Teacher training • Library collection on women and technology • Re-entry courses for women in technology • Database to acquire more female professors • Comparative research projects	• Summer school • Holiday courses in science and engineering fields • Entry courses for new students

Depending on the size of the group, summer students can choose between two or more curricula, which consist of one course of study each day. Once they have chosen a curriculum, they cannot change. This way participants encounter popular fields in natural sciences and engineering, with a comparatively high number of females as well as less attractive or less well known fields.

After enrolment on Monday, students are welcomed by, for instance, the equal opportunity officer, university president, vice-president, or city mayor. Choosing these prominent people is one way of demonstrating the importance of the programme to participants. Afterwards the summer students get to know each other in small groups, tutored by a female student. Later, these groups participate in the hands-on parts of the course together. This is followed by a guided tour giving a short overview of the university departments. The encounter programme of selected science and engineering branches begins. If possible, only one department is on the programme each day. Whilst the morning schedule is obligatory in all summer schools, the special courses or worksite tours in the afternoon in some of the programmes are voluntary.

Each programme day in a department offers hands-on activities as well as lectures, guided tours and panel discussions with female students and practitioners. Apart from the special programme, regular lectures for first semester students are also integrated in the programme. The summer school ends with a debriefing, a public presentation and a reception. During the following weeks, in some places the 'trainee students' can also participate in job shadowing.

A fundamental component of the summer school concept is the involvement of female tutors in the programme. Their impact as a role model is based on the fact that they are still quite close to the world experienced by participants. Other positive role models are the practitioners. The summer school coordinators try especially to recruit young alumnae, because experience shows that summer school students tend to relate to them more easily, than to female engineers in senior positions.

Recruitment and terms of admission
To inform potential participants about the summer school, flyers and posters are sent to regional secondary schools. The summer schools are also announced in a careers magazine which is distributed countrywide. Maths and science teachers are informed and, if possible,

189

Figure 2: A typical morning schedule of a summer school

	Group A	Group B
Monday, 8.00 – 13.30	Enrolment Lectures Guided tour in both universities	
Tuesday, 8.30. – 13.30	**European Transport Management** **Nautical Sciences** Fachhochschule	Physics University
Wednesday, 8.30. - 13.30	**Chemistry** University	**Civil Engineering (European) Civil Engineering Management** Fachhochschule
Thursday, 8.30. – 13.30	**Architecture** Fachhochschule	**Biology Mathematics** University
Friday, 8.30. - 12.00	**Informatics** University	Surveying Geodesy Fachhochschule
12.30 - 14.00	**Evaluation/reception/press conference**	

brief presentations are made in the schools. Former participants also recommend the summer school. A main source of information is the regional press.

Participants are accepted on the programme in the order that their applications are received. This guarantees diversity of background (e.g. school, hometown). Participation is free of charge, apart from accommodation (if necessary) and food. In order to make potential participants aware of the plans for the summer school as early as possible, the first information is provided through newspaper releases and an announcement to the secondary schools. Students who are interested are urged to get in touch with the coordinators quickly. Those who leave their address early are the first to receive the application form. Up to now this small advantage has guaranteed high motivation among participants. It underpins the perception that the summer school is something special and highly rated – although participation is free.

Research on the summer schools

To facilitate the evaluation of each programme, summer school students are asked to complete questionnaires before, during and after the event. The goal is to obtain information about the participants and their rating of the different programme modules and to learn more about the impact of the scheme.

The following are some of the results of the evaluation of nine summer schools involving 570 participants (Kosuch, 1995, 1996b, 1997; Tendler, 1998a):

- The average age of participants is between 19 and 20.
- About 80% are students in 11th and 12th grades in secondary school, which in Germany ends after 13 years of school.
- Approximately three quarters of the students come from the area and one quarter from other parts of Germany (these figures vary between different universities).
- During the last two years of secondary school students have to major in two subjects. Most participants combine one subject from the field of science and mathematics with a language or cultural studies. The second largest group is the one with two majors in science and mathematics, the smallest is with no majors in this field. This shows that the programme mainly attracts those young women who already have good prerequisites for technology-related professions, but also show an interest in non-technical fields.
- Basic interest in technical courses of study differs widely.
- Between 72% and 92% of the summer school participants could not refer to any role model concerning career decisions.

The feedback after participating in the encounter programme is positive:

- About 95% participate in the full programme, despite the fact that the science and engineering fields students show an interest in are combined with other technology subjects which they either do not know about or have not shown any interest in.

- 77% to 95% of the participants state that the summer school met their needs and expectations.
- The average grade which the students give the programme is between 1.8 and 2.2 (on a 6 point scale, where 1 means 'very good' and 6 means 'failed').

The impact, measured through self-assessment by the participants, is:
- the number of students who envisage choosing one of the branches of technology that they encountered during summer school increases in most cases;
- the knowledge of each single science and engineering field improved significantly;
- as regards vocational choices, the summer school supports changes in preferences. Students who, before participating, expressed a strong interest in well-known engineering fields with a comparatively high percentage of female students – such as architectural studies – afterwards stated newly acquired interests in lesser-known fields of study such as European civil engineering management or in fields where very few women are found, such as electrical engineering.

These changes in preference support the basic concept of the summer school schedule, which only allows a choice between two or more weekly programmes but not an individual combination of fields of preference.

The personal feedback statements made by summer school students often show enthusiasm and gratitude. They urge the organisers to offer the summer school again. But how did the participants benefit in the long run? What was the impact on their vocational choices? As regards the genuine impact of the intervention, a significant source of information is provided by the results of a study on the career decisions of former participants of the summer school 1995-1997 in Oldenburg that was carried out in 1998 (n=70) (Tendler, 1998b).

The results show that the summer school is successful in motivating young women to enrol in natural science and engineering courses.
- 74% of the participants who are currently university students, chose courses of study in natural science and engineering. 65% of the enrolled students chose a course of study that was encountered during the summer school.
- 27% of the university students enrolled in one of the universities in Oldenburg. Unfortunately the questionnaire did not inquire whether participants applied but were not accepted.
- 70% of former participants who are doing an apprenticeship, chose vocations that

qualify them for courses of study at the University of Applied Sciences (e.g. apprenticeship in construction drawing or in surveying).

The results of the study also show that the summer school helps students in their decision-making process towards enrolling in science and engineering.

- 75% state that they felt strongly supported in their pre-decisions and that the encounter programme drew their attention to new opportunities. Feelings of doubt and insecurity were reduced.
- 65% of those who are now university students and 74 % of the students in science and engineering say that they coped very well with the new situation as students in the first semester.
- In retrospect, 74% of the summer school alumnae consider it positive that the programme is mono-educational.

Implementation and dissemination of good practice

In Lower Saxony, Fachhochschule Oldenburg, the university of applied sciences, was the first to offer the technology summer school for women in 1995. Three years later in 1998 four standard universities and four universities of applied sciences had already followed their example. In cities where both types of universities are established – as is the case in Oldenburg – both institutions offer the summer school together. This year all the universities that were involved in both projects mentioned, participated in summer schools – with little or no project funding. In Oldenburg, both universities have declared that they will definitely offer the summer school in 2000. Thus the implementation was successful.

To disseminate and promote the summer school even more, the project released a programme manual (Arbeitsgruppe Sommerhochschule, 1999):

- to enable others to establish similar activities;
- to help reduce the costs by avoiding the 'reinvention of the wheel';
- to enable universities who already have experiences of the summer school to switch the main responsibility for the organisation between different departments each year.

The programme manual is based on experiences from nine summer schools with 570 young women. The organiser's kit contains, for example:

- guidelines (e.g. for developing the schedule or for writing press releases);
- checklists and timetables as an aid to planning and implementing the programme;

- background information (e.g. statistics, research results);
- sample material (such as sample letters, posters, schedules).

After the summer school manual was released and the impact of the results had been presented publicly in a final conference, the Minister of Science and Culture urged and encouraged other universities in Lower Saxony to establish summer schools for young women and recommended the project's action kit. This is especially important because of the tendency that once university departments start to see the success of the programme they want to change it into a co-educational programme. This year this occurred at one of the universities of applied sciences. The consequence was that only one female student applied and participated in the programme. This shows how important it is to keep it mono-educational for girls and young women.

Conclusion

The summer school has proved to be an effective means of improving the access of young women to science and engineering studies. In light of the Oldenburg experiences, one can encourage all universities with science and engineering departments to establish this kind of access support for young women.

    The project 'Motivating girls and young women to choose a technical career' has an impact on the percentage of women who are enrolled in these educational fields. Figure 3 shows the numbers at FH Oldenburg compared to the overall numbers in Germany. Between the winter semesters 1995/96 and 1997/98 there has been an increase in the percentage of female engineering students from an average of 7 % (1.2 % in electrical engineering and 11.9 % in regional planning). FH Oldenburg can report an even higher increase. In 1997/98 the percentage of women in engineering science was 3% above the average (2 % in surveying and geodesy, 5% in transport and nautical studies). The summer school is one, if not the core activity of the project responsible for that effect. To change the culture on campus towards a more inclusive climate, more universities should encourage young women to encounter and participate in natural science and engineering fields of studies.

Figure 3: Female students of engineering sciences in German universities (Percentage)

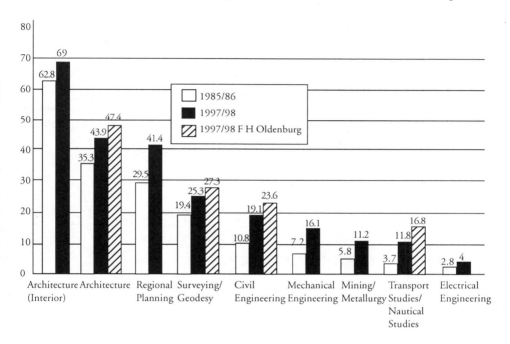

References

Arbeitsgruppe Sommerhochschule des Modellvorhabens 'Motivation von Frauen und Mädchen für ein Ingenieurstudium' (ed) (1999) *Leitfaden zur Organisation einer Sommerhochschule für Oberstufenschülerinnen,* FH Oldenburg.

Kosuch, R. (1995) *Sommerhochschule für Schülerinnen an der FH Oldenburg.* Unpublished Evaluation Report.

Kosuch, R. (ed) (1996a) *Berufsziel: Ingenieurin. Aufbruch in die/der Technik.* Weinheim Deutscher Studienverlag.

Kosuch, R.(1996b) *Sommerhochschule 1996 an der FH Oldenburg und der Carl von OssietzkyUniversität Oldenburg.* Unpublished Evaluation Report.

Kosuch, R. (1996c) 'Niemand will mehr Ingenieur werden' - doch vielleicht Ingenieurin? Motivierung für ein Ingenieurstudium durch die Veranstaltung einer Sommerhochschule in: Melezinek, A. and Kiss, I. (ed) *Bildung durch*

Kommunikation. Alsbach/ Bergstraße, Leuchturmverlag, 493-496.

Kosuch, R. (1997) *Sommerhochschule 1997 an der FH Oldenburg und der Carl von Ossietzky Universität Oldenburg*. Unpublished Evaluation Report.

Modellvorhaben 'Motivation von Frauen und Mädchen für ein Ingenieurstudium' (ed) (1996) *Broschüre zu den ersten Ergebnissen des Projektes*, brochure.

Tendler, H. and Wetzel, Chr. (1998a) *Sommerhochschule 1998 an der FH Oldenburg und der Carl vonOssietzky Universität Oldenburg*. Unpublished Evaluation Report.

Tendler, H. (1998b) *Auswertungsbericht zum Gemeinsamen Sommerstudienprogrammem der FH Oldenburg und der Carl von Ossietzky Universität Oldenburg*. Unpublished Evaluation Report.

20. The engagement of minority ethnic groups in higher education: experiences from the UK

Paul Taylor

Introduction

The purpose of this chapter is to explore a means through which it might be feasible to create an inclusive higher education, or rather a higher education that effectively engages with minority ethnic groups. The chapter argues that a major starting point should be the attempt to make the staff of higher education reflect the diversity that already exists, or is being aimed for, within the student body. It is therefore necessary to create an organisational culture within higher education institutions which recognises the value of cultural diversity and engages with minority ethnic groups. In this way potential students should be provided with an atmosphere and role models that may encourage them to become more engaged with higher education.

In order to explore these issues the chapter draws on two research projects. The first was a detailed case study of non-academic employment within one university which focused on the recruitment of minority ethnic groups (Johnson *et al*, 1996). The case study institution is in an area with a relatively high proportion of the local population from minority ethnic groups. The research involved interviews and focus groups with those involved in recruitment and representatives from other large local employers and community-based minority ethnic organisations. The second research project was a small scale investigation of academic career progression (Heward *et al*, 1995; 1997). This project interviewed sixteen senior academics within two contrasting subjects, law and biology. The choice of subjects was based upon the relatively high representation within both subjects at undergraduate level of both minority ethnic groups and women (Taylor, 1993). In addition the subjects were chosen to represent different subject cultures within higher education (Becher, 1990; Thomas, 1990).

Inclusion or Engagement

This chapter argues that processes of engagement need to be considered rather than those of inclusion. It examines the way in which the current culture of higher education tends to be one of exclusion and discrimination. Only through exploring the existing ways in which individuals, in particular those from minority ethnic groups, become (or are prevented from being) engaged with higher education is it possible to consider the most appropriate steps required for greater inclusivity and cultural diversity. The term engagement is used in preference to the usual oppositional term inclusion, which suggests a sense of passivity by those from minority ethnic groups. It also suggests that once groups are 'included' in higher education the need for further action ceases. Engagement is used to indicate processes by which members of minority ethnic groups become involved themselves or can be encouraged to become involved by others within higher education. Essentially engagement suggests a continuous process of action in which universities encourage and welcome those from minority ethnic groups, and minority groups themselves are actively engaged in the campus culture. The term aims to recognise some of the already notable achievements of those from minority ethnic groups (Taylor, 1992, 1993; Modood, 1993) and is also used to suggest it is the responsibility of majority groups already within higher education to become actively engaged with those from minority ethnic groups (Taylor, 1996).

Contextual issues

In common with other major organisations throughout the 1990s, universities in the UK have continued to develop equal opportunities and anti-discrimination policies (for example Williams *et al*, 1989; Heward & Taylor, 1992; CUCO, 1994; EOR,1995; Farish *et al*, 1995). These research studies have found university equality policies to focus much more on employment than student issues and a lack of policy links between the two roles of universities as employers and educators. The relatively slow rate of progress is partially a result of the reliance within UK legislation upon voluntary action meaning that the priority given to equality initiatives within universities can vary tremendously (EOR, 1995: p30). West and Lyon (1995) have suggested cost, both financial and in terms of personal diminution of power, may also hinder policy development.

There are major structural barriers to change in higher education. Morley argues that 'the conventional hierarchical, organisational structure of much of the academy lends itself to slowness in change and lack of opportunities for equality' (1994: p196). The study of academic careers forming part of this discussion also found structures in the sector which were likely to hinder progress in equality. It identified 'the importance of power structures and the significance of informal processes of stereotyping and informal networks of contacts' (Heward *et al,* 1995: p161) in maintaining processes of racial and gender differentiation. The departmental structure and autonomy within universities adds another level of complexity. Leicester and Lovell's research found patchy departmental practice 'arising from the commitment of individuals to one or another aspect of equal opportunities' (1994, p50), little co-ordination of activities and few departments with routine good practice integrated into other departmental policies. In effect equality policies are often 'added on' and potentially operating in conflict with other policies, rather than representing a coherent integrated approach (Taylor, 1998).

Recent studies of the academic profession have revealed some of the ways processes of inclusion and exclusion operate against particular groups. Halsey's (1992) study of 6,000 respondents found that association with Oxford and Cambridge and giving priority to research were significant in promotion to a chair. In a study of academics in both the USA and UK, Becher (1990) demonstrated how subject differences influence judgements of academics by 'gatekeepers' to the profession and the institution. Bourdieu (1988) also found subject differences to play a key role in the definition of promotion criteria in his study of academics in Paris. He too identified the key role of 'gatekeepers' and the importance of shared implicit assumptions which lay behind selection criteria and help to form a 'habitus' for different subjects within universities,,into which entrants have to fit.

Academic power also operates through more informal methods in order to advance or hinder the careers of others. Several studies have identified the key role played by networks within professions and the way these may operate to exclude women or minority ethnic groups (for example on the medical profession see Lorber, 1984 and Elston, 1980). The male domination of subject-based networks can operate to make women academics feel excluded (Bagilhole, 1993). The extent to which these networks also exclude those from minority ethnic groups was one factor explored in the research study of academic career progression. The position of members of minority ethnic groups and women in the academic profession is of particular importance for the education and professional socialisation of many other professional groups and it assumes greater significance given the expansion of higher education and the desire to create an increasingly more diverse student body (Ball & Eggins, 1989; Schuller, 1991; Tapper & Salter, 1992). If universities are able to overcome some of these barriers and create more integrated equality policies they may start to establish a more diverse staff. In this way they will have a greater diversity of staff resources in order to help engage with minority ethnic students and also offer potential students role models within the sector.

Exclusionary practice

The research on academic and non-academic recruitment in universities is based on a case study institution, located in a geographic area of relatively high minority ethnic representation (Johnson *et al*, 1996). In the surrounding region 8.2% of the local population are from minority ethnic groups whilst monitoring data unfavourably reveals that around 7% of applicants were from these groups. Other local employers tended to attract a more representative percentage of minority ethnic groups. Furthermore, monitoring data showed that levels of representation diminished at each stage of the selection process through shortlisting to appointment. The institutional data masks the numerous variations across the university in terms of occupational areas and departmental differences, some of which had major difficulties attracting applicants. It is sufficient to note that despite some variations the data provided a relatively consistent picture. White women most commonly had the highest success rates largely due to the types of jobs available. In some areas African-Caribbean men had success rates above those expected given their local representation. Despite the predominance of Asians amongst the local minority ethnic population these groups had consistently lower shortlisting and appointment rates. Furthermore the monitoring data for previous years indicated that the situation had worsened for minority ethnic applicants over time.

Key actors in the recruitment process were interviewed and identified issues explaining the processes underlying the monitoring statistics. The university's formal equal opportunities policy was welcomed by all respondents, however, its operation presented certain difficulties. As found by Leicester and Lovell (1994) departments did not feel involved with the policy. One head of department said 'we never get to see the feedback data, nor has the EO [equal opportunities] policy been effectively followed up'. Whilst the heads of department insisted they would not tolerate any discrimination they felt a lack of support in developing good practice from the personnel department. The lack of centrally provided equality training was often cited as evidence of the lack of commitment to the policy. Another department head felt there should be a more pro-active stance taken centrally and 'there should probably be a post within the personnel function dedicated to equal opportunities to facilitate positive action strategies'. This perception of a lack of support is likely to feed into all recruitment activities, including student recruitment.

Another major factor thought to be an explanation for the relatively poor recruitment data was the perceived exclusionary nature of the university. It was frequently suggested that the university had a very low profile locally and was little known amongst minority ethnic communities. One respondent's experience from another institution in the city suggested the 'university was another planet ... was a common perception'. There was also a lack of knowledge of available job opportunities, during interviews candidates often expressed their surprise that the university had other job opportunities besides academic ones. Representatives of community-based organisations also supported the view of the university being exclusionary. Part of this was due to the university's geographic location away from the heart of the city and was strengthened because the university was not thought to have sought relationships and contacts with minority community organisations. One community representative stated that the 'university is a very distant, élitist place ... people in the university don't know what goes on in [the city] ... they just don't seem interested'. These views are likely to have a negative impact on potential students from local minority ethnic groups for whom the university does not have a high profile and who may gain the impression that it does not seek to engage with the local population.

The cumulative effect of both the reduced chances of appointment and external impressions of the institution was clearly identified by another community representative: 'People feel it's a waste of time applying. What is there to motivate black people to apply for jobs? Often people are given the formality of an interview, but never appointed'. Clearly the more the institution is perceived as élitist and remote the worse its local image becomes and the more difficult it is to attract minority ethnic applicants. The lack of engagement therefore becomes self-fulfilling.

Processes of engagement

Examples from different departments in the case study revealed how processes of engagement can benefit recruitment. However, if these processes operate to the exclusion of minority ethnic groups they further hinder equality objectives, creating a downward spiral of perceptions. The case study usefully revealed engagement processes which could, with sufficient motivation, be utilised to help recruit minority ethnic groups, creating an alternative affect: an upward spiral of progress and achievement.

The external perceptions of the university were often challenged once individuals had joined the university. A number of respondents felt that within job details, insufficient emphasis was given to the relative merits of university employment. One head of department felt that 'technicians and secretaries probably have to trade off better conditions (such as access to summer holiday schemes and perhaps security and fringe benefits) against lower pay'. A commonly cited 'perk of the job', giving the university a competitive edge, was the facilities available within the university such as sports, arts, catering, library and for some employees the provision of free transport to and from work.

The significance of challenging perceptions was supported by findings from focus groups with minority ethnic members of university staff. These employees all expressed their happiness working at the university although some racial problems had been encountered by a very few members of the focus groups. They also tended to see the university as a good employer and particularly commented on the facilities available as a further positive attribute which displaced concerns about low income levels and poor career prospects. These 'perks' had also been known to the individuals prior to their application and had been a factor in determining their decision to apply to the university.

A key factor revealed by the focus groups was that of familiarisation which operated in two ways. Firstly, in relation to encouraging applicants, secondly, by overcoming recruiters' reservations. All of the minority ethnic staff participating in the focus groups had some previous contact with the university before applying for their first job there. Some had been former students, others had visited the university's recreational facilities or had accompanied friends or relatives to work. This process of familiarisation meant that they were not threatened by the perceptions of the university as an élitist employer and made them realise some of the potential perks.

The process of familiarisation overcoming recruiters' reservations was linked to the concern of many minority ethnic staff that managers held some form of racial prejudice which affected their recruitment decisions. Before being considered for employment many staff felt that it had been important for managers to have a 'taster' opportunity of their abilities, often using temporary contracts for the purpose. One member of staff stated that 'I applied seven times before I got this job ... I came here as a temp, then they appointed me ... because they knew me'. Another stated that 'if they know you, you've got a chance of getting a job'. The experience indicated is consistent with research that has found minority ethnic groups tend to take a longer and more arduous route to obtaining employment (Brennan & McGeevor, 1990).

This suggests a positive method of pursuing greater engagement with minority ethnic groups through more formal processes of familiarisation which could help overcome reservations and misunderstandings on both sides. One department within the university (hospitality) had previously held open evenings which provided an opportunity to talk to managers about available employment. These had been viewed as relatively successful at

encouraging new applicants and overcoming some of the misconceptions of both sides.
The experiences gained through staff recruitment suggest that targeted invitations to
open days, perhaps to local colleges with high proportions of minority ethnic students,
could overcome some of the perceptions of the university held by potential student
applicants.

Academic career progression

The study investigating academic career success sought to identify routes to power within
institutions (Heward *et al*, 1995, 1997) by considering Connell's idea (1985, 1991) of
the interaction of individual life histories and institutional structures. The two subjects
law and biology were chosen to reflect the different subject cultures. In addition, given
the concern of institutional structures, respondents came from both the old and new
university sectors (Wagner, 1989 and Schuller, 1991).

Within the academic profession the main currency which aids progress is that
of reputation. Peer evaluation of intellectual work, theses, publications, conference papers
and research applications form the basis of this reputation. Some respondents saw the
making of their own reputation as a conscious activity, others simply put it down to luck
and being in the right place at the right time. However, exploration of these 'lucky'
events often revealed them not to be just a matter of luck.

A key factor in the building of reputations was the ability to engage with the
subject culture. In biology a successful career was typified by movement between
internationally prestigious research centres involving long hours of laboratory work. Clearly
the ability to engage with this particular culture requires geographic mobility and domestic
support to overcome any caring responsibilities for family or relatives. In law success was
most commonly associated with the publication of a key teaching text, practical
involvement with the legal profession and a good teaching reputation. Engagement with
this particular culture therefore enables greater flexibility of working time and lower
levels of geographic mobility.

The respondents often cited the major role played by a significant mentor in
their success. The encouragement of a mentor gave respondents self-confidence and a
positive evaluation of their own abilities. For example one white professor of law described
the process through which he was promoted to a Readership. He was invited to attend a
colloquia on his particular specialism which was being organised by a senior member of
the profession whom he knew. The respondent explained that 'one of the professors who

was in the group had seen my book and heard me talk and said to somebody else 'This chap should have been promoted some time ago'. That person then fed it through to the Dean of [...] Law School who did something about it'. Mentors also acted as a means of introduction to informal networks within the subject culture in which the individual's ability became known. Another white professor stated that 'It's not the applications but the invitations that have been important'. Involvement in networks also resulted in being passed work which helped build a reputation. A professor of law said that a mentor of his 'suggested I should be made a reader. And in fact when he retired he handed me a number of things. So, for instance, I am one of the editors of a big professional book. I suspect the reason I was invited was because he suggested my name'.

Engagement with these important networks may be more problematic for those from minority ethnic groups. One respondent who was a research fellow in biology and a member of the Sikh community felt that there were difficulties in presenting his work at what he saw as the appropriate conferences. As a Sikh he said he often felt isolated socially and culturally. He was vegetarian, did not smoke or drink and therefore found that networking at conferences did not come easily. Given the two-way relationship required for successful engagement in networks this may help to explain why minority ethnic groups can become excluded.

Explanations for why white male dominated networks may not successfully engage with members of minority ethnic groups were also revealed. Members of minority ethnic groups were often seen in stereotypical ways and thought to lack the abilities necessary for an academic career. Such stereotypes are likely to disadvantage minority ethnic students and discourage individuals from becoming engaged with the academic profession. One Asian respondent in law felt that as an undergraduate he 'wasn't very bright because all these people were speaking so wonderfully with their public school accents'. It was not until receiving his exam results that he said he became aware of his true abilities. Stereotypes held by gatekeepers to the profession obviously can have a major effect on preventing minority ethnic groups entering academia. One white professor considered students from the local minority ethnic population to be 'diligent' and 'assiduous' but 'not to have an enquiring mind'. Another white professor in a department where one third of the students were from minority ethnic groups stated that the few minority ethnic applicants he had considered were 'not of the right calibre'. One minority ethnic respondent said that he was encouraged to think of himself as able but his evaluation of his own abilities had not been borne out by his labour market experience, where it took him a long time to obtain an academic post.

In summary, the research showed that the engagement of minority ethnic groups in the academic profession is reliant upon connecting with the power relations that exist within different subject communities. Gatekeepers and mentors are crucial to success which requires making a reputation, patronage and networking. A key difficulty to overcome for those from minority ethnic groups are the stereotypes held by gatekeepers which may marginalise, devalue or exclude them from routes towards inclusion and eventually power. These stereotypes held by some of the academic profession will also limit the ability of higher education to engage with minority ethnic groups. Whilst the lack of evident success of those from minority ethnic groups in the profession means a significant lack of role models which may discourage potential students who continue to see universities as elitist and exclusionary.

Conclusion

Both research studies identified a number of ways in which it may be possible to engage members of minority ethnic groups much more with higher education. Similar processes might usefully be used to create greater diversity amongst students. However, it is also essential to be aware of the internal processes that operate in ways which are likely to exclude minority ethnic groups. The combination of these internal exclusionary processes and external discrimination and disadvantage creates major barriers which need to be overcome.

Familiarisation is a key process, which was seen to benefit those from minority ethnic groups, and recruiters. This process might also be used to help student recruitment because it can overcome misconceptions about higher education. Misconceptions of élitism and exclusivity may prevent potential students making any contact with a university. Actively seeking the engagement of minority ethnic students in open days and other outreach activities can challenge such misconceptions. Through such familiarisation, recruiters may also have their prejudiced conceptions challenged.

The operation of informal networks helps to maintain some professional power, autonomy and control, often in opposition to management. The maintenance of this power relies upon exclusionary practice, mentoring and recommendation to control the careers of others. As such the value of trying to artificially create such networks remains questionable. At best institutionally supported networks for minority ethnic staff and students may indicate a level of commitment and offer a temporary solution. However, universities need to recognise the role of these networks in providing contact with others outside of the institution. The informal messages distributed by these networks may often be in opposition to the formal institutional ones.

In the long term, the aim of processes of engagement should be to make a more diverse higher education. Long-term organisational cultural change should be sought to ensure universities welcome and value diversity amongst staff and students. If more role models are visible within universities this should make higher education attractive to a greater diversity of staff and students. Indeed universities have a responsibility to aim for this as educators of other major professions.

References

Bagilhole, B. (1993) 'How to keep a good woman down: an investigation of the role of institutional factors in the process of discrimination against women academics' in *British Journal of the Sociology of Education*, 14.

Ball, C. and Eggins, H. (1989) (eds) *Higher Education into the 1990s: New Dimensions.* Milton Keynes, Open University Press.

Becher, A. (1990) *Academic Tribes and Territories.* Milton Keynes, Open University Press.

Bourdieu, P. (1988) *Homo Academicus.* Oxford, Polity Press.

Brennan, J. and McGeevor, P. (1990) *Ethnic Minorities and the Graduate Labour Market.* London, Commission for Racial Equality.

Commission on University Career Opportunity (1994) A *Report on Universities' Policies and Practices on Equal Opportunities in Employment.* London, CUCO.

Connell, R. W. (1985) *Teacher's Work.* Sydney, Allen and Unwin.

Connell, R. W. (1991) 'Live fast and die young: the construction of masculinity among young working-class men on the margin of the labour market' in *Australian and New Zealand Journal of Sociology*, 27.

Elston, M. (1980) 'Medicine', in A. Ward and R. Silverstone *Careers of Professional Women.* London, Croom Helm.

Equal Opportunities Review (1995) 'University academics: the equality agenda' in *Equal Opportunities Review,* No. 59, January/February.

Farish, M., McPake, J., Powney, J. and Weiner, G. (1995) *Equal Opportunities in Colleges and Universities: towards better practice.* Milton Keynes, Open University Press.

Halsey, A. H. (1992) *Decline of Donnish Dominion.* Oxford, Clarendon Press.

Heward, C. and Taylor, P. (1992) 'Women at the top in higher education: equal opportunities policies in action?' in *Policy and Politics*, 20(2).

Heward, C. Taylor, P. and Vickers, R. (1995) 'What is behind Saturn's Rings?: methodological problems in the investigation of gender and race in the academic profession' in *British Educational Research Journal*, 21(2).

Heward, C., Taylor, P. and Vickers, R. (1997) 'Gender, Race and Career Success in the Academic Profession' in *Journal of Further and Higher Education*, 21(2).

Johnson, M. R. D., Taylor, P., Roach, P. and Abbas, T. (1996) *The Recruitment of Ethnic Minority Staff: an analysis of recruitment to academic related and non-academic posts*, unpublished research report, Coventry, Centre for Research in Ethnic Relations.

Leicester, M. and Lovell, T. (1994) 'Equal opportunities and university practice; race, gender and disability: a comparative perspective' in *Journal of Further and Higher Education*, 18(2).

Lorber, T. (1984) *Women in Medicine*. London, Tavistock.

Modood, T. (1993) 'The number of ethnic minority students in British higher education: some grounds for optimism' in *Oxford Review of Education*, 12(3).

Morley, L. (1994) 'Glass ceiling or iron cage: women in UK academia' in *Gender, Work and Organization*, 1(4), October.

Schuller, T. (1991) (ed) *The Future of Higher Education*. Milton Keynes, Open University Press.

Tapper, T. and Salter, B. (1992) *Oxford, Cambridge and the Changing Idea of the University: the challenge to donnish dominion*. Milton Keynes, Open University Press.

Taylor, P. (1992) 'Ethnic group data and applications to higher education' in *Higher Education Quarterly*, 46(4), Autumn.

Taylor, P. (1993) 'Minority ethnic groups and gender in access to higher education' in *New Community*, 19(3), April.

Taylor, P. (1996) 'Overcoming Barriers to Higher Education Entry', in Egan, O. (ed.) *Minority Ethnic Groups in Higher Education*. Cork, Higher Education Equality Unit.

Taylor, P. (1998) 'The Equality Access Market: exploitation, add on or conflict?', paper presented at the 7th EAN conference, Tallinn, Estonia.

Thomas, K. (1990) *Gender and Subject in Higher Education*. Milton Keynes, Open University Press.

Wagner, L. (1989) 'Access and standards: an unresolved (and unreasonable?) debate', in C. Ball and H. Eggins (eds.) *Higher Education into the 1990s: new dimensions*. Milton Keynes, Open University Press.

West, J. and Lyon, K. (1995) 'The trouble with equal opportunities: the case of women academics' in *Gender and Education*, 7(1).

Williams, J., Cocking, J. and Davies, L. (1989) *Words or Deeds? A Review of Equal Opportunities Policies in Higher Education*. London, Commission for Racial Equality.

21. Examples of good practice from Czech higher education institutions in overcoming the social exclusion of people with disabilities

Vera Stastna

Introduction

The Czech Republic is one of the so-called Central and Eastern European countries in transition. In industrial societies success was measured in terms of an economic index; in the information and knowledge society it will be measured in terms of knowledge and the ability to deal with information. However, there are other aspects which are not necessarily mentioned but which keep us informed about the level of the society. One of these is the full integration of people with special needs, including access to higher education and related study opportunities.

Before the revolution in 1989 there were two different worlds in the Czech Republic – that of the 'handicapped' and that of 'normal' people. Those with severe disabilities were placed in institutions for social care, children who were able to stay with their families attended special schools (e.g. special schools for children with visual or hearing impairments). Their problems were not discussed in public, people with disabilities lived in artificial social isolation. Further, they had no practical possibility of living outside their social establishments - e.g. public places and accommodation were not accessible. After 1989 the situation began to change. Barrier-free access has been provided in streets, public buildings (including several university faculties), theatres, cinemas, pubs etc.; almost all traffic lights at pedestrian crossings in Prague and larger towns have been equipped with bleep signals for people with visual impairments. However, the social barriers still exist. People with disabilities have begun to fight for their rights and the opportunity to be integrated as full members of society. But society has not been prepared for social contact with people with special needs, including disabilities. Sometimes these people are seen as passive subjects of social care. Integration is still not understood as it should be – as a dynamic process, the 'top' form of socialisation, which means not only that people with disabilities are prepared for life in society, but also that society is prepared to accept them. For example, an 'inappropriate' attitude is the role of 'charity' in meeting special educational requirements. This kind of positive discrimination leads to the provision of minimum requirements for those with a disability.

I am not an expert on the integration of people with special needs and will therefore simply describe and comment on some examples I have seen and been moved by. I have selected examples from three different areas: centres aiding students with visual impairments; performing arts courses integrating deaf students and degree programmes in adapted physical activity. Other such examples where teachers and students seek ways to achieve integration without false charity and positive discrimination could be found.

Centres for visual impairment aids

The first examples are centres for assisting people with severe visual impairment, developed by the Charles University and the Czech Technical University in Prague. The problem of integration is not only a problem of educating children and young people with visual impairment, but it concerns people of any age with this disability and the whole society in which they live. The disability itself sets some limits but a very important issue is how individuals themselves perceive their visual impairment. Their perception of the impairment can be an obstacle to communication and accessing external assistance if it is required. If a person with a visual impairment is provided with the appropriate compensatory aids which enable communication, their education can be achieved without comprising standards. Modern electronic aids such as Optacon, Eureka, vocal output or Braille connected to a computer compensate for the visual disability and enable equal access to information. Moreover, communication with the aid of a computer is communication with a person without a disability and this is also very important for both parties. The Ministry of Education has accepted the philosophy of equal opportunities for higher education students and other people with visual impairment and provides funding for state of the art technical equipment in three centres.

1) The first of these is the Lab TEREZA at the Faculty of Nuclear and Physical Engineering at the Czech Technical University in Prague. This centre was developed in the early 1990s with the help of the TEMPUS programme. It is used for integrated higher education studies for students with visual impairments. It is at the disposal of students from other higher education institutions and students from secondary and primary schools too. The main aim, however, is to provide opportunities for studying

for a first or higher degree. The equipment is freely accessible to those who have some knowledge of how to use the compensatory aids. For those who are less experienced or have not used such equipment before, courses, usually lasting six months, are organised.

2) Lab CAROLINA at the Faculty of Mathematics and Physics at Charles University started in 1995. This lab mainly provides basic computer courses for people who are blind and visually impaired, and specialises in courses for the Internet and Wintalker, allowing vocal control of the operating system Microsoft Windows. The laboratory staff scan and print the books on a Braille printer. Those who have completed the basic course are welcome to use the lab at any time, others have to come during opening hours to benefit from the help of the staff.

3) The Institute for Basic Therapy for the Visually Impaired at the Faculty of Physical Education at Charles University has its roots in the Training Centre for basic rehabilitation therapy which was established in 1994, and in 1999 became an Institute. From 1995 to 1999 38 trainers in space orientation for the visually impaired were educated, and in order for them to maintain a high professional level, regular workshops and seminars have been organised. The staff of the institute are involved in teaching and thesis guidance at different faculties in Charles University and the Higher Professional Social School JABOK. They organise seminars for teachers from elementary schools for children with visual impairments and other public sector professionals. The staff regularly prepare contributions for a special radio programme for people with visual impairments. They have very good co-operation with Humboldt University and a Dutch institute for the visually impaired – Theofaan in Grave. The Institute has rebuilt an old laundry as a new educational centre where the students and trainers are taught. It is used for visually impaired learning, for family members of people with visual disabilities to become better acquainted with their needs and for various lifelong learning courses connected with this type of disability.

Thus it can be seen that from a tradition of isolation and special, minimal education, people with visual impairments can be assisted to be independent learners in mainstream universities.

VDN – Educational drama for the deaf

Another group of 'disabled' people is the deaf. The word 'disabled' is probably not the right one. Modern emancipatory tendencies have resulted in them being considered as a minority. Deaf people have their own clubs, pubs and sign language. An interesting study programme has been developed at Janacek Academy of Music and Dramatic Arts in Brno – 'Educational Drama for the Deaf' – VDN (The acronym has been developed from the Czech name of the programme *Vychovna Dramatika Neslysicich* and has three meanings. Beside the one already mentioned, the acronym also expresses *Velmi Dobry Napad* – in English 'A Very Good Idea' and *Vlastni Divadlo Neslysicich* 'Theatre of the Deaf'). The study programme was started in 1992 and the emphasis is on movement arts. After three years of study the graduates are awarded a bachelor's degree and are mainly engaged as teachers and tutors in elementary schools for children and young people with hearing impairments. There is a one-year extension course for those who are interested in theatre and wish to develop their movement and acting skills.

Throughout the three years a considerable part of the programme is devoted to movement training, acrobatics, classical and modern dance, tap dancing, juggling and work with props. In the subject 'theatre movement' the students learn the principles of mime and get to know the 'secrets and peculiarities' of this kind of theatre which uses so-called 'absolute communication'. In addition, students attend courses on graphic technique, working with masks, working with puppets and courses in make-up, self-reflexive psychology and speech therapy. Much attention is paid to developing sign language, the study of foreign languages and work with computers. Teaching practice and theatre practice also form part of the programme.

Since 1992 several interesting productions have been mounted, which the group is still performing. VDN have taken part in many festivals in the Czech Republic and have given guest performances in Slovakia, Austria, Poland, Germany, France, Great Britain, Belgium, Holland and Turkey. Furthermore, the group also participated in the EUROPALIA′ 98 festival in Brussels, the Czech Republic being the first post-communist country to present its culture at this festival.

Their repertoire includes productions for adults, such as *Genesis,* a production intended to demonstrate the aesthetic beauty and wealth of expression in sign language. They also have productions for children, including *ABC*, a production showing children the letters of the alphabet in a playful way. The children share in the creation of the letters together with the actors. The letters are written, spoken, and shown in the form of a finger alphabet. The performance is intended for children over four years old and everybody who likes movement, acrobatics and fantasy.

The sign interpreter is present at all theoretical and practical classes and at all events organised by the faculty. The whole study programme begins with an introductory course, where both hearing and deaf students are present. This informal integration is continued throughout the whole study period. The deaf students live and work together with the other students.

The theatre is a good opportunity for improving communication and removing some of the barriers between students with and without disabilities. The lack of communication is consequently linked with further possibilities for self-realisation, as it is not only a matter of disability, but is also a sign of a lack of interest on both sides, and of many surviving prejudices.

In 1998/99 a new accredited study programme was offered in the Faculty of Drama at the Academy of Performing Arts in Prague – the Integration Study Programme, which is strongly targeted towards communication. In this programme the students with and without disabilities meet. It is an opportunity for the personal development of the individuals involved.

The programme has been run for the first pilot year. The study group consisted of both Czech and international students (from Sweden, Italy, Iceland and Slovenia) from different faculties: drama, theatre, music, arts and practitioners; four of the students have disabilities. Some of the participants are full-time students, others are part-time. The programme was accredited by the Ministry of Education and it is possible to study for a bachelor's or master's degree. During the first year the students gave two public performances of an original production. They prepared an improvisation for 'Meeting the theatre schools', an event organised under the patronage of UNESCO in Rumania in July 1999. They have also taken part in several theatre workshops in Poland - Poznan and Wroclaw – and were invited to a conference in Slovenia on new methods and concepts in theatre in March 1999. A very interesting round table was organised at the Faculty of Drama in Prague, in co-operation with the Austrian Cultural Institute where the problems of disability were discussed with the students of the whole faculty.

The realisation of the project has already produced some interesting experiences. The greatest surprise was that although it was hardly possible to remove boundaries between people, they were restructured and became permeable. These boundaries were not between students with and without disabilities, but between the Czechs and foreigners, between men and women, between students and working participants, between actors and non-actors, etc. It was not always the same people who were in the position of being 'disabled' – this group was always changing. Such diversity can help a great deal in understanding the needs of others and contributes to changing perspectives. The openness of the group was also limited. The opportunity of joining the programme later only existed for a month, after that it would have disrupted the intensive work. This created a major difficulty as 'latecomers' could only watch. There were also disappointments – some of those who were a great help to the whole group left. Some did not manage all the school tasks, some left for different study activities. The most positive aspect was that solidarity predominated, misunderstandings and disagreements were resolved. There was a large developmental and creative potential in the group. In this example a potential disability has been transferred into an advantage, creating a new and exciting drama programme.

Study programme in Adapted Physical Activity

The third set of examples also fully correspond with the idea of 'combating social exclusion'. 'To combat' means 'to fight against' and a group of enthusiasts from the Faculty of Physical Culture of Palacky University in Olomouc has fought and is constantly fighting. However, some battles have already been won. Even before 1989 students with and without disabilities studied together at the faculty from time to time, but the real breakthrough was the full-time master programme in Adapted Physical Activity which was initiated in 1991.

The specific aspects of the professional training of students with special needs are not always easy, especially if the discipline is physical education, where there are some additional difficulties. A modification of some sport disciplines creates further problems as well as needing to ensure the safety of physical activities and overcome the problems of communication already mentioned.

This programme overcomes these difficulties and graduates of the study programme now work:
- as teachers and educators in schools, especially those where efforts are being made to integrate children with special needs in physical education;
- at schools for children with special needs, special (remedial) schools;
- in centres for special education;
- in recreational activity centres and clubs;

- in private establishments;
- as tutors for physical activities in institutions for social care;
- as counsellors for regional decision-makers, especially in connection with government policy on physical education and sport which is under way and should be agreed by spring 2000;
- in crisis centres;
- and in firms dealing with compensatory aids.

The idea for the study programme in adapted physical activities came from a teacher, who visited a similar scheme abroad. She witnessed integrated classes of students, both with and without disabilities being taught together. Similarly, she observed one teacher in a wheelchair, and a leader of a sport and scout camp who was also in a wheelchair.

Initially, a counselling and guidance centre was established at the faculty. Here, applicants and parents discuss all the positive and negative issues together with the technical aspects of the admission procedure, and potential courses of study are determined. The centre has contacts with secondary schools to help attract potential applicants, but any form of positive discrimination was rejected from the start, and admission is no guarantee that the student will successfully complete their studies. The requirements are strictly laid down, if necessary with some modifications, and students with disabilities have to try as hard as any of their peers. There is not a campaign to encourage students with disabilities to apply for these programmes; the number of students with special needs approximately corresponds to the percentage of such people in society and to the number of them interested in higher education in the field of physical activities. In absolute numbers - there are two deaf graduates who have already started working in schools and four deaf students studying at present, three students in wheelchairs and two who have each had a leg amputated.

The last fight was to gain recognition that the graduates also fulfil all the demands for qualified teacher status. The studies have been transformed into a credit system and the new Higher Education Act from 1998, particularly Article 21 'Make all possible provisions for equilibrating opportunities for studying at a higher education institution...', together with the Articles which facilitate the individualisation of study programmes, helped to win this battle. It is true that some students without disabilities oppose the adaptation of requirements, but there are also those that support the inclusive approach and, if necessary, they work voluntarily as personal assistants for their colleagues with disabilities. Sometimes the doctoral students take on the role of assistants. There is a significant difference between a first-year student with a disability (namely deafness) and a graduate. The graduates are independent and are not afraid to fight for their rights or to protect others.

The faculty has a wide international contact network, it is part of an ERASMUS project co-ordinated by the University of Leuven, and it co-ordinates a CEEPUS (Central European Exchange Programme for University Studies) network concentrated on adapted physical activities. Two students with disabilities will this year enjoy the benefits of the CEEPUS student mobility scheme, and study abroad.

The CEEPUS project was developed from regular CEEPUS networks and led to a more complex programme co-ordinated by the Faculty of Physical Culture of Palacky University in Olomouc. Partner universities are from Croatia, Poland, Slovakia, Slovenia and the Czech Republic. Co-operation has been established with Austria and Hungary. Each of the participating institutions has outstanding results in a special field – physiotherapy, dance therapy, special educational needs and teacher training. During the programme the participants visit several institutions in different countries to benefit from the maximum results achieved in the region. In the year 2000 a special co-ordination meeting is planned which should bring together teachers and students on the project, other experts and people with special needs. The presentation of the theoretical results of the project as well as sports competitions in adapted physical activities are being planned. In this final example, perceived disadvantages have again been turned into advantages, and exclusion has been overcome.

Conclusion

'Studying with Friends' is the CEEPUS motto, and helping as friends with our know-how and enthusiasm was the reaction of the CEEPUS community to the Kosovo crisis. The Central CEEPUS Office has been co-operating with the World University Service (WUS) and via their office in Tetovo/Pristina humanitarian aid organisations were contacted. Several fields of co-operation were established, with trauma alleviation at the top of the list. The Central CEEPUS Office took the initiative and developed a project. 'Of course there are various forms of post-trauma treatment and physical activity is one of them. No matter what trauma one has suffered, physical activities carefully calibrated to one's condition will help heal,' wrote the Secretary General of the CEEPUS programme. People from the CEEPUS network have practical experience in treating psychological trauma, as they successfully treated victims of the flood catastrophe in 1997. 'The plan was to organise and train special teams of network participants and to send them to Albania and Macedonia, where they were to train local staff who would then disseminate the know-how.' The actual needs of each destination were to be established by a detailed questionnaire designed by Ms. Valkova and mailed by the Central CEEPUS Office to all target destinations. A week-long preparatory course in Olomouc would brief the teams specifically for the tasks ahead. Vaccination costs and transportation would be covered by the Austrian Ministry of Science and Transport, each team member would also receive a special CEEPUS scholarship provided by his/her home country. One of the first target destinations was to be the Cegrane Camp, where the International Mercy Cooperation was planning to set up a day clinic for people with disablities.

The return of many refugees to Kosovo since the end of the NATO bombings has, of course, necessitated a revision of these plans. However, the needs still persist and so does CEEPUS enthusiasm. The Central CEEPUS Office is still in touch with the organisations it has been working with and once they have set themselves up in Kosovo we shall soon define new destinations, in Kosovo and in the neighbouring countries. We have also established direct contact with the Rector and the International Relations Office of the University of Pristina, which is preparing to take up work. 'Studying with friends and co-operating with friends from the region in their time of need is a contribution to help sow the seeds for future integration' (Central CEEPUS Office).

Let me conclude by changing a little the final words of the above quotation and extending them from their European context to cover the real integration of all people in society. 'Studying with friends and co-operating with friends even if they are slightly different and have different needs is a contribution to help sow the seeds for future integration in the whole society.'

References

Educational Drama of the Deaf - faculty materials, Faculty of Theatre, Janacek Academy of Music and Performing Arts.

Higher Education Act of 22 April 1998 (Act No. 111/1998 Code).

Pilatova, J. *The project 'Rozvoj komunikace'*. Project Report, 1 January 1999.

Pilatova, J. *'Intentions of the 'Integration Programme'*. March 1999.

Sorantin, E. *'CEEPUS and the Kosovo Crisis'*. Central CEEPUS Office, June 1999.

Stehlikova, E. Theatre review in *Divadelní noviny* (Theatre Newspaper).

Valkova, H. *'Combating Social Exclusion'*. May 1999.

Vangeli, N. *'Vyvoleni a postizeni'* in *Umeni a kritika,* 19 March 1999.

Part Six

The Way Forward

22. Policy, practice and theory: the role of higher education research in combating social exclusion

Liz Thomas and Robert Jones

In this chapter we argue that, in addition to actively engaging in strategies to not just *increase*, but to *widen* participation in post-compulsory education, higher education institutions (HEIs) should be undertaking research. Thus moving beyond knowledge *transfer* to knowledge *production*. It is only through the generation of knowledge that is accessible and useful to practitioners and policymakers, that solutions to promoting genuinely wider participation will be achieved. This is necessary to ensure that greater participation in education and lifelong learning is based on the premise of *'second chances, not second helpings'* (Woodrow, 1999: p12). We therefore review different approaches and conceptualisations to knowledge and research, and discuss the advantages of participatory action research.

The role of higher education in combating social exclusion – a 'positional' or a 'democratic' good?

It is commonly assumed that entry to, and successful completion of, a higher education course, accrues certain benefits to the graduate. These may be straightforwardly material, elevating the graduate to a higher income band, accelerating promotion and enhancing career prospects generally. Similarly, the graduate may experience the advantages brought by an increase in status and 'cultural capital'. The two may well often work together. The consumption of higher education to increase economic status is the outcome of viewing education as a 'positional' good[1] (see Jary & Thomas, 1999: p4). In contrast to these

comparatively instrumental outcomes of higher education study when it is conceived as
a positional good, it is possible to imagine other consequences for the learner too. For
example, self-fulfilment, personal development and the ability to question, challenge or
resist practices and attitudes that might otherwise have gone unacknowledged and which
may have conspired to subjugate the individual or group concerned. In this
conceptualisation, higher education can be viewed as a 'democratic' good, in which all
can share, and all can potentially benefit (*ibid*).

Expanding educational opportunities and participation, especially to 'non-
traditional' students, can also be used as a tool intended to reduce social exclusion. Social
exclusion moves beyond conceptualising social injustice in purely economic terms (see
for example, Marx,1976; Rawls, 1972; Dworkin, 1977; Sen, 1985). It embraces the lack
of ability of the socially excluded to exercise their social, cultural and political rights as
citizens. It therefore encompasses more than material deprivation:

> 'Social exclusion represents a qualitative restructuring constituting a change in
> the way people relate to each other, manifested by ever widening inequalities,
> spiralling levels of violence and a breakdown of social solidarity.'
> (Powell, 1999: p21)

Social inclusion therefore requires both economic and cultural change – economic
redistribution and cultural recognition. 'Education' therefore is well placed to span this
dual role of social inclusion, potentially offering economic and cultural advancement.
In our opinion, higher education and the access movement can only address social exclusion
fully if this role receives adequate attention and higher education is viewed as a democratic
good. Proposing policies and initiatives without challenging a narrow credentialist
framework of learning is self-defeating, (see Brill, 1999; Dore, 1976), serving to perpetuate
a form of education tailored to serve the needs of an economy and culture marked by
iniquitous divisions. As early as 1970 Ivar Berg portrayed the spiralling of educational
requirements as a 'race in which all run harder and nobody gains'. But, while we believe
the 'democratic' role of higher education is essential in challenging and overcoming social
exclusion collectively rather than individually, we feel it is also beneficial and necessary to
move beyond simply *knowledge transfer*. Not only should higher education play a direct
role in combating social exclusion through flexibility and innovation in its recruitment,
admission and teaching policies, but a key role must be research and *knowledge production*
in the field of widening participation and social inclusion. Given the pursuit of certain

theoretical and methodological directions we assert that higher education can widen participation, and simultaneously attack those aspects of society that function to exclude certain groups. It is to the role of higher education research that we now turn our attention.

A theoretical overview

In order to locate our claims theoretically we will begin by examining briefly two views of knowledge and research: Anthony Giddens' concept of 'reflexivity', and aspects of the work of Martyn Hammersley's ethnographic epistemology. The claim we try to substantiate throughout this first part of the discussion relates to our view that significant gaps exist between research and policy and practice. Although it may be difficult to separate the relationships between these three areas analytically, the second part of the discussion will try to address the disjuncture between research, practice and policy, drawing on strands of our own empirical studies. It is argued that a form of participatory action research (PAR) can be utilised to forge auspicious links between researchers and communities. This approach marks something of a departure from both the accounts of knowledge reviewed in the first part of our analysis. We will maintain however, that PAR offers a viable and potentially radical way to conduct empirical studies in the field of access, and, more significantly, is in itself inclusive and part of a broader learning process.

Links between research and policy and practice

It seems relatively safe to suppose that researchers in general, and particularly in the field of access, invest a degree of faith in the knowledge they produce, and believe that it will translate into practical measures and subsequently inform broader strategies. These may manifest themselves in comparatively small, localised initiatives, perhaps at the community or institutional level, or much more widely. More ambitious researchers may hope that their study's findings will percolate upwards to the national and international level and inform government and inter-state policy and implementation. There is no necessary reason why both outcomes cannot occur, although contribution to national and international policy-making by a single research team is likely to be minimal. But, whether we are referring to more immediate consequences of research at the local level or less direct ones at the wider level, in each case researchers rarely intend their work to be completely ineffectual. For example, Whyte (1991) argues that most researchers *expect* their research to have an impact on practice, and no researcher would argue that their

research is devoid of any practical significance, but it is up to 'others' to make the links
and to utilise the research findings.

'Recognising that the link between such social research and action is seldom
established, the mainstream researcher nevertheless assumes that good science
must eventually lead to improved practice. Here the important word is eventually.
How long must we wait before what mainstream researchers discover eventually
gets implemented in practice?'
(Whyte,1991: p8)

Approaches to knowledge and research: Giddens and Hammersley

We wish to examine Giddens' concept of reflexivity in relation to the utilisation of research
and knowledge. In Giddens' work reflexivity describes and explains knowledge and
knowledge production as a dynamic process, emerging from an interface between
researchers and the researched. For several reasons, however, the field of widening
participation may fail to achieve a state of reflexivity.

First it will be helpful to provide a working definition of reflexivity. Initially, we
should perhaps acknowledge that Giddens uses the term, in part, to refer to elements of
social and historical change regarding the ways in which social actors acquire and act on
knowledge. In this sense, its descriptive and explanatory potential may be restricted when
applied to mundane, less expansive contexts. Nevertheless, as we will see, the idea of
reflexivity in Giddens' work does suggest that knowledge production, and thus research,
have certain consequences which should be tangible at various levels from the macro to
the micro (i.e. from the international and national to the small group and individual
level). Central to Giddens' account is a distinction between traditional and modern cultures
(1990: pp36-38), and although reflexivity is said to be found in both, it is in the latter
that it becomes dominant. From this view, social actors are seen to be reflexive in so far
as they tailor their behaviour to fit that of their cultural milieu, and as Giddens states,
'...in pre-modern civilisations reflexivity is...largely limited to the reinterpretation and
clarification of tradition', (*op. cit*, p37). By contrast, modernity encourages an orientation
towards the future and change, resulting in much higher levels of reflexivity. Here '...social
practices are constantly examined and reformed in the light of incoming information',
(*op. cit*, p38).

Unlike traditional societies, modernity applies reason to spheres of life and culture which may previously have been unquestioned, allowing individuals (or 'lay-agents') to gain new knowledge and fashion their conduct accordingly. Needless to say, disciplines such as sociology are said to play a major role in this process. Research into the nature of institutions, associations and groups produces knowledge that is then drawn upon by lay-agents, and when acted upon, gives rise to a new situation that is once again studied. Giddens describes this process thus:

> The reflexivity of modernity, which is directly involved with the continual generating of systematic self-knowledge, does not stabilise the relations between expert knowledge and knowledge applied in lay-actions. Knowledge claimed by expert observers (in some part, and many varying ways) rejoins its subject matter, thus (in principle but also normally in practice) altering it.'
> (*op. cit*, p45)

This raises the question of whether or not there is sufficient evidence to suggest that such a process is endemic to the field of access and reducing social exclusion. If we look at parts of the national picture we may be able to begin to answer this dilemma. For instance, UK national statistics reveal a 33% API (Age Participation Index) in higher education, but this masks large disparities in, for example, participation by different socio-economic groups. 80% API for the highest socio-economic group, compared with 12% from the lowest. In an attempt to address such disparities the UK government has, as Alison Goddard (1999) reported, provided an extra 45,000 higher education places (15,000 of which are full-time). But, there seems to be little evidence to suggest that 'lay-agents' (i.e. potential entrants) have acted on this knowledge. Remarking on analyses from the Universities and Colleges Admissions Services (UCAS) statistics, the same article reveals that the number of applications for the academic year 1999-2000 has remained static.

Such figures should not on their own lead us to conclude that instances of reflexivity with regard to knowledge production and research in the field of access are so negligible as to be insignificant. They do, however, remind us of the enduring nature of, for example, class and socio-economic factors and barriers to social inclusion. These factors can and do inhibit the continuous process of reflexivity described by Giddens. It would seem that, in many ways, there is a 'material base' (with associated ideologies) that impedes the abilities of potential entrants to act on (or with respect to the preceding parenthesis, gather) knowledge and the findings of research.

Although, as was noted earlier, the concept of reflexivity is used by Giddens to theorise social and historical change, with regard to the role of knowledge we would like now to attempt to apply his concept to a contemporary micro level. If in the above, a reflexive relationship between access research and potential beneficiaries was not apparent, might it not be the case that at 'ground level' there exists a far greater degree of reflexivity? After all, practitioners and researchers may produce knowledge locally and proceed to disperse it in an ostensibly more direct fashion than is the case in the macro arena.

The range of factors that can encourage or constrain reflexivity in the local sphere are not inconsiderable in number or variation. Here though we will look at some of those that can lead to the opening up of gaps between research and practice. Martyn Hammersley has commented on some of these issues. Regarding the relationships that can often emerge in this context he remarks that:

> 'the attitudes of practitioners to the work of researchers is varied and complex. It is not uncommon for practitioners to claim that research is irrelevant to their work or that it misrepresents it or the problems they face.'
> (Hammersley, 1992: p74)

Relevance and validity constitute the two main concepts in Hammersley's attempts to establish his 'subtle realist' epistemology. We do not wish to engage with the strengths and weaknesses of this position here. Of more interest is the observation that sees the potential for tensions within the field of research. This is compounded when we introduce another 'tier' of stakeholders into this already potentially hierarchical structure, such as that of management or funding bodies. There may be less likelihood that such groups will advance a critique of findings and analyses on the grounds of their relevance to a particular field, but there is still room for conflict.

Perhaps the most familiar situation arises from the appetites of management and funding bodies for statistics and quantified data. Information collected in this form often seems to be granted a certain form of 'reverence' by these groups of stakeholders. While Martyn Hammersley (1996) has suggested that the practicalities of qualitative research often involve incorporating quantitatively directed tasks, such as measuring and counting, the researcher might not feel overly confident in attempting to collapse the distinction between the two approaches when answering to an impatient panel of assessors. In these settings common-sense assumptions can often appear rather entrenched. The routine of engaging with the quasi-positivism of the 'numbers game' (in whatever guise it may take) is not the only source of disagreement in the research field, however.

Depending on the character of the organisation in which the researchers are working there may be ad hoc attempts to direct attention to extraneous facets of an area of inquiry which, again, emanate not from practitioners but commissioning bodies or other external stakeholders. For example, if interim findings purport to detect weaknesses or problems regarding an institution's relationships with potential entrants, the focus of study may be encouraged to swivel round to emphasise, say, links with other agencies. Obviously, researchers will need to develop their own pragmatic responses, though the basic point remains; i.e. relationships which arise in and around the field can obstruct research and knowledge production. This will, in turn, hinder the establishing of reflexive processes whereby findings can be made public and used by lay-agents (i.e. potential entrants) to inform activity.

In summary, the emergence of reflexivity in the field of widening participation is forestalled at the macro level, and also confronted with difficulties in the local domain (where we might expect to find more direct links between researchers and the researched). A situation where researchers gather and collate information, which permits practices to be re-fashioned in its wake (and then, concomitantly, researched again), appears to meet a number of impediments. In the remainder of our discussion we will attend to the practice/research relationship. We have acknowledged that practitioner-researcher relationships can be problematic and in the following will propose a model for research and knowledge production, which can offer a solution to some of the more recurrent issues here. More saliently, the prototypical (and thus, somewhat tentative) framework we will advance will incorporate the 'researched' within the research process. The familiar distinctions between researchers, practitioners and researched will therefore be reworked, our aim being to induce as much laterality into the activity and structure of knowledge production as possible.

Participatory action research

We propose a participatory action research approach to overcome some of the limitations of traditional research and knowledge production. The epistemological justifications of participatory action research (PAR hereon) mark a point of departure with those of Anthony Giddens' reflexivity and Martyn Hammersley's subtle realism. This is not, however, to infer that these two positions are commensurable. For example, both operate with quite separate notions of 'truth'. Reflexive knowledge is an evanescent phenomena, constantly subject to modifications and adjustments as a result of modern social activity's transformational character. Conversely, Hammersley wishes to retain a form of the correspondence theory of truth (1992: p69). His dislike of knowledge theories that view truth as an overt social construction (c.f. *op. cit*, pp 45-48) would require a rejection of Giddens' conceptualisation of reflexivity. In addition, Hammersley propounds a comparatively sterile and seemingly ineffectual view of the products of research. He writes '...I suspect that most social research findings have (at best or worst) only an extremely weak influence on what they predict or describe', (*op. cit*, p51).

On one level PAR *can* be seen to stand quite close to Giddens' understanding of the relationships that underpin contemporary forms of knowledge. For example, although Kemmis and Wilkinson (1998) do not cite Giddens, their account of PAR's epistemology does appear to share important aspects of his account. Regarding the salience of social activity they note that this inevitably involves:

'...changing the objective conditions [which] changes the way in which a situation is interpretively understood, which in turn changes how people act on the 'external', 'objective' world, which means that what they do is understood and interpreted differently, and that others also act differently, and so on, in a dynamic process of reflection and self-reflection.'
(*op. cit*, p31)

PAR (and its reflexive orientation) begins to differ from Giddens' position when the role of the researcher is considered. We noted earlier that Giddens' notion of reflexive knowledge requires a distinction between the lay-agent and the knowledge producer. By contrast, PAR aims expressly at the practical conflation of the two. Paraphrasing Fals Borda, the role of PAR is to aim '...to help people to investigate reality in order to change it', (Kemmis & Wilkinson, 1998: p26). Not surprisingly there is a strategic aspect here too, as is evident when these researchers state that the approach attempts:

'...to make the research process into a politics which will in some definite ways supersede and reconstruct the pre-existing politics of the settings in which it is conducted – indeed it aims to be a process in which various aspects of social life in the setting (cultural, economic and political) can be transformed through collaborative action.'
(*op. cit*, p31)

Suffice to say, then, that PAR tries to steer an emancipatory course through research.

It may be helpful at this juncture to try to give some concrete examples of the form that PAR may take within the field of widening participation. Here we will draw briefly on our own involvement in a project funded by the Further Education Funding Council (FEFC). The project in question used FEFC funding to employ eight community link workers, whose broad brief was to forge connections between locales with traditionally low rates of participation in post-compulsory education, and their local further education colleges. The intention was to recruit the link workers from the communities in which they would be working, and, in this broad sense, the initiative can be seen to draw from the PAR approach. As link workers, the perception amongst community members would, it was hoped, be less likely to reject the option of further learning if someone conveyed the 'message' to them with close knowledge and understandings of the area. Link workers would also be acting in the capacity of researchers, collecting information both about the educational perceptions and requirements of the target communities, and the best ways to work with these groups to widen participation and promote social inclusion. Situated at the two local universities, and acting formally as evaluators of the project, we sought to work with the link workers to gather information, and collate details of effective strategies, to share these with other link worker colleagues.

The link workers revealed detailed and complex local knowledge of the target communities. For example, it was quickly apparent that successful educational provision would have to engage with the particular internal characteristics of each area, especially with regard to local 'political' issues, such as 'status' and standing within the community and other issues. We asked the link workers about some of their experiences in their work. The following quote reveals details of social inter-relations that mitigate against successful further education provision in the area.

'We had a lot of people showing interest in computers… and I said 'Yeah – great, do you want to go to Talbot to do it?' 'Oh no! We're not going there!' That's the hard part, you see, getting people to go to different [venues]… We've got three schools as bases, kind of thing…and there's two primary schools and a high school that can be used. [Talbot] is the only place where we could put on computers. But we've noticed parents don't want to go. We've got this conflict, you see. The Brownhills' parents don't want to go to Greenfields, the Greenfields' ones don't want to go to Brownhills…, and neither of them want to go to Talbot… It's very difficult. The Greenfields' parents think the ones at Brownhills are stuck up and the Brownhills' ones think the Greenfields' ones are too… slobbish.'

The link worker proceeded to explain these tensions as rooted in types of housing. Succinctly, the large council estate forming the community focused on by the college contains three types of tenants; those residing in private, ex-council houses, those in housing association homes, and those in accommodation still rented from the council. In the perception of some in the community, the hierarchy descends from the first to the third category. The corollary is that each category of housing has, associated with it, its 'own' educational establishment, and this is mirrored in further education for adults, to the point of them deferring the use of other venues. It is knowledge such as this that helps to explain low take-up rates, even with respect to courses set-up in response to needs specifically expressed by the target communities. We would argue this type of knowledge should therefore inform provision, and, perhaps more pertinently, can come only from those with close associations with the people concerned. It must be admitted that the project alluded to does not realise all the tenets of PAR as espoused by Kemmis and Wilkinson. In one sense, there is a danger that (regarding the above example) it is collusive with many aspects of contemporary culture and the current socio-economic climate. Might not the provision of courses along the lines implied by the link worker's synopsis serve to reinforce structures of class and status, which are but reflections of wider societal divisions? If so, then there is no guarantee that PAR offers any more efficacious means of attacking exclusion than other research approaches.

In our view, however, it still retains an inclusive and potentially radical orientation that invites us as practitioners, policy-makers and theorists in the field of widening participation to re-think and re-formulate the role of higher education and the researcher. It helps to show that although knowledge provision (we are thinking here of critical thought as contained in the various humanities disciplines) constitutes an indispensable and essential way to encourage awareness of practices that perpetuate subjugation, there is also a very important, and somewhat neglected, place for knowledge production too. This is particularly the case in the context of access research intending to reduce social exclusion.

References

Berg, I. (1970) *Education and Jobs: The Great Training Robbery.* Harmondsworth, Penguin.
Brill, H. (1999) 'The false promise of higher education', paper to the 69th Annual Meeting of the Eastern Sociological Society. Boston, 4-7 March 1999.
Dore, R. (1976) *The Diploma Disease: Education, Qualification and Development.* London, Allen & Unwin.

Giddens, A. (1990) *The Consequences of Modernity*. Cambridge, Polity Press.

Goddard, A. (1999) 'Access Bait Fails to Lure Poor', in *THES* 4th June 1999, p1.

Hammersley, M. (1992) *What is Wrong with Ethnography?* London, Routledge.

Jary, D. and Thomas, E. (1999) 'Widening Participation and Lifelong Learning: Rhetoric or Reality? The Role of Research and the Reflexive Practitioner', in *Widening Participation and Lifelong Learning*, 1(1):3-9.

Kemmis, S. and Wilkinson, M. (1998) 'Participatory Action Research and the Study of Practice', in Atweh, W., Kemmis, S. and Weeks, P. (eds) *Action Research in Practice*. London, Routledge.

Powell, F. (1999) 'Adult Education, Cultural Empowerment & Social Equality: the Cork Northside Education Initiative', in *Widening Participation and Lifelong Learning*, 1(1):20-27.

Whyte, W. F. (ed) (1991) *Participatory Action Research*. Newbury Park, California, Sage.

Whyte, W. F., Greenwood, D. J. and Lazes, P. (1991) 'Participatory Action Research: Through practice to science in social research', in Whyte, W.F (ed) *Participatory Action Research*. Newbury Park, California, Sage.

Woodrow, M. (1999) 'The Struggle of the Soul of Lifelong Learning', in *Widening Participation and Lifelong Learning*, 1(1):13-20.

Note

[1] 'Positional' goods have 'zero-sum' benefits, in which the benefits enjoyed by some are to the exclusion and cost of others.

23. Access: past, present and future

Robert Lemelin

These days, policies that encourage access to higher education are generally looked upon as positive developments. In earlier times access was approached differently. I want to say a few words about the successes of access as well as the problems from the standpoint of access education in the United States.

In 1774, in the American colony of Virginia, a group of leaders sent a communication to the American chiefs of the Six Nations tribes, inviting one Native American young man from each tribe to come to Virginia for a university education. The chiefs considered the offer solemnly and responded with this statement:

'Our ideas of this kind of education happen not to be the same as yours. We have had some experience of that education; several of our young people were formerly brought up at the colleges of the northern provinces; they were instructed in all your sciences; but when they came back to us, they were bad runners, ignorant of every means of living in the woods, unable to bear either cold or hunger, knew neither how to build a cabin, take a deer, or kill an enemy, spoke our language imperfectly; were therefore neither fit for hunters, warriors, or counsellors; they were totally good for nothing.'

Embedded in that response is one of the traditional tensions in access, the tension between the needs and values of a minority culture and those of a predominant culture.

In the United States we have had a long and varied tradition providing access to higher education. In the 17th and 18th centuries, given the isolation of many communities and the early state of development of the country, students often came to higher education underprepared and needing tutoring. College preparatory schools were founded and attached to higher education institutions to correct this shortcoming. The focus of these preparatory schools was to bestow the 'benevolence' of access.

By 1836, access was defined in terms of cultural assimilation, one legislator put the matter in this way. He wrote:

'Let us now be reminded, that unless we educate our immigrants, they will be our ruin. It is no longer a mere question of benevolence, of duty, or of enlightened self-interest, but the intellectual training of our foreign population has become essential to our safety, we are prompted to it by instinct of self-preservation.'

In the 19th century, the growth of technology and its need for trained technicians encouraged the founding of technical colleges which took on some of the responsibility for higher education. Students who had the price of tuition were admitted to the new colleges. When they were found underprepared they were given support for they represented the colleges' source of income. The first preparatory department in higher education was established in 1849. After the American Civil War the so-called land grant agricultural colleges also took on a role of providing access.

Early in the 20th century American admissions standards were established which helped sort out access opportunities. By 1913 junior and community colleges began to provide access to higher education. The larger American cities developed superior free colleges for the poor. The outstanding model for these colleges, City College of New York, produced Ira Gershwin, Bernard Malamud and Jonas Salk.

The GI Bill for World War II veterans opened higher education to a variety of social classes. Soon, free higher education became a social goal and California became a leader in this development. In the East by the late fifties, Connecticut, for instance, offered a state college education for $25 a semester, and even that fee would be remitted if it were a burden for the student.

The sixties saw the steady expansion of open admissions – anyone could try college, regardless of academic background or finances. As a result, new groups entered higher education, groups that would not have been invited before. These new students were poor, had deficits in basic skills, had very limited background knowledge, and few cultural experiences. Their problems as learners changed whole institutions in terms of tone and content. Gradually the 'benevolent' focus of earlier access gave way to a combined civil rights and social justice focus and access had thus been added to the political agenda.

Since then, after nearly 40 years of development and institutionalization, access programmes in higher education have had many successes. The provision of financial aid is solidly established; access by students with disabilities is the law. A canon of materials has been created; a vocabulary and rhetoric have developed; new specialities like basic writing and first-year experience have been established; new teaching strategies, like supplemental instruction and computer assisted instruction have been used; professional organisations and journals reporting research and practice have appeared. Access activities have become public policy and there are 35,000 access colleagues working in the United States, delivering their programmes at the cost of 1% of the national higher education budget. Finally, access has also generated income and renewal for higher education.

There are problems however. Access tries to prepare students for the mainstream culture, but it is expected to make adjustment for multi-cultural agendas. When students are inadequately prepared, programmes work with several limitations. The confrontation of high goals and minimalist standards needs to be addressed more fully in our forums. Instructors often wrestle with pre-college or pre-secondary school skills. Studies that measure the effectiveness of programmes settle for minimalist standards too often. The achievement of high quality access has been difficult. There are a multiplicity of different programmes and strategies, and knowing what works is not easy. Staff are not paid well nor do they hold a position of equality in their institutions, and they must learn nearly everything on the job. Attrition rates are too high. We try to do too much, too fast. Research lacks vigour. Theory has been neglected. Access has no convincing and useful enveloping theory or definition and goals are muddled.

Adding to these problems, Americans are becoming hesitant in their support of access. They may be unwilling to make society pay for the injustice of socially caused problems in learning. Affirmative action is under fire. City College of New York, the access leader, is dismantling its open admissions programmes.

The changes in our society are bound to affect access patterns. We are needing to absorb and use new knowledge, being created at enormous speed, to develop learning modes for the new knowledge, to transform our society from a consumer to a learning culture; to merge the work-world and the academic world.

Access programmes will need to address new injustices – as globalisation stirs the pot. We will be required to describe clearly what we know and what we do, to further institutionalise access and to elevate it within academe, to link access work with cognitive science, to test the philosophical assumptions of our practice more vigorously. We need to be aware that higher education access is linked to the earliest years of learning and to bring our work to bear on those years.

Other problems haunt our work. Cultural gaps between students and higher education remain enormous. There is often tension between the access student and the non-access faculty.

There is questioning about the responsibility for learning – student or institution – and the limitations of mass higher education's ability to transform high risk students. We perhaps should prepare – as Sweden has done – an international statement on the higher education learning rights for the new century.

Finally, Morwenna Griffiths in an article on social justice and education, connects access to higher education to two fundamental issues: the relationship of education to the good of society and the use of education for the development and well-being of the individual. The difficulty is to discover exactly what the good of the society and good of the individual are, and whether they conflict or merge. But, there is no mistaking that is where we in access should be – dealing with those two issues.

Index